The Monochrome Society

NEW FORUM BOOKS Robert P. George, Series Editor

A list of titles in the series
appears at the back of the book

A M I T A I   E T Z I O N I

The Monochrome Society

PRINCETON UNIVERSITY PRESS   PRINCETON AND OXFORD

Second printing, and first paperback printing, 2003
Paperback ISBN 0-691-11457-9

The Library of Congress has cataloged the cloth edition of this book as follows

Etzioni, Amitai.
The monochrome society / by Amitai Etzioni.
p.   cm. — (New forum books)
Includes index.
ISBN 0-691-07090-3 (cloth : alk. paper)
1. United States—Moral conditions.   2. United States—Social conditions.   3. Social
values—United States.   4. Social problems—United States.   I. Title.   II. Series.

HN90.M6 E79 2001
306'.0973—dc21   00-048323

British Library Cataloging-in-Publication Data is available

This book has been composed in Electra

Printed on acid-free paper. ∞

www.pupress.princeton.edu

Printed in the United States of America

10 9 8 7 6 5 4 3 2

To my multicultural, monochromic family.

CONTENTS

ACKNOWLEDGMENTS

I am indebted to Jennifer Ambrosino and Mary Wilson for editorial assistance and to Natalie Klein, Rachel Mears, and Joanna Cohn for research assistance. Professors Dennis Wrong and Eva Elizur made several very helpful comments on a previous version of this collection. Andrew Volmert greatly helped in final preparation of this volume.

All the chapters included in this volume were previously published essays, but all were modified, revised, or extended for the purpose of this volume. An earlier version of Chapter I, "The Monochrome Society," was published in *The Public Interest*, No. 137 (Fall 1999), pages 42–55. Chapter II, "Is Shaming Shameful?" was first published under the title "Back to the Pillory?" in *The American Scholar*, Vol. 68, No. 3 (Summer 1999), pages 43–50. Chapter III, "The Post-Affluent Society," was previously referred to as "Voluntary Simplicity," and was first published in the *Journal of Economic Psychology*, No. 19 (1998), pages 619–643. Chapter IV, "Can Virtual Communities Be Real?" written with my son, Oren Etzioni, Professor of Computer Science at the University of Washington, was first published in *The Information Society*, Vol. 15, No. 4 (October–December 1999), pages 241–248. A much shorter version appeared as an editorial in *Science*, Vol. 277 (July 18, 1997), page 295. When I revisited cyberspace two years after the joint essay was completed, I found significant new developments, which I recorded in "E-communities Build New Ties, but Ties that Bind" for the *New York Times* (February 10, 2000, page E7), and added here.

While the first four chapters are couched in less technical terms, the rest are written more in the terms employed by social scientists and social philosophers. "Suffer the Children" (Chapter V) is forthcoming in *The Good Society*. "Holidays: The Neglected Seedbeds of Virtue" (Chapter VI) was published in *Sociological Theory*, Vol. 18, No. 1 (March 2000), pages 44–59, under the title "Toward a Theory of Public Ritual." "Salem without Witches" (Chapter VII) was published in *Contemporary Sociology*, Vol. 29, No. 1 (January 2000), pages 188–195, as "Creating Good Communities and Good Societies."

"Social Norms: The Rubicon of Social Science" (Chapter XIII) is forthcoming in the *Law & Society Review*.[1] "Why the Civil Society Is Not Good Enough" (Chapter IX) was published under the title "The Good Society" in *The Journal of Political Philosophy*, Vol. 1, No. 1 (March 1999), pages 88–103. "Virtue and the State: A Dialogue between a Communitarian and a Social Conservative" (Chapter X), an exchange between myself and Robert P. George, Professor of Political Science at Princeton University, was published in *The Responsive Community*, Vol. 9, No. 2 (Spring 1999), pages 54–66. "Restoring the Moral Voice" (Chapter XI) first appeared in *The Public Interest*, No. 116 (Summer 1994), pages 107–113. The questionnaire that appears within the chapter was published in *The Public Perspective*, Vol. 8, No. 1 (December–January 1997), pages 67–68. "Cross-Cultural Moral Judgments" (Chapter XII) appeared as "Cross-Cultural Judgments: The Next Steps" in the *Journal of Social Philosophy*, Vol. XXVIII, No. 3 (Winter 1997), pages 5–15. (Readers interested in a more extensive treatment of the same subject, especially as it relates to deontology and ultimate values, will find this discussion in Chapter 8 of my book *The New Golden Rule*, published by Basic Books in

1997.) "Stakeholders versus Shareholders" (Chapter XIII) first saw the light of day as "A Communitarian Note on Stakeholder Theory" in the *Business Ethics Quarterly*, Vol. 8, Issue 4 (October 1998), pages 679–691.

INTRODUCTION

One theme runs through the chapters in this volume: the concern with social virtues and the social foundations on which they rest. The chapters deal with the ways societies determine what they consider virtuous, and with the tension between individual rights and social characterizations of the good. Above all, the chapters examine the social foundations and processes that make people better than they would be otherwise.

Many used to hold that virtues do not constitute a proper subject for a social scientist, and some still do. Social science was supposed to be value-free, to be scientific. However, there is nothing unscientific about finding the conditions under which virtue is nourished versus those in which it is undermined. Additionally, social science cannot be value-neutral. Whether it studies the relations between people of difference races, classes, genders, or nationalities, it inevitably deals with matters that entail value judgments. The same holds when the subjects of study are the alternatives society faces when dealing with those who violate its moral (and legal) precepts, and of course when the subject is the ultimate purpose of life in hyper-materialistic societies. Value judgments, though, should not be confused with being arbitrary declarations of one's values. The discipline of ethics is all about justifying the judgments we render. In this sense, these chapters cross the line between sociology and ethics (and maybe some other parts of social philosophy).

Why draw on the term "virtues" when social scientists often prefer to use the term "values?" Because values have acquired a rather relativistic connotation. Social scientists write about American values, Afrikaner values, and fascist values — as if they were all of a kind. A value is a value is a value. Virtues evoke a firmly anchored conception of the good. No one will speak of Nazi virtues, I hope. In effect, the term serves to flag that there are, as the Founding Fathers put it so well, some "self-evident truths." This is the way I use the term in the following pages.

The chapters are all Weberian in one limited sense: they assume that beliefs play an important role in history and society. Max Weber — whose work must be largely understood in the context of a grand and prolonged debate of European intellectuals with Karl Marx — did not maintain that economic and technological forces are unimportant. Weber merely was able to show that these forces are not dominant, but that they are only one of the factors that shape history and society. The other forces — values, moral commitments, shared understandings — define the area in which these chapters fall. To put it differently, the chapters assume that society cannot be understood or changed without attention to its and our normative facets.

The points made in the following chapters are made in two voices: that of the public intellectual and that of the academic. I have spent a lifetime trying to speak in both voices, addressing my colleagues while also reaching for a wider audience. While the voice changes as different audiences are addressed, the points do not. All speak to the condition of our society: the developments that brought us here, where these may carry us unless we change course, as well as where we might do well to stay the course.

The volume opens with an exploration of the relationship among racial and ethnic groups that make up American society. I turned to this subject when I read repeatedly that a considerable number of public leaders and colleagues believe that American society is in the process of being deeply transformed — from being a European-dominated society to one governed by a "majority of minorities." Black, Latino, and Asian Americans — I read — will become the majority of the country's population sometime after the year 2050 and will carry us in fundamentally new directions, compatible with their values and interests. I found that those who foresee such a turn are inadvertently racists, because they assume that people's pigmentation will determine their personal, social, and political views and actions. I show herein that the vast majority of all Americans, whatever their background or race, basically hail the same virtues and have the same dreams and aspirations. Moreover, far from growing apart, we are coming together through intermarriage and other processes to be discussed. America does not make homogenization a virtue, but neither does it employ apartheid of any kind or color. The record shows that, in American society, diversity continues to be well contained by unity. We are much more a monochrome society than a rainbow society, or one in which colors do not mix and there is no place for white (Chapter I).

A good society fosters a set of core virtues that defines that which it considers good. The good society is not a neutral one that leaves it up to its members to decide on their own whether or not they wish to pollute the environment, abandon their children, abuse their spouse, drink and drive, and so on. Some of these virtues are ensconced in law; others are only supported by informal social controls such as approbations for those who behave in line with the social norms and censure for those who violate them.

To sustain virtuous behavior, a good society relies more on its informal processes than on the law. As we have seen both during Prohibition and the recent war on drugs, unless most members of the society favor the behaviors the society considers virtuous, it is very difficult to make members of the society adhere to the social norms. Further, the more a society can rely on informal social processes, the less it must resort to the coercive tools of the state. Shaming members of the community who violate social norms is a major feature of the informal processes that keep people virtuous and out of jail. It is nevertheless rather poorly regarded. Hence, I set out to examine whether shaming people is shameful (Chapter II).

Sometimes it seems as if the only virtue we uphold wholeheartedly is getting richer, consuming ever more material goods and services. But numerous studies show that such a drive is utterly Sisyphusian: as people's income grows ever more, their contentment does not. Once their basic creature needs are well and securely sated, they aspire to enrich their social, cultural, and spiritual life. Affluent societies hence seem overdue for a reexamination of their purposes for the long run and of the sources of meaning in their members' lives, which might well lead to seeking to curb materialistic excesses. There are a few signs that such an examination may lead to a return of a moderate counterculture, what some have called "voluntary simplicity." Studying the matter, I found some rather surprising nascent developments that combine that old idea of "enough is enough" (and Maslow's ideas about moving up the hierarchy of human needs) with the transition to a knowledge-based economy. This economy seems to be increasingly governed by different laws than the industrial one — laws that might enable us, I was amazed to note, to escape scarcity to a significant extent and greatly enhance social justice. In this sense, less indeed can be more (Chapter III).

The spread of the Internet and the increasing amount of time people spend in cyberspace led several observers to be concerned about increases in atomization and isolation of modern living, coming on top of previous declines in community. To explore this subject I teamed up with a much younger person, one fully conversed with the digital world, a professor of computer sciences at the University of Washington, my son, Oren. We concluded that often the way in which the question is stated in this matter, as in so many others, affects the answer. The question has been often raised whether online communities could replace or duplicate offline ones. If the question is posed in this way, we concurred with those concerned with the negative social effects of cyberspace, the answer is in the negative. However, if one instead studies whether online communities have virtues all of their own, one finds that virtual communities can contribute to a rich social life, albeit in ways that differ from face-to-face ones. Off and online communities can fulfill the same basic social needs, although each has strengths and weaknesses of its own. Indeed, they can supplement one another rather well, and thus sustain and enrich interpersonal and communal life.

On revisiting the same questions but two years later in updating the original essay for publication in this book, I found numerous community-building developments in cyberspace that were not in place when we initially wrote our original article. I hence added those at the end of Chapter IV. The next step, we expect, will be adding audio and visual communications to text messages, which would make nonverbal feedback much easier and significantly further enrich online communities. The conclusion is not that there is nothing to be concerned about in cyberspace as far as social and communal life are concerned. However, cyberspace is becoming more community-friendly.

Communitarian thinking has been criticized as vague and bereft of specific policy implications. This is not a place to review the work of my colleagues, but numerous communitarian policy ideas have been presented over more than ten years in the communitarian quarterly I edit, *The Responsive Community*, ranging from sex education to gun control, from child care to organ donation.[1] Others are briefly indicated in my book, *The New Golden Rule*.[2] Furthermore, several are outlined in chapters included in this volume. One such discussion focuses on policies that concern the protection of children from material that is violent and vile in the media, including several that do not involve the state. These policies favor making devices such as V-chips and filters for computers available to parents and educators. Civil libertarians and libertarians have objected to these policies. Chapter V examines their arguments, their implications for liberal (in the political science sense of the term) theory, and argues from a communitarian viewpoint why these policies are justified.

My rather preliminary discussion of holidays in Chapter VI is aimed largely at encouraging my colleagues to dedicate more of their attention to this subject. More indirectly (and this may well take another publication) I hope to put an examination of the ways we celebrate on the national agenda. As I see it, the ways our holidays and rituals have been debased is a major cause of our current moral condition. Roughly two-thirds of all Americans hold that society is in a moral crisis. Asking what may be done about it has so far largely focused on the family, schools (especially on character education), and on the role of religion and spirituality in our personal and social life. An examination of the ways holidays and rituals have deteriorated and may be rejuvenated belongs in the same category of social forces and institutions — the seedbeds of virtue.

Social scientists have established that rituals (such as weddings, bar mitzvahs, and confirmations) and holidays are the occasions in which we reaffirm our moral commitments. During regular work days, our commitment to our virtues tends to run out as we rush about our business. Rituals and holidays are supposed to take us away from these daily routines and lead us to places where — often with our fellow citizens — we rededicate ourselves to that which is sacred, ennobling, spiritual. The chapter implies that this is often no longer the case for many of our rituals and holidays. For instance, Memorial Day was once a day on which Americans showed their appreciation for those who gave their lives for the country; the Fourth of July was once a day to express patriotism. For many Americans, these occasions have become little more than two more days on the beach. The move into cyberspace further contributes to the deterioration of our holidays. Cyberspace is in full swing 24 hours a day, seven days a week, 365 days a year. It knows no pause or break or holiday. One can shop, trade, or work in it at all times. Separating holidays from the daily routine now requires much greater effort and deliberate decision making than in the days when all workplaces, shops, and banks closed at least at some point.

That communities *can* foster virtues is a theme that runs through many of these chapters. The communities I refer to in Chapter VII and others therefore do not necessarily refer only to local or residential ones. The chapters encompass the full range of communities: small ones; communal attributes in large, even nation-size societies; and the beginning of still more encompassing communities, including regional ones (the European Union); and even a few, very preliminary touches of a world community. In a sense, all the chapters deal with how to make things more communitarian: from changing the forms of punishment to reach a deeper and more value-based consensus to using the Internet to build communities to exploring the foundations of a good society.

Professor Amy Gutmann raised the question whether there can be communities that are not oppressive, whether there can be Salems without witches.[3] My response is that contemporary communities, in our kinds of society, are much less overpowering than traditional ones used to be. Moreover, we have in place powerful correctives whose task is to ensure that communities will not violate people's rights. Obviously, these are not always effective. However, in an imperfect world, life sans communities may well cause much more harm than having occasionally to rein in communities that become overbearing. And we have in place — at least in principle — the forces that ought to serve to ensure that communities do not violate universal virtues, especially individual rights. These include all the structures and processes that back up the Constitution, especially the courts.

The concept of moral dialogues is introduced in Chapter VII and is revisited in others. It refers to dialogues that occur in both small and larger communities, in which shared characterizations of the good evolve. All communities have numerous values that are handed down to them from previous generations, but these are subject to constant editing by communal processes. I consider these dialogues of special importance for several reasons. First, they differ a great deal from the proceduralist and rationalist notion of reasoned deliberations. (That is, moral dialogues are a major concept that differentiates liberal from communitarian thinking.) Second, they are the processes through which social norms and behavior are recast without involving the state as a rule. And, finally, they provide ways to change our conceptions of what we consider our virtues to be, without losing them.

Social sciences provide a major tool that we can employ to understand and deal with the social realm. They help us to dissect and treat it. In the past, different social sciences each offered a rather distinct perspective on the world. But over the last few decades, the traditional division among sociology, economics, political science, psychology, and so on has become much less important as two languages of social science have been developed that cut across the traditional divisions. They might be referenced as the neoclassical paradigm (modeled after the assumptions of the dominant school of American economists) and the institutional paradigm. Thus a sociologist who draws on neoclassical terms and conceptions (for example in exchange sociology) has much more in common with colleagues from other social sciences who draw on the same paradigm (e.g., public choice in political science; law and economics among legal scholars) than with sociologists who rely on institutional concepts. The same holds for the other disciplines.

Recently, a small but important group of legal scholars who worked in the neoclassical paradigm (law and economics) discovered a concept long pivotal to the institutional paradigm, social norms (or mores). These are expressions of virtues, but on a less abstract and less general level. For example, assume that the expectation that you will spend time with your children is a norm, while respect for the family is a value. The legal scholars who rediscovered social norms differ significantly in the way they treat them. Some try more than others to incorporate social norms into the neoclassical paradigm; others begin to see the merit of the institutional paradigm. One may wonder why this is a matter one should consider to any great extent. The answer is that, like a prism, the way social norms are treated reveals volumes about alternative ways of thinking about the social world (Chapter VIII).

Over recent years, much attention has been paid to the civil society as the rich fabric of voluntary associations or intermediary bodies that stand between the state and the individual. The merits of the civil society are well known and need not be rehashed here. The question one faces, though, does it suffice to create and maintain a well- formed and nourished civil society to make for a good society, one that we find virtuous? Liberals may well point out that this is the wrong question, that society ought not to be formulated by a shared understanding of the good. Hence they might well prefer a civil society over the quest for a good society. Elsewhere, I spelled out the argument (following communitarian lines) why society requires shared formations of the good.[4] Here I studied which additional social structures and processes might help make the society into one that fosters virtues. One telltale sign is when we cease to view all voluntary associations as being of equal merit—the KKK and Hadassah, the Black Nation and the Urban League—and recognize that some are more in line with the virtues the society seeks to sustain than others. This and other indicators, and the issues raised by focusing on the good society beyond the civil society, are the subject of Chapter IX. This chapter led a dialogue between Professor Robert George and myself which seems to me to further clarify the issues and hence is appended in Chapter X.

Often, when I write about the moral condition of the country, the processes and structures that make a society better than it would be otherwise, some of my more progressive friends and colleagues cringe. The very terminology makes them uncomfortable. I tried to assuage their concerns in my discussion of the moral voice. I added a very preliminary questionnaire that might help study these matters empirically (Chapter XI).

Many increasingly recognize that the relativistic position—that notion that we should not judge others, especially the conduct of those in other culture—is not sustainable. There are several rather philosophical reasons scholars and others are abandoning relativism. I add a rather simple one: when we learn about sex slaves, the forced marriage of young girls to old men, the beheading of adulterous princes, or the amputation of the hands of thieves, moral responses do form in our hearts. The only choices we have are to leave them unexamined and be defensive about them, or freely acknowledge them and try to spell out the reasons we judge such conduct one way or the other. Neutrality is not an option. As we proceed, the question arises, on what grounds can we base such cross- cultural judgments? I grapple with this difficult question in Chapter XII.

Both supportive and critical reviewers of the chapter expressed surprise at the position repeatedly articulated here that one can combine a commitment to universal individual rights with fostering the particularistic virtues of a given community. While I realize that Asian communitarians and early communitarians have often viewed commitment to the values of communities as contrasting with individual rights, this opinion pushes them into an untenable position of cultural relativism because there is no cross-cultural foundation on which to base judgments. In contrast, I argue that communities must be contained, less they turn abusive. Individual rights are a major source of such containment.

The fact that universal and particularistic claims occasionally conflict of course does not invalidate either, nor does it constitute evidence that the two cannot be reconciled. On the contrary, I found here as elsewhere, that it is very productive to take as one's starting point that social virtues cannot be satisfactorily defined by relaying one paramount moral principle or "value" (e.g., liberty); that we best make our starting point that the characterization of social virtues requires squaring often partially incompatible principles. (This point has been much emphasized by Philip Selznick.)

A preliminary sense that a high respect for individual rights and particularistic community commitment can be reconciled can be gleaned from life in the early kibbutzim. Members had the full assortment of individual rights and a considerable core of rather strong, shared, community-specific normative commitments. Moreover, members learned to deal with conflicting demands. For instance, they realized that they were free to say everything on their minds, but that certain expressions would undermine the social world in which they live. (Free speech protects offensive speech but does not mandate it. Communities can frown on certain speech but as long as they do not ban it, they do not offend the right of free speech.) In other situations, members coped with conflicting demands by leaning in one or the other direction, as specific situations and considerations suggested. Thus on occasion, freedom of assembly came into conflict with the need of the members to work hard in the kibbutz's farm, and hence turn in early. As a result, when there were no burning issues on week-days, assemblies were cut short, or if the matters had agitated a good number of members, they were then deprived of sleep.[5]

In the two years I spent teaching at the Harvard Business School, no line I learned stayed with me more than the idea that "the corporation belongs to all who invest in it." These include of course not merely the shareholders, but all people who work long and hard for a corporation, and communities that provide corporations with various assets (e.g., tax exemptions). I hence joined others who explored the idea that corporations belong to all the stakeholders rather than merely to the shareholders. How far one can carry this idea, and whether it would make corporations more virtuous, remains an open question (Chapter XIII).

Amitai Etzioni
Washington, D.C., 2000

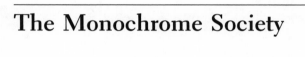

The Monochrome Society

I

The Monochrome Society

Various demographers and other social scientists have been predicting for years that the end of the white majority in the United States is near, and that there will be a majority of minorities. A 1997 CNN special program was devoted to the forthcoming majority of people of color in America.[1] That same year, President Clinton called attention to this shift in an address at the University of California at San Diego on a renewed national dialogue about race relations.[2] His argument was that such a dialogue is especially needed as a preparation for the forthcoming end of the white majority, which will occur somewhere in the middle of this century. In his January 2000 State of the Union address, Clinton claimed that "within ten years there will be no majority race in our largest state, California. In a little more than fifty years, there will be no majority race in America. In a more interconnected world, this diversity can be our greatest strength."[3] White House staffer Sylvia Mathews provided the figures as 53% white and

47% a mixture of other ethnic groups by 2050.[4] Pointing to such figures, Clinton asked rhetorically if we should not act now to avoid America's division into "separate, unequal and isolated" camps.[5]

Some have reacted to the expected demise of the white majority with alarm or distress. Arthur M. Schlesinger, Jr., decries the "cult of ethnicity" that has undermined the concept of Americans as "one people."[6] He writes, "Watching ethnic conflict tear one nation after another apart, one cannot look with complacency at proposals to divide the United States into distinct and immutable ethnic and racial communities, each taught to cherish its own apartness from the rest."[7] He also criticizes diversity and multiculturalism, arguing that "the United States has to set a monocultural example in a world rent by savage ethnic conflict; the United States must demonstrate 'how a highly differentiated society holds itself together.'"[8] James Q. Wilson writes, "The third condition [for democracy] is *homogeneity* . . . as Daniel P. Moynihan has observed, the deepest and most pervasive source of human conflict is ethnic rivalry."[9]

Dale Maharidge, a professor and journalist who has conducted hundreds of interviews concerning race, class, and ethnicity in California, has written about the end of the white majority in America in his book, *The Coming White Minority: California's Eruptions and America's Future*. He reports that sometime between the date of his book's publication in 1996 and the year 2000, California's population will have become less than 50% white. He writes, "'Minorities' will be in the majority," a precursor to the 2050 state of racial composition nationwide, when "the nation will be almost half nonwhite."[10]

Maharidge comments that his interviews, observations, and research have shown that, especially in California,

[W]hites are scared. The depth of white fear is underestimated and misunderstood by progressive thinkers and the media. Whites dread the unknown and not-so-distant tomorrow when a statistical turning point will be reached that could have very bad consequences for them. They fear the change that seems to be transforming their state into something different from the rest of the United States. They fear losing not only their jobs but also their culture. Some feel that California will become a version of South Africa, in which whites will lose power when minorities are the majority.[11]

Whites in California have demonstrated their fear of the "browning" of America by forming residential "'islands' that are surrounded by vast ethnic or transitional communities, as well as deserts, mountain wilderness, and the ocean," demonstrating, Maharidge predicts, "what the rest of America might become."[12] Whites and nonwhites alike also passed the anti-immigrant Proposition 187, which Maharidge links to these same fears about the end of the white majority. He warns, "California's electoral discord has emanated from whites. There is ample evidence that white tension could escalate. What will California be like in 2010, when nonwhites make up 60% of the population? . . . And how will California's actions influence the rest of the nation as non-Hispanic whites fall from 76% of the U.S. populace to just over half in 2050?"[13]

In contrast, John Isbister, a professor of economics at the University of California at Santa Cruz, asks us to ponder whether America is too white. He contends, "The decline in the white proportion is a healthy development for the country. . . . The principal case for a falling white proportion is simply this: it will be easier for us to transform a society of hostility and oppression into one of cooperation if we are dealing not with a majority versus several small minorities, but with groups of roughly equivalent size."[14]

ONE PEOPLE

As I see it, both views — that of alarm and that which celebrates the ending of the white majority and the rise of a majority of minorities — are fundamentally wrong because these positions are implicitly and inadvertently racist: they assume that people's pigmentation, or, more generally, racial attributes, determine their visions, values, and votes.[15] Actually, I claim and will show that very often the opposite is true.

The fact is that America is blessed with an economic and political system as well as culture and core values and much else that, while far from flawless, is embraced by most Americans of all races and ethnic groups. (To save breath, from here on, race is used to encompass ethnicity.) It is a grievous error to suggest that because American faces or skin tones may appear more diverse some fifty years from now, most Americans who hail from different social backgrounds will seek to follow a different agenda or hold a different creed than a white majority. While, of course, nobody can predict what people will believe or do fifty years hence, there is strong evidence that if they behave in any way that resembles current behavior of white, black, brown, yellow, red, or other Americans, they will share the same basic aspirations, core values, and mores. Moreover, current trends, during a period in which the nonwhite proportion of the population already has increased, further support the thesis that while the American society may well change, whites and nonwhites will largely change together.

A fair number of findings, we shall see shortly, support the thesis that American society is basically much more of one color — if one looks at conduct and beliefs rather than pigmentation and other such external, skin-deep indications.

A word about the inadvertent racism involved in the opposite position. To argue that all or most members of a given social group behave the way some do is the definition of prejudice.[16] This holds true not merely when one argues that all (or most) Jews, blacks, or those belonging to any other social group have some unsavory qualities, but also when one argues that all (or most) of a given group are antiwhite, alienated, and so on because some (often actually a small minority) are.

One may argue that while of course there is no direct correlation between race and political conduct, social thinking, and the values to which one subscribes, there are strong correlations. But is this true? Even if one controls for class differences? Or, is race but one factor among many that affect behavior? And if this is the case, might it be that singling out this biological given and unyielding factor, rather than paying full attention to all the others, reflects a divisive political agenda rather than social fact? Above all, are there significant correlations between being nonwhite and most political, social, and ideological positions? I turn now to findings supporting the thesis that there are many more beliefs, dreams, and views that whites and nonwhites of all colors share than those that divide them.

Some findings out of many that could be cited illustrate this point: A 1992 survey found that most black and Hispanic Americans (86% and 85%, respectively) desired "fair treatment for all, without prejudice or discrimination."[17] One may expect that this value is of special concern to minorities, but white Americans who took part in this survey felt the same way. As a result, the proportion of all Americans who agreed with the quoted statement about the importance of fairness was close to the above figures, at 79%.[18]

A poll of New York residents showed that the vast majority of respondents considered teaching "the common heritage and values that we share as Americans" to be "very important."[19] One may expect this statement to reflect a white, majoritarian value. However, minorities endorsed this position more strongly than whites: 88% of Hispanics and 89% of blacks, compared to 70% of whites agreed.[20]

A nationwide poll found that equal proportions of blacks and whites, 93%, concurred that they would vote for a black presidential candidate.[21] Another national poll found that "over 80% of all respondents in every category — age, gender, race, location, education, and income — agreed" with the statement that freedom must be tempered by personal responsibility.[22]

Far from favoring placing stress on different heritages, approximately 85% of all parents; 83% of African American parents; 89% of Hispanic American parents; and 88% of foreign-born parents agreed with the statement, "To graduate from high school, students should be required to understand the common history and ideas that tie all Americans together."[23]

And far from stressing differences in the living conditions and economic status of different groups, views about the nature of life in America are shared across racial lines. According to the National

Opinion Research Center's (NORC) 1994 General Social Survey, 70% of blacks and 60% of whites agreed that "the way things are in America, people like me and my family have a good chance of improving our standard of living."[24] Likewise, 81% of blacks and 79% of whites reported to NORC that "the quality of life is better in America than in most other advanced industrial countries."[25] And, 84% of all parents surveyed — 80% of foreign-born parents, 87% of Hispanic American parents, 73% of African American parents — agreed that "the U.S. is a unique country that stands for something special in the world."[26] Lawrence Otis Graham, an African American author, writing about African Americans, sums up the picture by stating, "Blacks, like any other group, want to share in the American dream."[27] The American dream, not some other or disparate one.

Close percentages of blacks (70%) and whites (65%), in a poll conducted in 1994, agreed that "the U.S. has made some or a lot of progress in easing black-white tensions in the past ten years."[28] In the same poll, 70% of whites and 65% of blacks said that "racial integration has been good for society."[29]

Sociologist Alan Wolfe finds in his middle-class morality project, which surveyed whites, blacks, Hispanics, Asians, Native Americans, and "others," that a striking majority of respondents disagreed or strongly disagreed with the statement, "There are times when loyalty to an ethnic group or to a race should be valued over loyalty to the country as a whole."[30]

Even in response to a deliberately loaded question, a 1997 poll showed that similarities between the races are much larger than differences. Asked, "Will race relations in this country ever get better?" 43% of blacks and 60% of whites replied in the affirmative.[31] (The pollsters tended to focus on the 17% who struck a different position rather than on the 43% who embraced the same one. The difference between 57% of blacks and 40% of whites who did not believe that race relations were going to get better was also 17%.)

While Americans hold widely ranging opinions on *what* should be done about various matters of social policy, people across racial and ethnic categories identify the same issues as important to them, and to the country. For instance in a 1996 survey, whites, African Americans, Latinos, and Asian Americans concurred that education was "the most important issue facing [their] community today."[32] Similarly, more than 80% of blacks, Latinos, and whites shared the belief that it was "'extremely important' to spend tax dollars on 'educational opportunities for children.'"[33] In another survey, 54% of blacks and 61% of whites ranked "increased economic opportunity" as the most important goal for blacks.[34] And 97% of blacks and 92% of whites rated violent crime a "very serious or most serious problem" in a 1994 poll.[35]

As we can see in Table 1, whites, African Americans, Latinos, and Asian Americans agreed about areas of life that had gotten worse or harder for "people like [them]" between 1985 and 1995. Between 45% and 55% agreed that public schools had worsened; 50 to 60% agreed that getting a good job was more difficult; between 48% and 55% within each group agreed that finding "decent, affordable housing" was tougher, and between 34% and 48% found it more challenging "for families like [theirs] to stay together."[36]

Table 1
Are the Problems of People Like You Getting Worse?

"During the past ten years, has XXX gotten better, worse, or stayed the same (OR become easier or harder) for people like you (OR families like yours)?" (Numbers given are the percentage of people in each category saying "worse" or "harder.")

	Whites	African Americans	Latinos	Asian Americans
	N = 802	N = 474	N = 252	N = 353
Public schools	55	57	45	47
To get good jobs	56	60	50	56
To find decent, affordable housing	55	49	55	48
For families like yours to stay together	45	48	40	34
Health care	44	39	30	30

Source: *Washington Post*/Kaiser Family Foundation/Harvard School of Public Health Survey Project, 1995: 75–76. Reprinted with permission.

More specifically, the following percentages said that each area was "worse" or "harder": public schools—whites 55%, African Americans 57%, Latinos 45%, Asian Americans 47%; getting good jobs—whites 56%, African Americans 60%, Latinos 50%, Asian Americans 56%; finding decent, affordable housing—whites 55%, African Americans 49%, Latinos 55%, Asian Americans 48%; for families like theirs to stay together—whites 45%, African Americans 48%, Latinos 40%, Asian Americans 34%.

Other problems that troubled America's communities highlighted points of convergence among the views of members of various racial and ethnic groups. "Between 80 and 90% of black, white, and 'other' Americans agreed that it was 'extremely important' to spend tax dollars on 'reducing crime' and 'reducing illegal drug use' among youth."[37] In addition, some shared public policy preferences emerged. Among whites, African Americans, Latinos, and Asian Americans surveyed by the *Washington Post*/Kaiser Family Foundation/Harvard School of Public Health Survey Project, between 75% and 82% of each group felt "strongly" that Congress should balance the budget. Between 30% and 41% were convinced that Congress should instate limited tax breaks for businesses; between 46% and 55% concurred that Congress should cut personal income taxes; between 53% and 59% agreed that Congress should reform Medicare (see Table 2).[38]

More specifically, the following percentages of each group felt "strongly" that Congress should take action on the following items: balance the budget—whites 82%, African Americans 79%, Latinos 75%, Asian Americans 75%; provide limited tax breaks for businesses—whites 39%, African Americans 41%, Latinos 41%, Asian Americans 30%; cut personal income taxes—whites 52%, African Americans 50%, Latinos 55%, Asian Americans 46%; reform Medicare—whites 53%, African Americans 58%, Latinos 59%, Asian Americans 58%. As well, 67% of all parents—68% of African American parents, 66% of Hispanic American parents, and 75% of foreign-born parents—told *Public Agenda* that the most important thing for public schools to do for new immigrant children was "to teach them English as quickly as possible, even if this means they fall behind in other subjects."[39]

Table 2
Policy Preferences for Congressional Action

"For each issue, please tell me if you think this is something Congress should do or should not do." (Numbers given are the percentage of people in each category saying "strongly feel Congress should do.")

	Whites	African Americans	Latinos	Asian Americans
	N = 802	N = 474	N = 252	N = 353
Limited tax breaks for businesses	39	41	41	30
Balance the budget	82	79	75	75
Cut personal income taxes	52	50	55	46
Reform the welfare system	83	73	81	68
Reform Medicare	53	58	59	58
Put more limits on abortion	35	32	50	24
Limit affirmative action	38	25	30	27

Source: *Washington Post*/Kaiser Family Foundation/Harvard School of Public Health Survey Project, 1995: 73–74. Reprinted with permission.

More African-Americans than whites or Hispanics thought that "the U.S. is the greatest country in the world, better than all others." However, the differences were small (African Americans 60%; whites 55%; Hispanic Americans 48%). The percentages were similarly close when respondents were asked to what extent they were proud to live under the American political system — 76% of whites, 73% of African Americans, 71% of Hispanic Americans said they were proud.[40]

All this is not to suggest that there are no significant differences of opinion along social lines, especially when matters directly concern race relations. For instance, many whites and many blacks (although by no means all of either group) take rather different views of the guilt of O. J. Simpson. One survey will stand for many with similar findings that could be cited: 62% of whites believed Simpson was guilty of the murders of which he was accused and acquitted, in contrast to 55% of African Americans who believed he was not guilty.[41]

Likewise, concerning affirmative action, 51% of blacks in a 1997 poll favored programs which "give preferential treatment to racial minorities," a much higher percentage than the 21% of whites who favored such programs.[42] And a very large difference appears when one examines voting patterns. For instance, in 1998, 55% of whites versus 11% of African Americans voted for Republican candidates for Congress.[43] And recent surveys have found several startling differences in the extent to which African Americans trust the government (Table 3).[44]

Still, if one considers attitudes toward the basic tenets of the American creed, the overwhelming majority of blacks are surprisingly accepting of them. A 1998 *Public Perspective* poll found that 54% of blacks and 66% of whites agreed with the statement, "In the United States today, anyone who works hard enough can make it economically." A 1994 national survey reported that 67% of blacks and 77% of

Table 3
Trusting the Government: Differences among African Americans and White Americans

Question	African Americans (%)	Whites (%)	Difference (%)
Some people say the CIA has been involved in importing cocaine for distribution in the black community. Do you think this is absolutely true, probably true, probably not true, or absolutely not true? (% responding true)	73	16	57
Some people say that HIV and AIDS are being used as part of a plot to deliberately kill African Americans. Do you think that this is absolutely true, probably true, probably not true, or absolutely not true? (% probably true and absolutely true)	62	21	41
Verdict [in the 1992 Rodney King trial] shows blacks cannot get justice in this country. (% agree)	81	27	54
Do you think blacks and other minorities receive same treatment as whites in the criminal justice system? (% no)	54	9	45

Source: Robert C. Smith and Richard Seltzer, *Contemporary Controversies and the American Radical Divide.* (Lanham, Md.: Rowman & Littlefield, 2000), 86, 88, 121, 128.

whites agreed that "a basic American belief has been that if you work hard you can get ahead—reach your goals and get more," was still true. Most blacks (77%) said they preferred equality of opportunity to equality of results (compared to 89% of whites). When it came to "Do you see yourself as traditional or old-fashioned on things such as sex, morality, family life, and religion, or not?" the difference between blacks and whites was only 5%. When asked whether values in America were seriously declining, the difference was down to one percentage point.

A question from an extensive national survey conducted at the University of Virginia by James Davison Hunter and Carl Bowman asked: "How strong would you say the U.S. decline or improvement is in its moral and ethical standards?" Twenty-three percent of blacks and 33% of whites said there was a strong decline, while 40% of blacks and 38% of whites said there was a moderate decline, and 29% of blacks and 24% of whites said the standards were holding steady.[45] When asked "How strong would you say the U.S. decline or improvement is in the area of family life?" 18% of blacks and 26% of whites said there was a strong decline, while 42% of blacks and 40% of whites saw a moderate decline, and 31% of blacks and 25% of whites said family life had held steady.[46] Roughly the same percentages of blacks and whites strongly advocated balancing the budget, cutting personal income taxes, reforming the welfare system, and reforming Medicare.[47] Percentages were also nearly even in responses to questions on abortion and marijuana.[48]

Hunter and Bowman found that "the majority of Americans do not . . . engage in identity politics—a politics that insists that opinion is mainly a function of racial, ethnic, or gender identity or identities rooted in sexual preference."[49] While there are some disagreements on specific issues and policies, this study found more similarities than discrepancies. Even when asked about such divisive issues as the direction of changes in race and ethnic relations, the similarities across lines were considerable. Thirty-two percent of blacks, 37% of Hispanics, and 40% of whites felt these relations were holding steady; 46%, 53%, and 44%, respectively, felt they had declined. (The remainder felt that they had improved.)[50] That is, on most issues, four out of five — or more — agreed with one another, while those who differed amounted to less than 20% of all Americans. There is no anti-anything majority here, nor is there likely to be one in the future.

Similarly, 81% of blacks, like 71% of all Americans, in a 1998 survey thought that blacks and whites "generally get along fairly well."[51] When asked in 1994, "When today's/your children reach your age, do you expect that race relations will have improved, will have worsened, or will be about the same as today?" a close 48% of blacks and 51% of whites concurred that relations would be better.[52] In 1998, the Gallup Organization found a similar position among whites and blacks (60% of whites and 54% of blacks agreed) that only a few white people dislike blacks. Only 5% of blacks and 2% of whites said that "almost all white people dislike blacks."[53]

Notably, nearly half of both blacks and whites want to set racial questions aside as much as possible. In a 1995 survey for *Newsweek*, Princeton Survey Research Associates found that 48% of blacks and 47% of whites agreed that the Census Bureau should stop collecting information on race and ethnicity "in an effort to move toward a more color-blind society — even if it becomes more difficult to measure progress on civil rights and poverty programs."[54]

As already suggested, many pollsters and those who write about their findings, tend to play up small differences and downplay large similarities. During my days at Columbia University's Bureau of Applied Social Research we were advised to use the "fully-only" writing device. Thus, we would write that fully, say 9% agreed with whatever we wanted to play up, while only 43% disagreed. It should hence be stressed that in most of the figures cited above the differences among the races are much smaller than the similarities. On most issues there are no findings that could be considered, even by a far-fetched interpretation, to show a "white" versus a "black" position, nor a single position of any group of people of other colors. That is, none of these findings suggest — in fact, they directly contradict — that race determines a person's views, values, or votes.

Most interestingly, *differences among social groups that include both blacks and whites are often larger than differences among races.* For instance, sociologist Janet Saltzman Chafetz concludes her study of such differences with the statement that "in any dimension one wishes to examine — income, education, occupation, political and social attitudes, etc. — the range of difference within one race or gender group is almost as great as that between various groups."[55] A 1994 Kansas City study showed that "income differences between age groups in a given race are greater than income differences between entire races."[56] While much has been made of the digital divide, Alan Westin — the most systematic surveyor of this field — reports that differences in the use of computers and the Internet are larger between men and women than between the races.[57]

Rather little attention has been paid in this context to the fact that while African Americans are the least mainstreamed group, there is a growing black middle class, many members of which have adopted lifestyles and aspirations similar to those of other middle-class Americans — and which diverge from those of other black Americans. For instance, a 1998 *Wall Street Journal* public opinion poll showed differences within distinct classes of a single race to be greater than differences among those races, on several, albeit not on all, key issues. For instance, 82% of middle-class whites and 70% of non-middle-class whites reported satisfaction with their personal finances (a disparity of 12%), while 74% of middle-class blacks and 56% non-middle-class blacks reported such satisfaction (a difference of 18%). The differences of 12% and 18%, respectively, are higher than the differences in opinion between the races (8% difference between middle-class whites and blacks, and 14% difference between non-middle-class whites and blacks).[58] (William Julius Wilson is among the scholars who have pointed out the significance of class differences when studying racial differences.)

I am not suggesting that race makes no difference in a person's position, feelings, or thinking. And one can find polls, especially in response to single questions, that show strong racial influence. However, race does not *determine* a person's response and often, on all important matters, Americans of different social backgrounds share many convictions, hopes, and goals, even in recent years, as we see the beginning of the decline of the white majority. Moreover, each racial group is far from homogeneous in itself. Differences within each group abound, further contradicting any notion of a nonwhite united majority facing a unanimous white group, a view often promoted by champions of identity politics.

RACE: A SOCIAL CONSTRUCTION

Many social scientists call into question the very category of race drawn on by those who foresee increasing racial diversity. Alain Corcos, author of several books on genetics, race, and racism, notes that "race is a slippery word," one that is understood in varying manners at various times, one without a single definition we may readily grasp. He writes, "Race is a slippery word because it is a biological term, but we use it every day as a social term. . . . Social, political, and religious views are added to what are seen as biological differences. . . . Race also has been equated with national origin. . . . with religion . . . with language."[59]

The diversity of characteristics by which race is and has been defined points to its unsatisfactory quality as a tool for categorizing human beings. Both anthropological and genetic definitions of race prove inadequate, because while each describes divisions among the human population, each fails to provide reliable criteria for making such divisions. As Corcos notes, they "are vague. They do not tell us how large divisions between populations must be in order to label them races, nor do they tell us how many there are."[60] Importantly, "These things are, of course, all matters of choice for the classifier."[61]

Considering the biology of race, Corcos notes that biological divisions do not hold up. "Geographical and social barriers have never been great enough to prevent members of one population from breeding with members of another. Therefore, any characteristic which may have arisen in one population at one time will be transferred later to other populations through mating."[62] Corcos further chronicles scientific and social scientific attempts to categorize humans into races by such sundry methods as craniology and evaluating skin coloring, nose size and shape, and other physical characteristics. Despite these efforts, "Scientists have been unable to classify humanity into races using physical characteristics such as skin color, shape of nose or hair, eye color, brain size, etc. They also have been unable to use characteristics such as blood type or other genetic markers."[63]

Social anthropologist Audrey Smedley, professor at Virginia Commonwealth University, shares these observations. She admits there are apparent biophysical differences among humans, but reminds us that "race originated as the imposition of an arbitrary value system on the facts of biological (phenotypic) variations in the human species."[64] That is, she suggests race is imposed from *without*, not generated from within. Race "was the cultural invention of arbitrary meanings applied to what appeared to be natural divisions within the human species. The meanings had social value but no intrinsic relationship to the biological diversity itself."[65]

Racial categories are learned rather than innate. Like other cultural traditions such as food, clothing, and musical preferences, racial categories are passed from generation to generation. Psychological anthropologist Lawrence Hirschfeld finds "that children as young as three have a complex understanding of society's construction of racial categories. Children do not sort people into different races based only on physical differences. . . . Society's 'racial' assignments provide more of a signature of 'other' than do physical differences. For children, race does not define the person."[66]

To put these concepts in plainer language: at first it seems obvious that there are black, brown, yellow, and white people. But upon second thought, we realize that there are great differences within each group, even if we choose to focus on, for example, skin color rather than on, say, manners. And, these differences do not parallel one another. That is, persons with darker skin are not necessarily short (or tall), and so on. Race, which has been magnified in recent decades by identity politics, is but one imprecise social category, one that does not define human conduct any more than numerous other social attributes (especially income), and often to a much lesser extent.

Particularly telling is that many groups once considered separate races 100 years ago are no longer so viewed today. The classification changed in law, public policy, the press, and in the public mind. Jewish, Slavic, Irish, Polish, and many other ethnic groups were considered races in 1910 in the United States. Matthew Frye Jacobson refers to the category of race as "fabricated" in his aptly titled book, *Whiteness of a Different Color: European Immigrants and the Alchemy of Race*.[67] A DNA study conducted by Howard University found that some 30% of all black males tested had some white DNA.[68]

Especially important for the future "monochrome-ness" of American society is the way Hispanic Americans come to view themselves and to be characterized by others. The special significance of this development, surprisingly infrequently discussed, is that Hispanics constitute the fastest-growing, major American social group due to high levels of immigration, high rates of childbirth, and because the group is gaining in political self-awareness and experience. Given that the number of African Americans is growing much more slowly (mainly because there is very little immigration from Africa), and that this group already has a relatively high level of political presence and hence less room to grow in this area, Hispanics are very likely to overtake African Americans in the next decade as the leading non-European group in American society.

As a result, in the next decades, we are quite likely to stop talking about a black and white society, one in which Hispanics are not mentioned at all or only as an afterthought, as countless books and essays did in the recent past, and instead focus on the relationship between European Americans and Hispanic Americans. The picture that is going to emerge from such a change in perspective will be deeply affected by the way Hispanics are depicted.

Some attempts have been made to define Hispanics as a separate race — a brown one. If such a characterization had caught on, it would have increased divisiveness in America; fortunately, from the viewpoint of those who favor a monochrome society, most Americans and the media continue to view Hispanics as an ethnic group rather than a race.

Attempts to change the social construction of Hispanics, however, continue. Instead of simply treating them as one white group among others (groups that differ in their features, for instance, many immigrants from the Middle East are quite "dark," but are viewed as whites in contemporary America), continuous attempts are being made to classify Hispanics as something different—and to lump them with the nonwhite groups. Thus, recent press reports employed the category "non-Hispanic whites," who are projected to lose their majority in July 2001 in California, and in later years all over America.[69]

There is of course no God-given or scientific reason to classify Hispanics as different from other white ethnic groups. Indeed, the category of "non-Hispanic whites" reflects a mixture of the ways statistics are kept (which themselves reflect normative and political pressures) and an ideological agenda, although those who use this term do not necessarily subscribe to it or are even aware of this agenda. (As Orlando Paterson says, "These are all basically political decisions, the census always just reflects changing attitudes.")[70]

The ways Hispanics come to see themselves in the near future is the single most important factor in determining to what extent America will continue to be a primarily monochrome society. If Hispanics view themselves largely as white, continue to share basic American values, and recognize that they are not all of one kind (just the way other white groups are not), America's diversity will not overwhelm its essential unity. If Hispanics view themselves as if they were a racial minority, of one kind, and increasingly ally themselves with those African Americans who seek social and normative separateness (which by itself is a declining number), maintaining a monochrome America will be seriously challenged.

"ASIAN AMERICANS" AND "LATINOS"?

The very notion that there are social groups called "Asian Americans" or "Latinos" is largely a statistical artifact (reflecting the way social data are coded and reported), promoted by some ethnic leaders, and a shorthand the media find convenient. Most so-called Asian Americans do not see themselves, well, as Asian Americans, and many resent being labeled this way.[71] Many Japanese Americans do not feel a particular affinity to Filipino Americans, Pakistani Americans, or Korean Americans.[72] And the feeling is rather reciprocal. As Professor Paul Watanabe, from the University of Massachusetts, an expert on Asian Americans and himself an American of Japanese descent, puts it: "There's this concept that all Asians are alike, that they have the same history, the same language, the same background. Nothing could be more incorrect."[73]

William Westerman of the International Institute of New Jersey complains about Americans who tend to ignore the cultural differences among Asian nations, which reflect thousands of years of tradition. He wonders how the citizens of the United States, Canada, and Mexico would feel if they were all treated as indistinguishable "North Americans."[74]

The same holds for the so-called Latinos, including three of my sons. Americans of Hispanic origin trace their origins to many different countries and cultures.[75] Eduardo Diaz, a social service administrator, puts it this way: "There is no place called Hispanica. I think it's degrading to be called something that doesn't exist. Even Latino is a misnomer. We don't speak Latin."[76] A Mexican American office worker remarked that when she is called Latina it makes her think "about some kind of island."[77] Many Americans from Central America think of themselves as "mestizo," a term that refers to a mixture of Central American Indian and European ancestry. Among those surveyed in the National Latino Political Survey in 1989, the greatest number of respondents chose to be labeled by their country of origin, as opposed to "pan-ethnic" terms such as "Hispanic" or "Latino."[78]

A recent extensive survey comparing Mexican, Puerto Rican, Cuban, and Central/South American attitudes and political behavior found numerous differences among these groups. Support for legal abortion ranged from 32% (Central/South Americans) to almost double that (60%, Puerto Ricans). In response to a question about party affiliation, the percentage of Hispanics identifying themselves as Republicans ranged from 12% (Central/South Americans) to 34% (Cubans).[79] Large differences were also found in the rate to which different Latino groups became United States citizens, which reflected differences in their feelings both about their country of origin and their willingness to become Americans. The percentages of those who had become citizens ranged from 53% (Cubans) to 26% (Central/South Americans).[80]

Another study found that:

> Just as majorities often disdain minorities, minorities often dislike one another, sometimes more harshly than majorities. For example, an early 1990s Harris poll found that 46% of Hispanic Americans and 42% of African Americans agreed that Asians are "unscrupulous, crafty, and devious in business," whereas only 27% of whites thought so. Fully 68% of Asians and 49% of African Americans agreed that Hispanics tend "to have bigger families than they are able to support"—as did 50% of whites. Some 33% of Hispanics and 22% of Asians believed that African Americans, "Even if given a chance, aren't capable of getting ahead"—in contrast to 12% of whites. And "when it comes between choosing between people and money, Jews will choose money," thought 54% of African Americans, 43% of Hispanics and 35% of Asians, but only 12% of non-Jewish whites.[81]

The significance of these and other such data is that far from seeing a country divided into two or three hardened minority camps, we are witnessing an extension of a traditional American picture: Americans of different origins identifying with groups of other Americans from the same country, at least for a while, but not with any large or more lasting group.

Far from there being a new coalition of nonwhite minorities soon to gain majority status (something President Clinton points to and Jesse Jackson dreams about as a rainbow, one that contains all colors but white), the groups differ greatly from each other — and within themselves.

To reiterate, on numerous issues, the differences among various minority groups are as big or bigger than those between these groups and "Anglo" Americans. For instance, while fewer Cuban Americans agree with the statement that U.S. citizens should be hired over non-citizens than Anglos (42% of Cubans compared to 51% of Anglos), other Hispanic groups agree more strongly than Anglos (55% of Puerto Ricans and 54% of Mexican Americans).[82] Quotas for jobs and college admissions are favored only by a minority of any of these four groups studied, but Cubans differ from Mexicans and Puerto Ricans more (by 14%) than from Anglos (by 12%).[83]

The fact that various minorities do not share a uniform view, which could lead them to march lockstep with other minorities to a new America (as some on the left fantasize) is also reflected in elections. Cuban Americans tend to vote Republican, while other Americans of Hispanic origin are more likely to vote for Democratic candidates.[84] Americans of Asian origin also cannot be counted on to vote one way or another. First-generation Vietnamese Americans tend to be strong anti-Communists and favor the Republican party, while older Japanese and Chinese Americans are more often Democrats, and Filipino Americans are more or less equally divided between the parties. (Of the Filipino Americans registered to vote, 40% list themselves as Democrats, 38% as Republicans, and 17% as independent.)[85]

THE LESSONS OF "NONWHITE" STATES AND CITIES

Some social scientists argue that we can learn about the future, in which nonwhite majorities will prevail, by examining the states and cities in which minorities already comprise the majorities. For instance, Peter Morrison, former head of the Population Research Center at RAND, suggests that one can see the future in cities that have a majority composed of minorities.[86]

One clear way to examine the impact of the rise of nonwhite majorities is to study election results. They show, as did the survey data cited above, that people of a given racial background often do not vote for a candidate of their color — and above all, that nonwhite groups often do not jointly support any one candidate of any one color or racial background. Any suggestion that race or ethnicity determines for whom one casts one's vote is belied by the facts. For example, Peter Skerry notes that "when first elected to the San Antonio City Council in 1975, [the popular Henry] Cisneros was the candidate of the Anglo establishment and received a higher proportion of Anglo than Mexican votes cast."[87]

We often encounter the future first in California.[88] In a 1991 Los Angeles election for the California State Assembly, Korean American, Filipino American, and Japanese American groups each ran their own candidate, thus splitting the so called "Asian American" vote, not deterred by the fact that they thereby ensured the election of a white candidate.[89]

In some cities that contain nonwhite majorities, we find white, black, and Hispanic mayors alternating, despite only relatively small changes in the composition of the city population. For instance, in Los Angeles, which is roughly 64% nonwhite (specifically, nearly 40% Hispanic, 14% black, nearly 10% Asian, and 0.5% American Indian according to the 1990 census),[90] Tom Bradley, an African American, served as mayor for 20 years, until 1993, when the citizens elected Richard Riordan, a white politician. New York City and San Francisco also have in recent years alternated between white and black mayors without witnessing any dramatic changes in the racial and ethnic backgrounds of those who inhabit those cities.

New York City, comprised of approximately 29% blacks, 24% Hispanics, and 7% Asians and Pacific Islanders, (nearly 60% nonwhites),[91] elected the white Ed Koch, then chose the African American David Dinkins, followed by a white mayor, Rudolph Giuliani.[92] San Francisco, a city made up of roughly 55% minorities (approximately 11% black, 30% Asian, 14% Hispanic, and 0.5% American Indian),[93] was served by three white mayors from 1976 through 1995, but elected the African American Willie Brown in 1996. Dallas, which is about 30% black, 21% Hispanic, and 2% Asian, had no African American mayor until 1995.[94] Philadelphia, long served by white mayors, elected Wilson Goode to serve between 1984 and 1992 as the city's first African American mayor. Goode was followed by the white Edward Rendell in this city of nearly 40% blacks, 6% Hispanics, and 3% Asians. The fact that cities like Washington, D.C. (nearly 66% black)[95] and Detroit (nearly 76% black)[96] tend to elect black mayors is beside the point, because neither comprises a coalition of minorities but one minority, and the only one that usually envisions itself as a single group.

Additionally, Virginia, in which whites outnumber minorities significantly (1.5 million minorities and 4.8 million whites), has elected a black governor. L. Douglas Wilder served from 1989 to January 1994.[97] In the rural and conservative Second District of Georgia, a two-thirds white voter majority reelected Sanford D. Bishop, Jr., an African American Democrat, to serve as their representative.[98] The state of Washington, comprised of only 4.5% Asian Americans, elected Gary Locke in 1996, putting in office the first Asian American governor in the mainland United States.[99] While one can find counter examples, the examples listed here indicate that the majority of minorities does not necessarily elect people of color, nor does the white majority necessarily elect white officials. Moreover, I expect more blurring in the future rather than less, given all the various vectors discussed in this analysis.

INTERMARRIAGE AND THE RISE OF "OTHERS"

Last but not least, the figures used by those who project a majority of minorities or the end of a white majority are misleading. These figures are based on a simplistic projection of past trends. How simplistic these projections often are can be quickly gleaned from the Census projection that the number of Native Americans will grow from

2,433,000 in 2000, or approximately 1% of the total population to 4,405,000, or approximately 1% of the total population by the year 2050, and to 6,442,000, or approximately 1% of the total population by the year 2100.[100] That is, 100 years and *no* change.

This tendency to depict the future as a continuation of the past is particularly misleading because it ignores the rapidly rising category of racially mixed Americans, the result of a rising number of cross-racial marriages and a rejection of monoracial categories by some others, especially Hispanic Americans.

One out of twelve marriages in 1995 (8.4%) were interracial/ethnic marriages. Intermarriage between Asian Americans and whites is particularly common; marriages between Hispanic Americans and whites are also rather frequent, while marriages between whites and blacks are the least common. In 1998, out-marriage by Hispanics of all generations totaled 16.7%, while non-Hispanic Asians out-married at a rate of 15% and non-Hispanic blacks out-married at a rate of 5%.[101]

Intermarriage between black and other Americans is less common, but also rising. "In 1990, 84% of all married black people over the age of 65 were in both-black marriages, but only 53% of married blacks under 25 were," according to the Statistical Assessment Service.[102] And the Census Bureau finds that over the past 20 years, the number of marriages between blacks and whites has more than quadrupled, increasing from 65,000 in 1970 to 296,000 in 1994.[103] From 1960 to 1997, the percentage of all marriages that were interracial grew from 0.4% to 2.3%.[104] Similarly, researchers Douglas Besharov and Timothy Sullivan found that the number of black-white marriages constituted 1.7% of all marriages in 1960, but represented 6% of all marriages in 1990.[105] A study from the University of Michigan reports that in the 1940s about 2% of black men married white women, whereas by the 1980s about 8% did so. And while in the 1940s about 1% of married black women had married interracially, in the 1980s that figure had reached nearly 3%.[106] The number of inter-marriages also increases with each subsequent generation living in the U.S. In the mid-1990s, slightly under 20% of first-generation Asian American women were intermarried, as opposed to slightly under

30% of the second generation and slightly over 40% of the third generation. Slightly under 10% of first-generation Hispanic women were intermarried, contrasting sharply with percentages in the mid-20s and mid-30s for second and third-generation women, respectively. Black intermarriage rates were much lower, even though there was an increase overall — no figures were over 5%.[107]

The trend toward intermarriage is strongest among the young; 30% of married Asian Americans have married outside the group, as have 16% of Hispanics and 11% of blacks in this age group.

"This is the beginning point of a blending of the races," predicts William Frey, a sociologist at the State University of New York at Albany. It is likely "that in these households racial or ethnic attitudes will soften," he says in *American Demographics* (Nov. 1999), as families realize that they can embrace many cultures without losing any one facet of their identity.[108]

About half of third-generation Mexican Americans marry non-Hispanic whites; even higher numbers of Asian Americans do the same.[109] Gregory Rodriguez has provided figures on this phenomenon, as shown in Figure 1.[110]

Altogether, since 1970, the proportion of marriages among people of different racial or ethnic origin increased by 72%. The 1990 Census noted 1.5 million interracial marriages.[111] Some put the number of children of mixed-race parents at 3 million, not including Hispanic mestizos and black Americans who have European or Native American ancestry.[112]

Another indication of some blurring of the lines among the races in American society can be gleaned from the fact that in the 1990 Census, 4%, or 9.8 million Americans, chose to classify themselves as "others," i.e., not members of any particular racial group. In a Census 2000 practice run, this number had increased to 5.4% of the sample.[113] The increase from 4 to 5.4% may seem minor, but given the size of the population, many hundreds of thousands are involved.

Even if the trends already cited do not accelerate and continue only at the present pace, the figures for 2050 may read something like

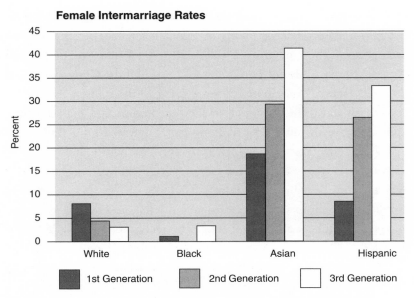

Female Intermarriage Rates

Legend: 1st Generation | 2nd Generation | 3rd Generation

(Categories: White, Black, Asian, Hispanic)

Figure 1: Female intermarriage rates. From: "Newcomers to America: The Successful Integration of Immigrants into American Society," National Immigration Forum, Washington, D.C., with permission.

the following: 51% white; 14% multiracial; 35% minorities. Far from dividing the country still further, the rise of the "others," along with the fact that more and more Americans will be of mixed heritage, with divergent backgrounds, will serve to blur the racial lines. That is, while there may well be more Americans of non-European origin, a growing number of the American white majority will have a Hispanic daughter- or son-in-law, an Asian stepfather or stepmother, and a whole rainbow of cousins. If one must find a simple image for the future of America, Tiger Woods, or Hawaii, as I see it, seems more appropriate than a view of a country in which Louis Farrakhan and his followers and the Aryan Nation are threatening one another.

Regrettably, identity politics led the U.S. Census Bureau to drop the category of "other" from its 2000 Census. This in turn makes it more difficult for Americans of mixed background, or those who wish to forgo racial labels, to declare themselves as what I would like to call "All Americans."[114] Because the way the Census constructs its categories affects the way many others do—for instance, those overseeing admissions to colleges—the category of other or multiracial Americans may well not gain as fast as it would if the Census followed its 1990 format. This in effect forces at least 10 million Americans into racial categories they seek to shed or modify, and makes American society seem more divided along racial lines than it actually is.

There are strong sociological reasons to argue that the U.S. Census reintroduce a nonracial category. (Others have suggested that this category be named "multiracial.") Inclusion of such a category would allow millions of Americans who are not, and do not see themselves as, members of any one race to be recognized as people with a blended heritage, reflecting the mixed heritage of America itself.

At issue is how we view ourselves as a nation. Are we going to continue to be divided by race? Or will we welcome the blurring of the lines that divide the races?

The number of Americans who refused a monoracial category grew from about 2.5 million in 1970[115] to 9.8 million by 1990.[116] If the 2000 Census had allowed, it is very likely that many more would have chosen the nonracial category. The main reason: rapidly increasing intermarriages.

The children of these couples are the main source of the continued increase in "multiracials." In addition, other Americans object to being racially categorized, or change their minds during their lifetime. The children of a couple I know—he black, she white—viewed themselves as white in primary school, black as adolescents, and now one passes as white and the other as black. What is gained by forcing such people to officially declare themselves one or the other?

The Census yielded to pressure from identity politics. It releases its data in two forms. One, a straightforward account; the other, "modified."[117] Here it reconfigured the statistics by re-boxing 9.8 million "other" Americans into monoracial categories!

Informal conversations with colleagues at the Census Bureau indicated that the Office of Management and Budget (which reviews all official questionnaires), yielded to pressure from several minority leaders. For instance, Ibrahim K. Sundiata from Brandeis University, who maintained that the "other" category reflects a drive to undermine black solidarity.[118]

Other African American leaders worried that the category of "other" would decrease the number of blacks in the nation's official statistics, and thus undermine the enforcement of antidiscrimination statutes and numerous social programs based on racial statistics. The NAACP and the Asian American Legal Defense and Education Fund, have disapproved of watering down nonwhite groups.[119]

As Gregory Rodriguez, a social researcher, states, "Some black groups, such as the NAACP and the Black Leadership Forum, a national coalition of the leaders of major civil rights organizations, are encouraging people to check just one box this year [2000]. The nuances and complexities of the multiracial future may be too threatening to the stark civil-rights era perspective forged in the segregationist past."[120]

Representative Carrie Meek (D-Fla.) explained: "The multiracial category would cloud the count of discrete minorities who are assigned to a lower track in public schools . . . kept out of certain occupations and whose progress toward seniority or promotion has been skewered."[121] Karen Narasaki, executive director of the National Asian Pacific American Legal Consortium, said the civil rights groups "won less on the strength of our intellectual arguments, and more on our political strength. OMB backed down."[122]

Whatever the motives, the 2000 Census instead will allow Americans to mark as many racial categories as their hearts desire — as long as they define themselves racially. The battle is already on as to how the results will be counted. African and Asian American groups demand that anyone who marks their race in any combination be counted as fully theirs. The Census has not yet announced its pleasure.

Only if the Census Bureau were to release the information referring to blended Americans as "multiracial" (or "nonracial," best as "All American"), would it encourage the nation to view itself as less divided. There are several indications that the country is ready for widespread changes in our social categories and thinking. Georgia and Indiana have already required government agencies to use the multiracial category. In California there is an Association for Multi-Ethnic Americans,[123] and Ohio, Illinois, Georgia, Indiana, and Michigan have introduced legislation to create a multiracial category on college applications.[124]

The notion that everybody who has any features shared by many African Americans and less common in other groups is black is particularly troubling. Colin Powell, of all people, articulated it when he objected to Tiger Woods considering himself All American, stating: "In America . . . when you look like me, you're black." Such views mirror the position of the American South (and South African apartheid) that everyone who has one drop of black blood, is all black. (Malcolm X quipped, "That must be *mighty* powerful blood.")[125] As Michael Lind says, "We're back to the one drop rule . . . I'm disgusted with the whole thing. This census should have been the first one not to identify people by race."[126] To reiterate, all concerned would be better off if we moved away from such rigid and immutable categorizations of people.

FURTHER MODERATION OF RACIAL AND ETHNIC LEADERSHIP

Predicting the political attitudes of leaders is especially difficult, surely as compared to demographic trends. One reason is that these attitudes are affected by many considerations including the conditions of the economy and which party controls the White House and Congress. However, for the following reasons I expect a secular trend of continued moderation from minority leadership over the next decades. (There will of course be exceptions, but I am speaking of the general pattern.) The part of moderation I am focusing on here is the one relevant to the issue at hand; the move from separatism and identity politics to "normal" interest group politics, that implicitly accept the basic societal framework.

One of the main reasons is the relative decline of African Americans in the total demographic and political picture. The Census Bureau has projected that the African American population, which currently, in the year 2000, makes up approximately 13% of the total U.S. population, will grow to approximately 15% in 2050, where it will remain steady to 2100.[127] In contrast, the Hispanic population, which currently makes up approximately 12% of the total U.S. population, is projected to rise to approximately 24% of the total U.S. population in 2050 and approximately 33% in 2100.[128] The Hispanic population is going to grow more rapidly because there is every reason to expect much more immigration of Hispanic origin than from Africa. (One should also note that whatever immigration there is from the West Indies and Haiti, these immigrants do not necessarily see themselves as African American or even part of one black community.)

The relative increase of the role of Hispanics versus blacks is significant because so far "minorities" has been largely identified in people's minds with blacks. Indeed, very often reference to race relations still evokes the term black and white while other groups are not mentioned at all or only as a second thought. This will change in the future as Hispanics continue to grow in relative size as well as in political awareness and organization.

The difference is especially relevant because blacks have been much slower to intermarry and otherwise be absorbed into the American society than other minorities. And on average, their leadership has been less moderate and more given to identity politics than the leaders of other groups. However, black leadership recently has been becoming less confrontational. (Compare, for instance, the speeches of Reverend Al Sharpton and Louis Farrakhan in recent years to a decade earlier.) There are numerous reasons for this trend. Not least of them is the rapid increase in the proportion of blacks that are middle class who, on average, tend to be more moderate than other blacks. The black middle class has grown significantly since the advent of the civil rights movement, and has "quadrupled since the '60s, doubling in the '80s alone."[129] In 1998, 40% of blacks defined themselves as middle class.[130] And, as Henry Louis Gates, Jr., states, "We don't have to pretend any longer that 35 million people can ever possibly be members of the same economic class. . . . Nor do they speak with one single voice, united behind one single leader. As each of us knows, we have never been members of one social or economic class and never will be."[131]

One may wonder whether Hispanic leadership in the future may be driven to less moderate identity politics. This is of course hard to predict. However, one notes that there will be also a growing Hispanic middle class and there is no obvious reason to expect that their tendency to intermarry and move up the economic and social ladders will slow down significantly. In contrast, Asian American leaders have tended, on average, to be so local and conservative in their orientation that they may well move a bit toward identity politics. Such a move, however, would still leave them rather moderate by comparison to many earlier African American leaders.

All said and done, while identity politics may well not end, one can expect — with the dethroning and simultaneous moderation of large parts of the African American leadership of minorities — identity politics to subside to a considerable extent. This would be of considerable significance for the future of the monochrome society because it would serve to make it not merely a demographic trend and one evident among the members of various social groups, but also encompass the orientation of the leadership, which in turns affects the way we see ourselves and each other.

Another reason several African American leaders object to a multiracial category is that race data are used for the enforcement of civil rights legislation in employment, voting rights, housing and mortgage lending, health care services, and educational opportunities.[132] These leaders fear that the category could decrease the number of blacks in official statistics, and thus undermine efforts to enforce antidiscrimination statutes and undercut numerous social programs based on racial quotas.

WHAT IS A RACE ANYHOW?

One may wonder if the number of Americans involved is large enough to justify what at first seems like a tempest in a teapot. The underlying reason is that one tends to underestimate the number of Americans who might qualify for the new category because one assumes that only those of a mixed racial heritage may fall into the All American box. Actually, there are considerable differences in color and other racial features within all racial groups, which makes the question of who is in versus out much more flexible than it often seems. For instance, many dark-skinned Hispanics who do not see themselves as black, and many light-skinned African Americans who do not wish to pass as white, would be free to choose the new category.

One should also note that those who study race professionally, especially physical and cultural anthropologists, strongly object to the concept of racial categorization. They point out that no single gene can be used to differentiate one race from another; moreover, indicators from blood types to texture of hair vary a great deal both among and within groups considered to be of one race. Indeed, the American Anthropological Association passed a resolution stating that "differentiating species into biologically defined 'race' has proven meaningless and unscientific."

THE MERITS OF A NEW CATEGORY

Dropping the whole social construction of race does not seem in the cards, even if the most far-reaching arguments against affirmative action and for a "color-blind" society win the day. However, there are strong sociological reasons to favor the inclusion of a multiracial category in the 2010 Census.

Introducing a multiracial category has the potential to soften racial lines that now divide America by rendering them more like economic differences and less like caste lines. Sociologists have long observed that a major reason the United States experiences relatively few confrontations along class lines is that Americans believe they can move from one economic stratum to another. (For instance, workers become forepersons, and forepersons become small business owners, who are considered middle class.) Moreover, there are not sharp class demarcation lines in this country as there are in England; in America many workers consider themselves middle class, dress up to go to work, and hide their tools and lunches in briefcases, while middle-class, super-liberal professors join labor unions. A major reason confrontations in America occur more often along racial lines is that color lines currently seem rigidly unchangeable.

If the new category is allowed, if more and more Americans choose this category in future decades, as there is every reason to expect given the high rates of intermarriage and a desire by millions of Americans to avoid being racially boxed in, the new Census category may go a long way in determining if America in the next century will be less caste-like and more class-like, a society in which differences are blurred.

Skeptics may suggest that how one marks a tiny box on the 2000 Census form is between one's self and the keepers of statistics. But, as this sociologist sees it, if the multiracial concept is allowed into the national statistics, it will also enter the social vocabulary. It will make American society less stratified along racial lines, less rigidly divided, and thus more communitarian.

THE ULTIMATE QUESTION

At stake is the question of what kind of America we envision for the longer run. Some see a complete blur of racial lines with Americans constituting some kind of new hybrid race. *Time* ran a cover story on the subject, led by a computer composite of a future American with some features of each race, a new, rather handsome breed (almond-shaped eyes, straight but dark hair, milk chocolate skin). This would take much more than a change in racial nomenclature, but it could serve as a step in that direction.

Others are keen to maintain strict racial lines and oppose intermarriage; these same people often seek to maintain the races as separate "nations." (The term nation is significant because it indicates a high degree of tribalism.) In a world full of interracial strife, this attitude — however understandable its defensive nature in response to racial prejudice and discrimination — leaves at least this communitarian greatly troubled. The more communitarian view seems to be one in which those who seek to uphold their separate group identities will do so (hopefully viewing themselves and being viewed as subgroups of a more encompassing community rather than as separate nations), but those who seek to redefine themselves will be enabled to do so, leading to an ever larger group that is free from racial categorization.

If a multiracial category is included further down the road, maybe in the 2010 Census, we may wish to add one more category, that of "multi-ethnic" origin, one which most Americans might wish to check. Then we would live to recognize the full importance of my favorite African American saying: We came in many ships but we now ride in the same boat.

MULTICULTURALISM OR AMERICAN CREED?

All this suggests that foreseeable changes in America's demography do not imply that the American creed is being or will be replaced by something called "multiculturalism."[133] Roberto Suro reminds us that we do not need to divest ourselves of plurality in order to achieve harmony. Suro writes,

> Americans have never thought of themselves as a single people as the Germans do. Although white, English-speaking Christians of European ancestry have set most of the norms for American society, there is still no sense of a *Volk* (a group that shares a common ancestry and culture and that embodies the national identity). Ideas, not biology, are what generate oneness and ho-

mogeneity in the United States, and so long as faith in those ideas has remained strong, the country has shown an extraordinary capacity to absorb people of many nationalities.[134]

The American creed always has had room for pluralism of subcultures, of people upholding some of the traditions and values of their countries of origin, from praying to playing in their own way. But American pluralism should be bound by a shared framework if America is to be spared the kind of ethnic tribalism of the type that — when driven to extremes — has torn apart countries as different as Yugoslavia and Rwanda, and has even reared its ugly head in well-established democracies such as Canada and the United Kingdom (where Scottish separatism is on the rise).

The social, cultural, and legal elements that constitute the framework that holds together the diverse mosaic are well known.[135] They include a commitment by all parties to the democratic way of life, to the Constitution and its Bill of Rights, and to mutual tolerance.[136] The mosaic is further fortified by a strong conviction that one's station in life is determined by hard work and saving, by taking responsibility for one's self and one's family. And, most Americans still share a strong sense that while we are different in some ways, in more ways we are joined by the shared responsibilities of providing a good society for our children and ourselves, one free of racial and ethnic strife, and providing the world with a model of a country whose economy and polity are thriving.

11

Is Shaming Shameful?

Young drug dealers, caught for the first time peddling, should be sent home with their heads shaved and without their pants instead of being jailed, was a suggestion I cautiously floated. My liberal friends rolled their eyes and stared at me with open dismay. When I tried to explain that if the same youngsters are jailed they are likely to graduate more hardened criminals than when they entered the stockades, that rehabilitation in prisons is practically unknown, and young people are often abused in jails, one of my friends stated that the next thing I would suggest would be to mark people with scarlet letters. The others changed the subject.

A recent tragedy brought the merit of shaming back into public and scholarly discussion. I was a member of a panel of lawyers and academics who were asked by National Public Radio to discuss the raping and murder of a seven-year-old girl in a women's bathroom at a Las Vegas casino.[1] The media attention this time was not focused on the father, who left his child roaming the casino at 3:30 A.M., or on the rapist-assassin Jeremy Strohmeyer, but on the friend of the assassin, one David Cash. He accompanied Mr. Strohmeyer to the ladies' room but did nothing to try to stop the savaging of Sherrice Iverson or to inform the police after the act.

In reaction, outraged Congress member Nicholas Lampson drafted a Good Samaritan act that imposes severe punishments on those who do not stop a sexual crime against a child when they could do so at little risk to themselves, or who do not report such offenses to public authorities. UCLA law professor Peter Aranella, who joined the NPR conversation, argued that the punishment was too severe and suggested instead that a shorter jail sentence should suffice. Ms. Elizabeth Semil from the National Association of Criminal Defense Lawyers, also on the panel, was even more critical of the Good Samaritan draft act. She pointed out, "Punitive legislation, criminal legislation, isn't the proper response."[2] She also speculated, "whether making it criminal to fail to act is good public policy. In other words, is it going to assist in solving the problem? And my response to that is: absolutely not."[3] A typical letter to the editor of the *Sacramento Bee* opined, "I realize this is a popular issue, but the consequences of a law of this nature are terrifying. . . . Americans would be required to function as part of the government apparatus. . . . Maybe you know someone who takes cash in their business, but doesn't necessarily tell the IRS. You may go to jail for not turning that person in."[4] A commentator in Bergen, New Jersey's *Record* holds forth, "As much as I'd like to encourage compassion and community, I think it's too late to legislate such morality."[5]

I, too, wondered if Americans should and could be turned into a nation of police informers, a role often despised not merely by their fellow citizens but even by the police themselves. And yet there is a strong sense that Mr. Cash behaved poorly (or worse) and others must do better. One looks for ways good Samaritans may be fostered but in some less punitive way, one that entails no jail terms.

I suggested shaming. Instead of jailing future Cashes, the law should require that the names of *bad* Samaritans be posted on a web site and in advertisements (paid for by the offenders) in key newspapers. Such posting would remove any remaining ambiguities concerning what society expects from people who can help others when there is no serious risk to their well-being. Those with a weak conscience or civic sense would be nudged to do that which is right by fearing that their names will be added to the list of bad Samaritans, their friends and families will chide them, and their neighbors will snicker.

While there are no statistics on the matter, it seems that judges have recently turned to shaming more often than a decade or two ago, as a middle course between jailing offenders and allowing them to walk off scot-free. Those convicted of driving under the influence of alcohol in Fort Bend County, Texas, must place "DUI" bumper stickers on their car.[6] A child molester in Port St. Lucie, Florida was ordered by a judge to mark his property with a sign warning away children.[7] The same judge ordered a woman convicted of purchasing drugs in front of her children to place a notice in the local newspaper detailing her offense.[8] Stephen K. Germershausen was ordered to place a four-by-six inch ad in his local Rhode Island newspaper, accompanied by his photo, stating, "I am Stephen Germershausen, I am 29 years old. . . . I was convicted of child molestation. . . . If you are a child molester, get professional help immediately, or you may find your picture and name in the paper."[9] A Tennessee judge sentenced a convicted defendant to confess his crime of aiding in the sale of a stolen vehicle before a church congregation.[10] Syracuse puts embarrassing signs in front of buildings owned by slum lords, and Des Moines publishes their names in newspapers.[11]

Far from being widely hailed as a more humane and just way of punishing offenders and deterring others, judicial shaming has raised waves of criticism that put to shame my friends' reactions to my proposals. Nadine Strossen, president of the American Civil Liberties Union (ACLU), was rather gentle: "I'm very skeptical when criminologists and sociologists say that the best way to rehabilitate someone is to isolate him and put some sort of scarlet letter on him. We need to integrate criminals back into our community."[12] The ACLU's Mark

Kappelhoff states that, "Gratuitous humiliation of the individual serves no societal purpose at all . . . and there's been no research to suggest it's been effective in reducing crime."[13] Judge Nicholas Politan, of the U.S. District Court (N. J.), wrote similarly that:

> Societies have often used branding or close equivalents thereto as means of making certain persons or groups of persons easily identifiable and thus, easily ostracized or set apart. . . . A clear example of such branding, justified by a social purpose wrongfully deemed acceptable by the populace, was the requirement in Nazi Germany that Jews wear the Star of David on their sleeve so that they might easily be identified. . . . This Court must determine whether Megan's Law and its attendant notification provisions amount to a branding of registrants with a 'Mark of Cain' or a 'Scarlet Letter,' thus rendering them subject to perpetual public animus.[14]

Law professor Evan Cherminsky is also concerned about shaming, claiming "the real measure of how civilized we are is the way we choose to punish people. It's not civilized to tell somebody 'you're going to sit in the stocks and we're going to throw stones at you.'"[15] Carl F. Horowitz, Washington correspondent for *Investor's Business Daily*, attacks shaming, which he writes includes public hanging, beheading of drug dealers, blacklisting, and boycotts.[16]

When I faced similar challenges from a class I teach at George Washington University, I suggested an examination of shaming suffers if one labels all punitive measures one disapproves of and seeks to shun, as shaming. True or pure shaming entails only *symbolic acts* that communicate censure, ranging from relatively gentle acts such as according a student a C+ or sending a disruptive kid to stand in the classroom's corner, to such severe measures as marking the cars of convicted repeat drunk drivers with glow-in-the-dark "DUI" bumper stickers. Shaming differs sharply from many other modes of punishment — public flogging, Singapore style, for instance — in that the latter inflict bodily harm, rather than being limited to psychic discomfort.

While shaming has some untoward consequences of its own, it is relatively light punishment, especially if one takes into account that most other penalties shame in addition to inflicting their designated hurt.

I also stressed that shaming is morally appropriate or justified only when those being shamed are acting out of free will. To the extent that people act in ways that the law or prevailing mores consider inappropriate, but cannot help themselves from doing so (such as when those with a mental illness defecate in the streets or scream their head off at 3 A.M.), chiding them is highly inappropriate. These individuals are to be helped, removed if need be, but certainly not shamed.

When I tried to advance similar arguments on NPR, Ms. Semil would not have any of it; she instead would rely on education, celebrating those who conduct themselves as good Samaritans rather than punishing those who do not. She said, "Instead of thinking about ways in which we can shame people, let's think about ways in which we can honor or hold up examples of the many heroes that we read about every week who risk their lives to save others; in other words, teaching by positive example children and adults that, indeed, this kind of behavior is rewarded and respected and admired."[17]

Such suggestions show that one's assessment of shaming is highly colored by one's assumption of human nature. Ms. Semil belongs to the sanguine camp that believes that people can be convinced to conduct themselves in a virtuous manner solely by means of praise, approbations, and words of encouragement, or by drawing on non-judgmental responses, allowing the goodness of people to unfold. For those who share this view, shaming is not merely cruel but also unnecessary punishment; indeed, punishment in general is antisocial. Many of those who hold this view of human nature tend also to believe that people are good by nature; if they misbehave, either the demands imposed on them are unjust or their behavior reflects distorting forces which they neither caused nor are able to control (for instance, that they were abused by their own parents).

I file with those who hold that a world of only positive reinforcements, while in theory very commendable, is not within human reach, and that hence a society must—however reluctantly—also employ some forms of punishment. Granted, we should first determine if the social demands are fair and reasonable, and to what extent we can rely upon positive inducements in given situations. But, at the end of the day, some form of disincentive—hopefully sparing and mostly of the gentle kind—cannot be avoided. Or, as Judge Ted Poe, a strong proponent of shaming penalties, puts it, "a little shame goes a long way. Some folks say everyone should have high self-esteem, but that's not the real world. Sometimes people should feel bad."[18]

An often overlooked feature of shaming, I should add, is that it is deeply democratic. Shaming reflects the community's values, and hence cannot be imposed by the authorities per se against a people. Thus, if being sent to the principal's office is a badge of honor in a person's peer culture, no shaming will occur in that situation. A yellow star, imposed to mark and shame Jews in Nazi Germany, is worn as a matter of pride in Israel. Thus, people are better protected from shaming that reflects values that are not shared by the community than from other forms of punishment, punishment that can be imposed by authorities without the specific consent of those who are governed.

Critics raise the question of whether shaming is superior to evoking guilt or vice versa, and whether the two are as separate as has been assumed.[19] This is a highly complex matter that deserves separate treatment. This essay merely deals with the normative and related issues raised by deliberate shaming as public policy.[20]

Critics are also quick to turn the communitarian tables on those who seek to use community to shame offenders by pointing out that communitarians have shown that communities are waning. Legal scholar Toni M. Massaro argues in *Michigan Law Review* that shaming will be cogent and productive only if five conditions coexist.

> First, the potential offenders must be members of an identifiable group, such as a close-knit religious or ethnic community. Second, the legal sanctions must actually compromise potential offenders' group social standing. That is, the affected group must concur with the legal decisionmaker's estimation of what is, or

should be, humiliating to group members. Third, the shaming must be communicated to the group and the group must withdraw from the offender — shun her — physically, emotionally, financially, or otherwise. Fourth, the shamed person must fear withdrawal by the group. Finally, the shamed person must be afforded some means of regaining community esteem, unless the misdeed is so grave that the offender must be permanently exiled or demoted.[21]

But, Massaro adds, the "cultural conditions of effective shaming seem weakly present, at best, in many contemporary American cities."[22]

While granting that it is unfair to say that "Americans have no commonly shared instincts about crime or about shame," Massaro believes that "American subculturism, or cultural pluralism, is pronounced enough to make broad conclusions about our moral coherence suspect, and thus to undermine the likely effectiveness of widespread government attempts to shame offenders, absent significant decentralization of criminal law authority and the delivery of formal norm enforcement power to the local subcultures."[23]

Massaro and others who draw on communitarians' arguments do not take into account that while communities clearly are much weaker now than they were in, for instance, colonial days, they are not powerless, especially in smaller towns and in what have been called urban villages, numerous ethnic concentrations in big cities that form rather strong communities, e.g., Chinatown in New York City. Otherwise shaming would be no punishment at all. People are, however, very reluctant — ashamed — to drive around with a DUI marker on their car or to place ads in their town newspaper that contain their picture, apologizing for their offenses. Indeed, an accountant, who was sentenced to stand in his neighborhood with a sign "I embezzled funds" seemed deeply distraught when interviewed, and mused that he might have been better off if he had instead accepted a jail sentence. Hardly indifference. A woman convicted of welfare fraud in Eau Claire, Wisconsin preferred to be jailed than wear a sign admitting, "I stole food from poor people."[24]

In arguing about these matters with liberal criminologists, I picked up a useful distinction between two kinds of shaming, one that isolates and is to be avoided, and one that reintegrates offenders into communities and is to be preferred.[25] Liberal criminologists worry that once a person is shamed, he will be cut off from his community and withdraw into himself or worse, into a criminal subculture, and hence will be unlikely to be rehabilitated. Instead, criminologists suggest dealing with crimes in a way that restores people to good standing in their communities. The measures they favor include face-to-face meetings of the offenders and the victims "facilitated" by community members; the offenders making amends (for instance, rebuilding a fence their car demolished); and closure, a ritual of reconciliation and forgiveness, all of which restore the offender to full membership in the community. David Karp, a criminologist, adds, "These efforts may be through social services or local economic efforts to change the social conditions of the offender's neighborhood."[26]

Reintegrative shaming may well be the best shaming there is, although the jury is out on whether it can be made to work, especially for offenders who are members of different communities than their victims, such as gang members. In effect, any kind of shaming will work only if it is couched in the reference terms of the community of the offenders — or if these terms can be changed as shaming occurs.

The history of our country offers some lessons on the working of shaming, mainly what happens to a good thing when it is driven much too far. Most importantly, history teaches us the significance of the particular context. In colonial America shaming was very common, not merely one tool of punishment among others but a major one. Indeed, historians report it often worked so well, no prisons were deemed necessary in some colonies — for instance, there were no prisons in South Carolina.[27] (This, however, applied only to white people; slaves were treated much more savagely.)

One reason shaming was so powerful during colonial times is that it took place in communities that were much smaller, tightly knit, and moralistic than any known to us today in this country. Historian Lawrence M. Friedman describes these communities as "little worlds on their own, cut off from each other" and "small-town life [was] at its most communal — inbred and extremely gossipy."[28] Another historian, Roger Thompson, writes that communities in Massachusetts were "well stocked with moral monitors who did not miss much in the goldfish-bowl existence of daily life."[29] Single people, who moved into colonies, were required to board with someone, so that the community could better keep an eye on them.

In contrast, today many Americans are members of two or more communities (for instance, at work and where they reside) and psychologically can shift much of their ego involvement from a community that unduly chastens them to another. While it was not practical for most individuals to escape from one community to another during colonial times, today the average American moves about once every five years, and in the process chooses which community he or she is willing to subject themselves. Moreover, privacy at home is much greater, and the moral agenda of most communities is almost incomparably shorter.

In short, the colonial era shows us how little we now seek to shame and how limited our ability to shame actually is. (Amy Gutmann, a liberal philosopher at Princeton University, once quipped that "communitarian critics want us to live in Salem, but not to believe in witches."[30] As I see it, we communitarians should, shamelessly, plead guilty as charged. We do favor communities in which moral mores are upheld without witch hunts, and maintain that in our kind of society this is possible.)

The purest form of shaming was 'admonition.' Law professor Adam Hirsch described it as follows: "Faced with a community member who had committed a serious offense, the magistrates or clergymen would lecture him privately to elicit his repentance and a resolution to reform. The offender would then be brought into open court for formal admonition by the magistrate, a public confession of wrongdoing, and a pronouncement of sentence, wholly or partially suspended to symbolize the community's forgiveness."[31]

Writes Lawrence Friedman, "The aim was not just to punish, but to teach a lesson, so that the sinful sheep would want to be back to the flock."[32]

The emphasis on reintegrative justice should appeal to the progressive criminologists who seek to restore it, although for others it may evoke the image of a Soviet or Chinese trial. Having witnessed one of these, what offended me most was not the shaming per se but the kind of matters people were shamed for, having conceived a second child and listening to the BBC.

While pure (merely symbolic) shaming was employed in the colonial era and long thereafter, often it was mixed with other forms of punishment such as fines, whipping, and worse.
Stocks and pillories combined holding people up for public ridicule with confining their movements, exposing them to the elements, and at least a measure of physical discomfort.

Friedman describes another common shaming measure, which was to make a culprit guilty of stealing money wear for six months, "a 'Roman T, not less than four inches long and one inch wide, of a scarlet colour, on the outside of the outermost garment, upon the back, between the shoulders, so that all times to be fully exposed to view, for a badge of his or her crime.' A robber had to wear a scarlet R; and a forger, a scarlet F, 'at least six inches long and two inches wide.'"[33] But, unlike the DUI signs today, the wearing of these insignia was proceeded by a public whipping in a considerable number of cases.

All said and done, it is easy to see why shaming as practiced in earlier periods or in other kinds of societies has left it in ill-repute. We had best think about shaming in terms of how different our much more liberal and tolerant society may adapt it to our needs rather than be swayed by an anachronistic image.

Most important, one must not evaluate any social policy in itself but must compare it to others. The existing criminal justice system jails millions of people, about half of them for nonviolent crimes mainly dealing in controlled substances. Offenders are incarcerated for ever longer periods, in harsher conditions, with fewer opportunities for parole. Still, the system rehabilitates very few, and the recidivism rate is very high. And the system imposes high charges on taxpayers. A year in jail costs the public about the same as a year at one of our nation's most costly colleges. Ergo, society is keen to find some new, more effective, more humane, and less costly modes of deterrence. Whether it works, and for which kinds of offenders, we are about to find out, that is, if our well-meaning progressive friends will allow us to proceed.

III

The Post-Affluent Society

VOLUNTARY SIMPLICITY CHARACTERIZATION

The idea that the overarching goal of capitalist economies needs to be changed and that achieving ever-higher levels of consumption of products and services is a vacuous goal, has been with us since the onset of industrialization. It has often taken the form of comparing the attractive life of the much poorer, pre-industrial artisan to that of the drudgeries of the "richer" industrial assembly-line worker.

In more recent times, criticism of consumerism was common among the followers of the counterculture. They sought a lifestyle that consumed and produced little, at least in terms of marketable objects. They sought to derive satisfaction, meaning, and a sense of purpose from contemplation, communion with nature, bonding with one another, mood-altering substances, sex, and inexpensive products.[1] Over the years that followed, a significant number of members of

Western societies embraced a much attenuated version of the values and mores of the counterculture. For example, studies by Ronald Inglehart beginning in the early 1970s found that "the values of Western publics have been shifting from an overwhelming emphasis on material well-being and physical security toward greater emphasis on the quality of life."[2] These "quality of life" factors form what Inglehart calls "postmaterialist values," and include the desire for more freedom, a stronger sense of community, more say in government, and so on. The percentage of survey respondents with clear postmaterialist values doubled from 9% in 1972 to 18% in 1991, while those with clear materialist values fell more than half from 35% to 16% (those with mixed commitments moved more slowly, from 55% to 65%).[3] These trends were reported for most Western European countries.[4]

Personal consumption, however, continued to grow. For example, in the United States, between 1980 and 1990, per capita consumer spending (in inflation-adjusted dollars) rose by 21.4%. The portion of consumer spending devoted to dispensable ("luxury") items, such as jewelry, toys, and video and audio equipment, rose in the same period from 6.78% to 8.63%.[5] Meanwhile, the personal savings rate of Americans fell from 7.9% in 1980 to 4.2% in 1990, and has remained near or below this level ever since.[6]

Still, the search for alternatives to consumerism as the goal of capitalism continues to intrigue people. I focus here on one such alternative, referred to as "voluntary simplicity." Among those who have employed this term, or have conducted relevant studies are Robert Paehlke, a professor of environmental and resource studies at Trent University in Ontario, Canada; Juliet Schor, a professor of economics at Harvard University;[7] and Dorothy Leonard-Barton, of the Harvard University Business School.[8] "Voluntary simplicity" refers to people choosing—out of free will rather than by being coerced by poverty, government austerity programs, or imprisonment—to limit expenditures on consumer goods and services and to cultivate non-materialistic sources of satisfaction and meaning.

As I already have suggested, the criticism of consumerism and the quest for alternatives are as old as capitalism itself. However, the issue needs revisiting for several reasons. The collapse of noncapitalist economic systems has led many to assume that capitalism is the superior system and, therefore, to refrain from critically examining its goals. But capitalism has defects of its own. The rise of religious fundamentalism in the Islamic world, not merely in countries such as Iran and Afghanistan but also in countries such as Algeria and Turkey, reflects deep concerns about the vacuousness of the materialistic world. Recent developments in former communist countries also indicate that many find that capitalism does not address spiritual concerns — the quest for transcendental connections and meanings — that all people have.[9] And pockets of young people, opinion makers, and others in the West have revealed similar yearnings.

Furthermore, as so many societies with rapidly rising populations now seek affluence as their primary domestic goal, the environmental, psychological, and other issues raised by consumerism are being faced on a scale not previously considered. For instance, the undesirable side effects of intensive consumerism that once were chiefly a concern of highly industrialized societies are now faced by hundreds of millions of Chinese, Indians, and Koreans, among others. Air pollution caused by massive use of cars ranks high among these.

Finally, the transition from consumption tied to satisfaction of what are perceived as basic needs (secure shelter, food, clothing, and so on) to consumerism (the preoccupation with gaining ever-higher levels of consumption, including a considerable measure of conspicuous consumption of status goods), seems to be more pronounced as societies become wealthier. Hence, a reexamination of the goals and lifestyles of mature capitalist societies is particularly timely. Indeed, this may well be an environment particularly hospitable for voluntary simplicity.

This examination proceeds first by providing a description of voluntary simplicity, exploring its different manifestations and its effects on competitiveness should the need and urge to gain ever-higher levels of income be curbed. It then considers whether greater income, and the additional consumption it enables, produces greater contentment. This is a crucial issue because it makes a world of difference to the sustainability of voluntary simplicity whether it is deprivational (and hence requires strong motivational forces if it is to spread and persevere), or whether consumerism is found to be obsessive and maybe even addictive. In the latter case, voluntary simplicity would be liberating and might become self-propelling and sustaining.

The answer to the preceding question, and hence to the future of voluntary simplicity as a major cultural factor, is found in an application of Abraham Maslow's theory of human needs discussed later in this chapter. It finds further reinforcement by examining the "consumption" of a growing *sub*category of goods whose supply and demand is not governed by the condition of scarcity in the postmodern era. The chapter closes with a discussion of the societal consequences of voluntary simplicity for the environment and for social justice.

Voluntary Simplicity: Three Variations

Voluntary simplicity is observable in different levels of intensity. It ranges from rather moderate levels (in which people downshift their consumptive, rich lifestyle, but not necessarily into a low gear), to strong simplification (in which people significantly restructure their lives), to holistic simplification.

DOWNSHIFTERS

One quite moderate form of voluntary simplicity is practiced by economically well-off and secure people who voluntarily give up some consumer goods (often considered luxuries) they could readily afford, while basically maintaining their rather rich and consumption-oriented lifestyle. For example, they "dress down" in one way or another: wearing jeans, inexpensive shoes, and T-shirts, and driving beat-up cars.

The rock star Bruce Springsteen is reported to dress in worn boots, faded jeans, and a battered leather jacket and is said to drive a Ford.[10] The CEOs of major corporations, including Microsoft's Bill Gates, Novel's Eric Schmidt, and Intuit's Scott Cook, appear annually at the highly regarded World Economic Forum at a posh ski resort in Switzerland, without ties and wearing unadorned sweaters.[11] David and Ellen Siminoff, a Silicon Valley power couple — he directs the investment of billions; she is a vice president at Yahoo! — rarely attend charity parties, and prefer to stay at home. She likes to wear khakis and T-shirts. Richer than most power couples they "take pride in their relatively modest tastes and inconspicuous consumption."[12] They drive the least expensive luxury cars on the market (a Lexus and a Mercedes), and they make do without a second vacation home or private planes.[13]

Henry Urbach reports that, "there has been a turn away from . . . the 'overdesign' of the 1980s toward a world of 'simple' things. Instead of snazzy plates designed by architects, we have white dinnerware from Pottery Barn. In place of Christian Lacroix poufs and Manolo Blahnik pumps, we want Gap t-shirts and Prada penny loafers. We like sport-utility vehicles, stainless-steel Sub-Zero refrigerators, Venetian blinds, retro electric fans, sturdy wooden tables — anything plain. Extravagance has surrendered to a look that is straightforward, blunt, unadorned."[14] And Pilar Viladas writes, "in architecture and design today, less is more again. Houses, rooms and furnishings are less ornate, less complicated and less ostentatious than they were 10 years ago. Rather than putting their money on display, people seem to be investing in a quieter brand of luxury, based on comfort and quality."[15]

Often this pattern is inconsistent and limited in scope, in that a person adhering to the norms of voluntary simplicity in some areas does not do so in many others. This moderate form of voluntary simplicity is illustrated by those who wear an expensive blazer with a pair of jeans, or drive a jalopy to their fifty-foot yacht.

David Brooks notes that to those who are wealthy, rejecting the symbols of success is acceptable only "so long as you can display the objects of poverty in a way that makes it clear you are just rolling in dough."[16] This should not be surprising, for there are no widely recognized symbols of voluntary simplicity, and most people still desire to be recognized as successful by their community.

Downshifting is not limited to the very wealthy. Some professionals and other members of the middle class are replacing elaborate dinner parties with simple meals, potluck dinners, take-out food, or social events built around desserts only. Some lawyers are reported to have cut back on the billing-hours race that drives many of their colleagues to work late hours and on weekends in the quest to reach ever-higher levels of income and to incur the favor of the firms for which they work.[17] Faith Popcorn, an observer of mass-market behavior, termed the trend "cashing out." She found that more and more people are leaving the corporate world, which they believe does not appreciate them.[18] Some businesses are fostering a limited degree of voluntary simplicity. For instance, in several workplaces there is one day (often Friday) in which employees are expected to "dress down." In other workplaces, especially on the West coast, employees may dress down any day of the week.

There seems to be no evidence that social scientists would find satisfactory to show that downshifting is widely practiced or that it has risen in some affluent societies. Some data do, however, point in these directions. Asked "days per week I can dress casually at my job," 52% of Americans in 1997 answered "any day;" 18% at least one day a week; and only 27% agreed with the statement "can't dress casually at work."[19]

A study by the Merck Family Fund in 1995 found that 28% of a national sample of Americans[20] (and, according to another survey, 10% of the sampled executives and professionals),[21] reported having "downshifted," or voluntarily made life changes resulting in a lower income to reflect a change in their priorities, in the preceding five years. The most common changes were reducing work hours, switching to lower-paying jobs, and quitting work to stay at home,[22] which might — but does not necessarily — correlate with downshifting. The same survey also found that 82% of Americans felt that people buy and consume more than they need, suggesting that voluntary simplicity is viewed as commendable but is not widely followed. Another survey, conducted in 1989, which also focused on sentiments rather than on changes in behavior, found that three out of four working Americans would like "to see our country return to a simpler lifestyle, with less emphasis on material success."[23]

This group includes people who have given up high-paying, high-status jobs as lawyers, business people, investment bankers, and so on, to live on less — often much less — income. One former Wall Street analyst restricts his spending to $6,000 a year. In another case, both members of a couple quit their jobs as high-paid executives in the telecommunications industry, and now live only on their savings — about $25,000 per year — and spend their time writing and doing volunteer work.[24] The *New York Times* reports, "Choosing to buy and earn less — to give up income and fast-track success for more free time and a lower-stress life — involves a quiet revolt against the dominant culture of getting and spending. Enough small revolts are now taking place, researchers say, to make [the] phenomenon . . . a major and growing trend of the 90's."[25]

Strong simplifiers also include a large number of employees who voluntarily choose to retire before they are required to do so, opting for less income and lower pension payouts in order to have more leisure time. While it is clear that the aggregate number of people who retire early is increasing, some of this increase may well be involuntary as a result of forced retirement and downsizing. It is not known what the proportion of voluntary versus involuntary retirement is.[26] However, informal interviewing, including among this author's colleagues, suggests that a significant proportion of this increase is voluntary.

Ideas associated with voluntary simplicity are ideologically compelling, if not necessarily reflected in actual behavior. In 1989, a majority of working Americans rated "a happy family life" as a much more important indicator of success than "earning a lot of money" — by an unusually wide margin of 62% to 10%.[27] In a 1998 poll, 80% of respondents said that they would not sacrifice most family time to be rich.[28] Also, numerous women and some men prefer part-time jobs, even if better paying full-time jobs are open to them. A major reason they are willing to reconcile themselves to earning a lower income seems to be the ability to dedicate more time to their children and to be at home when their children are there.[29] People who switch to new careers that are more personally meaningful but less lucrative also fall into this category. For instance, a 1997 source reports that "a growing wave of engineers, military officers, lawyers, and business people . . . are switching careers and becoming teachers."[30]

People who voluntarily and significantly curtail their incomes tend to be stronger simplifiers than those who only moderate their lifestyle, because a significant reduction of income often leads to a much more encompassing "simplification" of lifestyle than selective downshifting of select items of consumption. While it is possible for both an affluent person to cease working altogether and still lead an affluent lifestyle, and for someone who does not reduce his or her income to cut spending drastically, one must expect that as a rule, those who significantly curtail their income will simplify more than those who only moderate their consumption. Once people reduce their income, unless they have large savings, a new inheritance, or some other such nonwork-related income, they obviously de facto commit themselves to adjusting their consumption.

People who adjust their lifestyle only or mainly because of economic pressures (having lost their main or second job, or for any other reason) do not qualify as voluntary simplifiers on the simple grounds that their shift is not voluntary. One can argue that some poor people freely choose not to earn more and keep their consumption level meager. To what extent such a choice is truly voluntary and how widespread this phenomenon is are questions not addressed here. The discussion here focuses on people who had an affluent lifestyle and chose to give it up, for reasons explored below.

In contrast, people who could earn more but are motivated by pressures such as "time squeeze" to reduce their income and consumption do qualify, because they could have responded to the said pressure in means other than simplifying (for instance, hiring more help).[31] Moreover, there seems to be some pent-up demand for voluntary simplicity among people who report they would prefer to embrace such a lifestyle but feel that they cannot do so. *Gallup Poll Monthly* reports that 45% of Americans feel they have too little time for friends and other personal relationships, and 54% feel they have too little time to spend with their children.[32] Twenty-six percent of Americans polled said they would take a 20% pay cut if it meant they could work fewer hours.[33] Presumably, these people face, or at least feel they face, only two choices: keep their current job or possibly face prolonged unemployment.

THE SIMPLE-LIVING MOVEMENT

The most dedicated, holistic simplifiers adjust their whole life patterns according to the ethos of voluntary simplicity. They often move from affluent suburbs or gentrified parts of major cities to smaller towns, the countryside, farms, and less affluent or less urbanized parts of the country — the Pacific Northwest is especially popular — with the explicit goal of leading a "simpler" life. A small, loosely connected social movement, sometimes called the "simple-living" movement, has developed. It is complete with its own how-to books, nine-step programs, and newsletters, although reports suggest that "many persons experimenting with simpler ways of living said they did not view themselves as part of a conscious social movement."[34]

This group differs from the downshifters and even strong simplifiers not only in the scope of change in their conduct but also in that it is motivated by a coherently articulated philosophy. One source of inspiration is *Voluntary Simplicity*, written in 1981 by Duane Elgin, which draws on the traditions of the Quakers, the Puritans, transcendentalists such as Emerson and Thoreau, and various world religions to provide philosophical underpinnings to living a simple life.[35] This philosophy is often explicitly anticonsumerist. Elgin, for example, calls for "dramatic changes in the overall levels and patterns of consumption in developed nations," adding that "this will require dramatic changes in the consumerist messages we give ourselves through the mass media."[36] In 1997, the Public Broadcasting Corporation ran a special called *Affluenza*.[37] Its purpose was to provide a treatment for an "epidemic" whose symptoms are "shopping fever, a rash of personal debt, chronic stress, overwork and exhaustion of natural resources." Another source defined the signs of "*affluenza*" as "1. The bloated, sluggish and unfulfilled feeling that results from efforts to keep up with the Joneses. 2. An epidemic of stress, overwork, waste and indebtedness caused by dogged pursuit of the American Dream. 3. An unsustainable addiction to economic growth. 4. A television program that could change your life."[38] It promised a follow-up on "better living for less," which came out in 1998 and was titled, *Escape from Affluenza* and was hosted by Wanda Ubanska, co-author of *Simple Living*.[39] The Center for a New American Dream publishes a quarterly report on the same issues called simply *Enough!* Jessie O'Neill, granddaughter of a former president of General Motors, has founded and directs the Affluenza Project, an organization that shows people how to have healthy relationships with their limited funds.[40]

While one can readily profile the various kinds of simplifiers, there are no reliable measurements that enable one to establish the number of simplifiers of the three kinds or to determine whether their ranks are growing. One recent publication estimates, though, that nearly one out of four adult Americans — 44 million — are "cultural creatives," who rank voluntary simplicity high among their values.[41]

A Comparative Note

Voluntary simplicity is not a phenomenon limited to contemporary American society. Indeed, while there seems to be no relevant comparative quantitative data, voluntary simplicity seems to be somewhat more widespread in Western Europe, especially on the continent, than in the United States. (Great Britain, in this sense, is somewhere between Western Europe and the United States.) Many Europeans seem to be more inclined than Americans to sacrifice some income for more leisure time, longer vacations, and visits to spas, coffee shops, and pubs. This is reflected in these countries' labor laws (which in turn reflect not merely power politics but are also an expression of widely held values), that provide for extensive paid vacation times, early weekday closing hours for shops, the closing of shops on Sundays and parts of Saturdays, subsidies allowing thousands to pursue university studies for many years, as well as extensive support for cultural activities.[42] The aggregate result is that Western European societies produce less and consume less per capita than American society in terms of typical consumer goods and services, but have more time for leisure and educational and cultural activities that are more compatible with voluntary simplicity than the American society.

By contrast, consumerism is powerful and gaining in many developing countries as well as former communist societies where it is a rather recent phenomenon. In these societies the pursuit of washing machines, sexy lingerie, and other luxury goods seems to be all the rage. From China, we hear that "Westernization and consumerism are rushing in so rapidly that even the Chinese . . . are amazed. . . . American democracy is nowhere present, but American consumerism is everywhere."[43] In Russia, it is reported that "a new wave of commercialism [is] sweeping the Russian capital;" one popular store in Moscow has brisk sales of $1,290 gold and silver seraphim, $529 music boxes, and $1,590 plastic yule trees during the Christmas shopping season.[44] Consumerism is thriving in Vietnam, where Honda motorbikes, mobile phones, fax machines, and TVs are now popular in the cities.[45] These days, in the once backward country of Burma, "you can buy and rent laser discs . . . young people drive sports cars[and] jewelry shops are bustling."[46] And "despite their obvious affinity for Americana . . . Israelis increasingly are questioning whether the dizzying construction of U.S.-style shopping malls and American franchise shops is right for Israel,"[47] though they have long lost most of their pioneering spirit and have picked consumerism with a vengeance. In short, there are strong differences in the extent to which voluntary simplicity is embraced in various societies, affected by myriad economic, cultural, and social factors not explored here. A few hypotheses stand out. I turn to explore those next.

PSYCHOLOGICAL IMPLICATIONS

The answer to the question of whether voluntary simplicity can be sustained and greatly expanded depends to a significant extent on whether voluntary simplicity constitutes a sacrifice that people must be constantly motivated to make, or is in and of itself a major source of satisfaction, and thus self-motivating. To examine this issue the discussion next explores to what extent the opposite of voluntary simplicity—ever-higher levels of income and consumption—is a source of contentment. It then expands the answer by drawing on Maslow's observations about the hierarchy of needs.

Income and Contentment

Consumerism is justified largely in terms of the notion that the more goods and services a person uses, the more satisfied a person will be. Early economists thought that people had a fixed set of needs, and they worried about what would motivate people to work and save once their income allowed them to satisfy their needs. Subsequently, however, it was widely recognized that people's needs can be artificially enhanced through advertising and social pressures, and hence they are said to have if not unlimited, at least very expandable consumerist needs.

In contrast, critics have argued that the cult of consumer goods—of objects—has become a fetish that stands between people and contentment, one that prevents people from experiencing authentic expressions of affection and appreciation by others. Western popular culture is replete with narratives about fathers (in early ages), and recently of mothers as well, who slaved to bring home consumer goods, but far from being appreciated by their children and spouses found, often only late in their life, that their families would have preferred another lifestyle. It seems that many families might well have welcomed it if the "bread" winners would have spent more time with them and granted them affection and appreciation—or expressed their affection and appreciation directly, through presence and attention, and symbolic gestures such as hugs—rather than expressing such feelings by working long and hard and providing their families with monies or goods. Arthur Miller's play, *Death of a Salesman*, first published in 1949, is a telling example of this genre. In 1997, Neil Simon was still belaboring this story in his play, *Proposals*.

Social science findings, which do not all run in the same direction and have other well-known limitations, on the whole, seem to lend support to the notion that higher income does not significantly raise people's contentment — with the important exception of the poor. For instance, Frank M. Andrews and Stephen B. Withey found that the level of one's socio-economic status had meager effects on one's "sense of well-being" and no significant effect on "satisfaction with life-as-a-whole."[48] And Jonathan Freedman discovered that levels of reported happiness did not vary greatly among the members of different economic classes, with the exception of the very poor who tended to be less happy than others.[49]

Figures 2 and 3 show the results of a longitudinal study of the correlation between income and happiness.[50] Figure 2 represents the results of interviews conducted in 1971 to 1975; Figure 3 represents

Figure 2: Income and well-being for 1971 to 1975. From: Ed Diener, Ed Sandvik, Larry Seidlits, and Marissa Diener, "The Relationship between Income and Subjective Well-Being: Relative or Absolute?" *Social Indicators Research* 28 (1993): 204, with kind permission from Kluwer Academic Publishers.

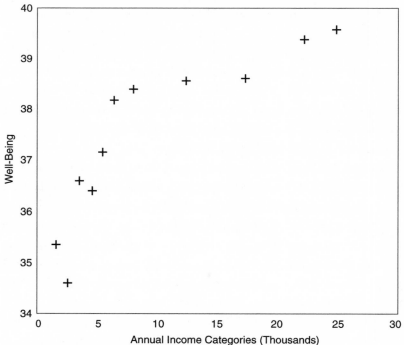

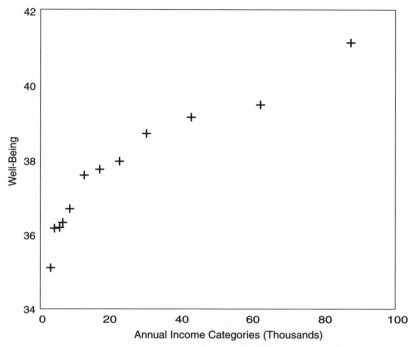

Figure 3: Income and well-being for 1981 to 1984. From: Ed Diener, Ed Sandvik, Larry Seidlits, and Marissa Diener, "The Relationship between Income and Subjective Well-Being: Relative or Absolute?" *Social Indicators Research* 28 (1993): 205, with kind permission from Kluwer Academic Publishers.

interviews with the same individuals carried out in 1981 to 1984. These figures demonstrate two things: first, at low incomes the amount of income *does* correlate strongly with happiness, but this correlation levels off soon after a comfortable level of income is attained; and second, during the decade that passed between the interviews, the individuals' incomes rose dramatically (note the change in the x-axis categories) but the levels of happiness did not (the y-axis categories are nearly the same). These figures are included to emphasize the point that voluntary simplicity as an avenue for contentment is mainly a road that may be traveled by those whose basic needs are met, rather than the poor or near poor.

Additional evidence suggests that economic growth does not significantly affect happiness (though at any given time the people of poor countries are generally less happy than those of wealthy ones). David G. Myers reports that while per capita disposable (after-tax) income in inflation-adjusted dollars almost exactly doubled between 1960 and 1990, 32% of Americans reported that they were "very happy" in 1993, almost the same proportion as did in 1957 (35%). Although economic growth slowed since the mid-1970s, Americans' reported happiness was remarkably stable (nearly always between 30 and 35%) across both high-growth and low-growth periods. Moreover, in the same period, rates of depression, violent crime, divorce, and teen suicide have all risen dramatically.[51] During a visit to Japan in 1999, I was told by a colleague that in the period in which the Japanese gross domestic product increased five times, the percentage of Japanese who stated that they were happy increased by a mere two percent.

Richard Easterlin commented on this phenomenon in his mid-1990s study that followed up on his groundbreaking 1973 study of the correlation between income and happiness. His question was, "Will raising the incomes of all increase the happiness of all?" His answer was simply "No."[52] He explained this by quoting Karl Marx: "A house may be large or small; as long as the surrounding houses are equally small it satisfies all social demands for a dwelling. But if a palace rises beside the little house, the little house shrinks into a hut."[53] In other words, any happiness that a person feels due to a rise in income is quickly offset by a rise in average income of those around them, which he discusses in relation to the aforementioned Japanese example.[54]

Amartya Sen showed that people who live in poorer countries often have a better quality of life than those who live in more affluent societies.[55] He joined others who questioned whether the GDP was a sound measurement of well-being and suggested the need for a much more encompassing measure. Presumably, as more people realize that happiness lies down other roads than a relentless pursuit of material goods, they become more inclined to volunteer to lead a simpler life.

Psychological studies make even stronger claims: that the *more* concerned people are with their financial well-being, the *less* likely they are to be happy. One group of researchers found that "highly central financial success aspirations . . . were associated with less self-actualization, less vitality, more depression, and more anxiety."[56] A survey from the late 1990s showed that people ranked material possessions low on their list of the things that matter in life. The top picks were "to have a happy family life" (50%), "to live in freedom" (34%), "to have good health" (30%), and "to be faithful to my religion" (23%). Just 8% chose "to have a good standard of living." In fact, when asked to pick two things that mattered least in life, "to have a good standard of living" was the top choice with 25% of the vote.[57]

Robert Frank argues in his 1999 book, *Luxury Fever*, that "money fails to satisfy in an era of excess" because now instead of trying to keep up with the Joneses, which is hard enough, we are trying to keep up with the Gateses — which is nearly impossible.[58]

Robert Lane summarizes the results of several studies as follows: "Most studies agree that a satisfying family life is the most important contributor to well-being. . . . The joys of friendship often rank second. Indeed, according to one study, an individual's number of friends is a better predictor of his well-being than is the size of his income. Satisfying work and leisure often rank third or fourth but, strangely, neither is closely related to actual income."[59] Lane further reports that increases in individual income briefly boost happiness, but the additional happiness is not sustainable because higher income level becomes the standard against which people measure their future achievements.[60] Benjamin Friedman, in an article in the *New York Review of Books*, explained that in the late 1950s and early 1960s a widely publicized study indicated that, on average, citizens of poor countries were no less satisfied with their lives than those in rich countries. Twenty-five years later, a similar study showed the happiness of a country's citizens to be far more in line with the per capita income. In other words, citizens of rich countries were happier than those of poorer ones. Friedman writes,

> The most plausible explanation for this puzzling change is that while people in the pre-television era mostly compared them-

selves to their fellow countrymen, and felt either satisfied or frustrated depending on whether their own circumstances matched what they saw at close hand, once a new generation grew up watching TV it began to see things differently. Today almost everybody, almost everywhere is familiar with at least the external appearance of middle-class living standards in the world's advanced postindustrial democracies. And most people want to be part of whatever will give them access to that way of life.[61]

Another indication that people do not find deep satisfaction in higher levels of material consumption can be seen in that after almost a decade of prosperity and peace, full employment and a soaring stock market, longer life spans and rising levels of health, Americans were full of a large variety of "low-grade" anxieties. These ranged from a fear of a Y2K meltdown to flesh-eating bacteria, genetically modified food to nuclear war. These were reported to "pop up anew, frights to fill the void."[62]

These and other such findings raise the following question: If higher levels of income do not buy happiness, why do people work hard to gain higher income? The answer is complex. In part, high income in capitalistic consumerist societies "buys" prestige; others find purpose, meaning, and contentment in the income-producing work per se. There is, however, also good reason to suggest that the combination of the artificial fanning of needs and cultural pressures maintain people in consumerist roles when these are not truly or deeply satisfying.

Voluntary simplicity seems to work because consuming less, once one's basic creature-comfort needs are taken care of, is not a source of deprivation, so long as one is freed from the culture of consumerism. Voluntary simplicity represents a new culture, one that respects work per se (even if it generates only low or moderate income) and appreciates modest rather than conspicuous or lavish consumption. But it does not advocate a life of sacrifice or service (and in this sense is rather different from ascetic religious orders or some socialist expressions as in kibbutzim).

Voluntary simplicity builds on the understanding that there is a declining marginal satisfaction in the pursuit of ever-higher levels of consumption. And it points to sources of satisfaction in deliberately and willingly avoiding the quest for ever-higher levels of affluence and consumption as well as making one's personal and social project the pursuit of other purposes. These purposes are not specifically defined, other than that they are not materialistic. Indeed, just as some find satisfaction intrinsically in work and savings rather than in purchasing power, so some voluntary simplicity followers find satisfaction in the very fact that they have chosen (without being forced to choose) a simpler lifestyle and are proud of their choice. Moreover, as they learn to cultivate other pursuits, simplifiers gain more satisfaction out of lifelong learning, public life, volunteering, community participation, surfing the Internet, sports, cultural activities, and observing or communing with nature. They discover, as Elgin puts it: "Voluntary simplicity [is] a manner of living that is more outwardly simple and inwardly rich."[63]

In each of these areas, some downshifters and even full-blown simplifiers slip back into consumerism, as they are subject to incessant promotions by marketers and peer pressure. Thus, Internet surfers may feel that they "need" to update their computer every other year or purchase various bells and whistles; and those engaged in sports feel they "need" a large variety of expensive, ever-changing, fashionable footwear, clothing, and equipment to enjoy their sport of choice. But others find that they can keep consumerism under control. They enjoy touch football, a well-worn pair of sneakers, or take pride in their beat-up car.

An area that needs further study is the tendency of consumerism, when restrained, to leave a psychological vacuum that needs to be filled.[64] Those who try to wean themselves off consumerism often need support, mainly in the form of approval of significant others and membership in voluntary simplicity groups and subcultures. For instance, they may need to learn gradually to replace shopping with other activities that are more satisfying and meaningful. While some find shopping a chore, among the affluent, shopping is a major recreational activity, often done with peers (if not for actual consumption but for collection and display purposes, anything from expensive knickknacks to antiques). Numerous teenagers and many tourists also shop as a major recreational activity. Indeed, one must expect that for people who draw satisfaction from shopping per se, to curtail this activity may initially evoke an anxiety of unoccupied time and they need help if they are to develop a taste for other activities. Long-term consumers are, from this view, no different from couch potatoes who are about to learn the joys of jogging.

The obsessive nature of at least some consumerism is evident in that people who seek to curb it find it difficult to do so. Many people purchase things they later realize they neither needed nor desired, or stop shopping only after they have "maxed out" their credit. In short, the fact that many in affluent societies have not yet embraced voluntary simplicity may not be due to the fact that it is not intrinsically satisfying but because obsessive consumption cannot be stopped cold, and transitional help may be required. Most important, conversion is most likely to be achieved when consumerism is replaced with other sources of satisfaction and meaning.

Maslow, the Haves and the Have-nots, and Voluntary Simplicity

Thus far this chapter has explored how difficult it is to sustain voluntary simplicity, given that it is common to assume that a high level of materialistic consumption is the main source of satisfaction driving people to work in capitalist societies. The evidence, while not all of one kind, tends to suggest that higher income does not lead to higher levels of satisfaction. Indeed, there is reason to suggest that the continued psychological investment in ever-higher levels of consumption has an addictive quality. People seek to purchase and amass ever more goods whether they need them (in any sense of the term) or not. It follows that voluntary simplicity, far from being a source of stress, is a source of profound satisfaction. This point is further supported by examining the implications of Maslow's theory for these points.

The rise of voluntary simplicity in advanced (or late) stages of capitalism, and for the privileged members of these societies, is explainable by a psychological theory of Abraham Maslow,[65] who suggests that human needs are organized in a hierarchy. At the base of the hierarchy are basic creature comforts, such as the need for food, shelter, and clothing. Higher up are the need for love and esteem. The hierarchy is crowned with self-expression. Maslow theorized that people seek to satisfy lower needs before they turn to higher ones, although he does not deal with the question of the extent to which lower needs have to be satiated before people move to deal with higher-level needs, or the extent to which they can become fixated on lower-level needs.[66]

Some have suggested that Maslow's theory has been disproved because people seek to satisfy their needs not in the sequence he stipulated or even all at once. This may well be the case, but the only issue relevant here is if people continue to heavily invest themselves in the quest for creature comforts long after they are quite richly endowed in such goods And, if in the process, their nonmaterial needs are neglected (even if they are not completely ignored). Western culture leaves little doubt that Maslow's thesis, if formulated in this way, is a valid one.

Maslow's thesis is compatible with the suggestion that voluntary simplicity may appeal to people after their basic needs are well– and securely satisfied. Voluntary simplicity is thus a choice a successful corporate lawyer, not a homeless person, faces; an option for Singapore, not Rwanda. Indeed, to urge the poor or near poor to draw satisfaction from consuming less is to ignore the profound connection between the hierarchy of human needs and consumption. It becomes an obsession that can be overcome only after basic creature-comfort needs are well– and securely sated.

This point is of considerable import when voluntary simplicity is examined not merely as an empirical phenomenon — as a pattern for social science to observe and dissect — but also as a set of values that has advocates and that may be judged in terms of the values' moral appropriateness. As I see it, the advocacy of voluntary simplicity addresses those who are in the higher reaches of income, those who are privileged but who are fixated on the creature-comfort level; it may help them free themselves from the artificial fanning of these basic needs and assist them in moving to higher levels of satisfaction. The same advocacy addressed to the poor or near poor (or disadvantaged groups or the "have-not" countries) might correctly be seen as an attempt to deny them the satisfaction of basic human needs. Consumerism, not consumption, is the target for voluntary simplicity.

Consumerism has one often observed feature that is particularly relevant here. Consumerism sustains itself, in part, because it is visible. People who are "successful" in traditional capitalist terms need to signal their achievements in ways that are readily visible to others in order to gain their appreciation, approval, and respect. They do so by displaying their income by buying themselves (or, in earlier days, their wives) expensive status goods, as Vance Packard demonstrated several decades ago. For example, James A. Finkelstein, founder of online luxury purveyor Luxuryfinder.com reported in late 1999 of his great difficulty in keeping $995 Pashmina shawls, $335 Pashmina pillows, and caviar costing $1,150 per 500 grams in stock. Other super rich fly their palm trees from Southampton to Palm Beach every winter to keep them warm. Still others fly linens to Paris for dry-cleaning; bills can run upwards of $6,000 a month.[67]

People who are well socialized into the capitalistic system often believe that they need income to buy things they "need." (Or that without additional income they "cannot make ends meet.") But examinations of the purchases of those who are not poor or near poor show purchases of numerous items not needed in a strict sense of the term, but needed to meet status requirements ("could not show my face"). This is the sociological role of Nike sneakers, leather jackets, fur coats, jewelry, fancy watches, expensive cars, and numerous other such goods — all items that are highly visible to people who are not members of one's community, whom one does not know personally. These goods allow people to display the size of their income and wealth without attaching their accountant's statement or income tax returns to their lapels.

In such a culture, if people *choose* a job or career pattern that is not income-maximizing, and if they voluntarily embrace simplicity, they have no established means of signaling that they have *chosen* such a course rather than having been forced into it; that they have not failed in the eyes of the capitalist society. There are no lapel pins stating "I could have, but preferred not to." *Voluntary simplicity responds to this need for status recognition without expensive conspicuous consumption by choosing lower—cost, but visible, consumer goods that enable one to signal that one has chosen, rather than been coerced into, a less affluent lifestyle.*

This is achieved by using select consumer goods that are clearly associated with a simpler life pattern and are as visible as the traditional status symbols *and/or* cannot be afforded by those who reduced consumption merely because their income fell. For instance, those who dress down as part of their voluntary simplicity often wear some expensive items (a costly blazer with jeans and sneakers) or stylistic and far from inexpensive dress-down items (designer jeans), as if to broadcast their voluntary choice of this lifestyle. (Which specific consumption items signal voluntary simplicity versus coerced simplicity changes over time and from one subculture to another.) Brooks refers to this practice as "conspicuous non-consumption."[68] In this way, voluntary simplifiers can satisfy what Maslow considers another basic human need, that of gaining the appreciation of others, without using a high—and ever-escalating—level of consumption as their principal means of gaining positive feedback.

A major development being brought about by technological innovations makes it more likely that voluntary simplicity may be expanded, and that the less privileged and have-nots may gain in the process. In considering this development, I first discuss the nature of nonscarce objects and then turn to their implications for the reallocation of wealth.

Voluntary Simplicity in the Age of Knowledge

Developed societies, it has been argued for decades, are moving from economies that rely heavily on the industrial sector to economies that increasingly draw upon the knowledge industry.[69] The scope of this transition and its implications are often compared to that which those societies experienced as they moved from farming to manufacturing. One should note that there is a measure of overblown rhetoric in such generalizations. Computers are, for instance, classified as a major item of the rising knowledge industry rather than traditional manufacturing. However, once a specific computer is programmed and designed, a prototype tested and debugged, the routine fastening of millions of chip-boards into millions of boxes to make PCs is not significantly different from, say, the manufacturing of toasters. And while publishers of books are now often classified as part of the knowledge industry and computers are widely used to manufacture books, books are still objects that are made, shipped, and sold like other nonknowledge industry products. Recognizing that some of the claims of knowledge enthusiasts are overblown is not to deny that a major transformation is taking place, but merely to note that its pace and scope are much slower and less dramatic than was originally expected.

The main significance of the rise of the knowledge age is that the resulting shrinking of scarcity greatly enhances the opportunity for large-scale expansion of voluntary simplicity. This following particularly important point is surprisingly rarely noted: *Unlike the consumer objects that dominated the manufacturing age — cars, washing machines, bicycles, televisions, houses (and computers) — many knowledge "objects" can be consumed, possessed, and still be had by numerous others, that is shared, at minimal loss or cost.* Hence, in this basic sense, *knowledge defies scarcity*, thus reducing scarcity, which is a major driving principle behind industrial capitalist economies. Compare, for instance, a Porsche to a software program, say Pretty Good Privacy (PGP)[70] (or a minivan to a folk song). If an affluent citizen buys a particular Porsche (and all other billions of traditional consumer objects), this Porsche — and the resources that were invested in making it — is not available to any others (if one disregards friends and family). Once the Porsche is "consumed," little of value remains. By contrast, the software program (and a rising number of other such knowledge objects) can be copied millions of times, enjoyed by millions at once and at the same time, and it will still be available in its full, original glory.

True, sharing (copying, downloading) knowledge has some minimal costs, because it requires some nonknowledge "carrier." Sharing knowledge entails using some limited material base, a disk, a tape, or some paper. Even when the process is completely electronic, one needs an instrument—a radio, for instance—to access the item involved (e.g., listening to a lesson). Typically, however, the costs of these material carriers are minimal compared to those of most consumer goods. While many perishable goods (consumer objects such as food or gasoline) are low in cost per item, one needs to buy many of them repeatedly to keep consuming them. In contrast, "knowledge" objects such as language tapes or CD-ROMs can be enjoyed numerous times and are not "consumed" (eaten up, so to speak). In that sense, knowledge objects have the miraculous quality of the bush Moses saw in Sinai: it burned but was not consumed.

One may raise questions here about intellectual property and the problems that arise when people copy items of knowledge without rewarding the creators. However the copyright to much knowledge has, so to speak, long expired, from the "rights" to the ancient Greek philosophers to those of Copernicus. And much is handed out free on the Internet for one reason or another.

Many items of culture that are largely composed of symbolic arrangements of words, tones, or colors, have a similar feature and hence should be treated as part of the knowledge sources of satisfaction. Thus, a 99-cent edition of Shakespeare issued on poor paper in India, is not less enjoyable than a fancy, leather-bound one issued in the West. Millions of students can read Kafka's short stories, solve geographical puzzles, and study Plato, without any diminution of these items. Thus, millions can learn to play chess, and the game is not diminished. Chess played by prison inmates, using figures made of stale bread, is not less enjoyable than a game played with rare, ivory hand-carved pieces. (One may gain a secondary satisfaction from the aesthetic beauty of the set and from owning such an expensive set, but these satisfactions have nothing to do with the game of chess per se.)

That is, *these sources of satiation are governed by laws that are the mirror opposite of those laws of economics that govern oil, steel, and other traditional consumer objects from cellular phones to lasers.*

Similarly, bonding, love, intimacy, friendship, contemplation, communion with nature, certain forms of exercise (Tai Chi for instance, as distinct from the Stairmaster), all can free one, to a large extent, from governing laws of capitalistic economies and from scarcity. Many of these "acts" are, in effect, governed by the religious notion that to give is to receive (as in the case of love). I mean this quite technically and not at all in a preachy manner. Those who extend love to their spouse, friends, dog, are much more likely to be loved back than those who merely seek to be loved. The same holds for friendship, and—in a more complicated way—for working in a soup kitchen or other deeds of social service. (I am not suggesting that there is an exact proportionality but a positive correlation between giving and receiving, in these realms).

In effect, from this viewpoint, the relationship-based sources of satisfaction are superior to knowledge objects because in the kinds of relationships just enumerated, when one gives more, one often receives more, and thus both sides (or, in larger social entities such as communities, all sides) are "enriched" by the same "transactions." Thus, when two individuals get to know one another as people and become "invested" in one another during rituals such as dating, neither is lacking as a result, and often both are richer for it. (This important point is often overlooked by those who coined the term "social capital" to claim that relations are akin to transactions.) Similarly, parents who are more involved with their children often (although by no means always) find that their children are more involved with their parents, and both draw more satisfaction from the relationship. Excesses are far from unknown—for example, when some parents attempt to draw most of their satisfaction from their children—and sharply asymmetrical relations, in which one side exploits the other's dedication or love, also exist. Nonetheless, mutual "enrichment" seems much more common.

The various sources of nonmaterialistic satisfaction listed here were celebrated by the counterculture of the 1960s. However, voluntary simplicity differs from the counterculture in that voluntary simplicity, even by those highly dedicated to it, seeks to combine a reasonable level of work and consumption to attend to creature-comfort needs, with extra satisfaction from higher sources. The counterculture tried to minimize work and consumption, denied attention to basic needs, and hence became unsustainable. To put it more charitably, it provided an extreme, path-blazing version for the voluntary simplicity that followed. While voluntary simplicity is much more moderate than the lifestyle advocated by the counterculture — as a result of fostering satisfaction from knowledge rather than consumer objects — the need to work and shop is notably reduced. As a result, voluntary simplicity frees time and other scarce resources for further cultivation of nonmaterialistic sources of satisfaction, from acquiring music appreciation to visiting museums, from slowing down to enjoy nature to reacquiring a taste for reading challenging books.

One should note that none of the *specific* sources of nonmaterialistic satisfaction are necessarily tied to voluntary simplicity. One can engage in a voluntarily simple life without enjoying music or nature, being a bonding person or a consummate chess player, an Internet buff or a domino aficionado. However, voluntary simplicity does point to the quest for *some* sources of satisfaction other than the consumption of "traditional," scarce goods and services. This statement is based on the elementary assumption that people prefer higher levels of satisfaction over lower ones; hence if greater satisfaction is not derived from ever-increasing levels of consumption, their "excess" quest will "yearn" to be invested elsewhere. It follows that while the specific activities that serve as the sources of nonmaterialistic satisfaction will vary, some must be cultivated or voluntary simplicity may not be sustainable.

SOCIAL CONSEQUENCES OF VOLUNTARY SIMPLICITY

The shift to voluntary simplicity has significant consequences for society at large, above and beyond the lives of the individuals that are involved. A promising way to think about them is to ask what the societal consequences would be if more and more members of a society, possibly an overwhelming majority, were to embrace voluntary simplicity. These consequences are quite self-evident for the environment and hence need to be only briefly indicated; they are much less self-evident for social justice and thus warrant further attention.

Voluntary Simplicity and Stewardship toward the Environment

There can be little doubt that voluntary simplicity, if followed on a large scale, would significantly enhance society's ability to protect the environment. Moreover, if a significant number of people recast their lives according to the tenets of voluntary simplicity, even if they merely downshift rather than deeply recast their consumption, they are still likely to conduct themselves in ways that are more congenial to the environment than they were when they followed a life of conspicuous consumption.

First of all, voluntary simplifiers use fewer resources than individuals engaged in conspicuous consumption. Simple means of transportation, such as bicycles, walking, public transportation, or even cars that are functional but not ostentatious use significantly less energy, steel, rubber, and other scarce resources than the cars often favored today. People who choose to restore old buildings or move to the countryside tend, with notable exceptions, to use fewer scarce resources than those who build for themselves ostentatious residences with expansive living rooms, extensive gardens even in hostile environments (for instance, green lawns next to the sea or in the desert), and so on. And, of course, the more one purchases fashionable clothing or appliances, the more often these items will be discarded while still fully functional, which "burns up" some more scarce resources. In short, simplifiers act in ways that are environmentally friendly.

In addition, voluntary simplifiers are more likely than others to recycle, build compost heaps, and engage in other civic activities that favor the environment. This is the case because simplifiers draw more of their satisfaction out of such activities than out of consumption.

Indeed, studies show that being committed to voluntary simplicity strongly correlates with being most apt to install insulation, buy solar heating equipment, and engage in other energy-saving behaviors.[71]

Elgin's *Voluntary Simplicity* is rife with environmental concerns. Indeed, he frequently uses the terms "voluntary simplicity" and "ecological living" interchangeably.[72] Other books on simple living also stress the connection between cutting back on consumption and helping the environment including Alan Durning's *How Much is Enough?* and Lester W. Milbrath's *Envisioning a Sustainable Society*.[73]

The converse correlation holds as well. As people become more environmentally conscious and committed, they are more likely to find voluntary simplicity to be a lifestyle and ideology compatible with their environmental concerns. It should be noted, though, that while the values and motives of environmentalists and voluntary simplifiers are highly compatible, they are not identical. Voluntary simplifiers bow out of conspicuous consumption because they find other pursuits more in line with their psychological needs, while still ensuring that their basic creature-comfort needs are well– and securely sated. Environmentalists are motivated by concerns for nature and the ill-effects of increasing usage of scarce and nonrenewable resources. Despite these different motivational and ideological profiles, often one and the same person is both a simplifier and an environmentalist. At the very least, those who have one inclination are supportive of those who have the other.

Voluntary Simplicity and Equality

The more broadly and deeply voluntary simplicity is embraced as a lifestyle by a given population, the greater the potential for realization of a basic element of social justice — that of basic socio-economic equality. Before this claim is justified, a few words are needed on the meaning of the term equality, a complex and much-contested notion.

While conservatives tend to favor limiting equality to legal and political statutes, those who are politically left and liberal favor various degrees of redistribution of wealth in ways that would enhance socio-economic equality. Various members of the left-liberal camp differ significantly in the extent of equality they seek. Some favor far-reaching, if not total, socio-economic equality in which all persons would share alike in whatever assets, income, and consumption are available, an idea championed by the early kibbutz movements. Others limit their quest for equality to ensuring that all members of society will at least have their basic creature comforts equally provided, a position championed by many liberals. The following discussion focuses on this quest for socio-economic, and not just legal and political, equality. At the same time it is limited to creature-comfort equality rather than on a more comprehensive equality. (The debate about whether or not holistic equality is virtuous, and if it entails undercutting both liberty and the level of economic performance on which the provision of creature comforts depends is an important subject. However, this subject need not be addressed until basic socio-economic equality is achieved, and this has proven, so far, to be an elusive goal.)

If one seeks to advance basic socio-economic equality, one must identify forces that will propel the desired change. Social science findings and recent historical experiences leave little doubt that espousing ideological arguments (such as pointing to the injustices of inequalities, fanning guilt, and introducing various other liberal and socialist arguments that favor greater economic equality), organizing labor unions and left-leaning political parties, as well as introducing various items of legislation (such as estate taxes and progressive income tax) — did not have the desired result. Surprisingly little wealth redistribution occurred in democratic societies. The most that can be said in favor of these measures is that in the past they helped prevent inequality from growing bigger.[74]

Moreover, in recent years, many of the measures, arguments, and organizations that championed these limited, rather ineffective efforts to advance equality could not be sustained, or have been successful only after they greatly scaled back their demands as far as socio-economic equality is concerned.[75] Worse from the viewpoint of advocates of equality, for various reasons that need not be explored here, economic *inequalities* have increased in many parts of the world. The former communist countries, including the Soviet Union and China —

where a sacrifice of liberties was once associated with a meager but usually reliable provision of creature comforts — have acquired a socio-economic system that tolerates a much higher level of inequality, and one in which millions have no reliable source of these comforts. Numerous other countries, which had measures of socialist policies, from India to Mexico, have been moving in the same direction. And in many Western countries social safety nets are under attack, being shredded in some countries and merely lowered in others. All said and done, it seems clear that if basic socio-economic equality is to be significantly advanced, it will need to be helped by some new or additional force.

Voluntary simplicity, if more widely embraced, might well be the most promising new source to help create the societal conditions under which the limited reallocation of wealth needed to ensure the basic needs of all could become politically possible. The reason is as basic and simple as it is essential: To the extent that the privileged (those whose basic creature comforts are well-sated and who are engaging in conspicuous consumption) can find value, meaning, and satisfaction in other pursuits that are not labor- or capital-intensive, could be expected to be more willing to give up some consumer goods and income than they would be otherwise. The "freed" resources, in turn, could then be shifted to those whose basic needs have not been sated, without undue political resistance or backlash.

The merits of enhancing basic equality in a society in which voluntary simplicity is spreading differ significantly in several ways from those that are based on some measure of coercion. First, those who are economically privileged are often those who are in power, who command political skills, and who can afford to buy political support. Hence, to force them to yield significant parts of their wealth has often proven impractical, whether or not it is just or theoretically correct.

Second, even if the privileged can somehow be made to yield significant portions of their wealth, such forced concessions leave in their wake strong feelings of resentment. These have often led those who are wealthy to act to nullify or circumvent programs such as progressive income taxes and inheritance taxes, or to support political parties or regimes that oppose wealth reallocation.

The preceding analysis suggests that when people are strongly and positively motivated by nonconsumerist values and sources of satisfaction, they are less inclined to consume beyond that needed to satisfy their basic needs and are more willing to share their "excess" resources. Voluntary simplicity provides a culturally fashioned expression for such inclinations and helps to enforce them, and it provides a socially approved and supported lifestyle that is both psychologically sustainable and compatible with basic socio-economic equality.

In short, if voluntary simplicity is more extensively embraced by those whose basic creature comforts have been sated, it might provide the foundations for a society that accommodates basic socio-economic equality much more readily than societies in which conspicuous consumption is rampant.

IV

Can Virtual Communities Be Real?

with Oren Etzioni

In this study of communities we combine the perspectives of sociology and computer science to compare face-to-face (f2f) and computer-mediated communications (CMC) from the viewpoint of their respective abilities to form and sustain communities. We also identify a third type of community — a hybrid — that is based on a combination of f2f and CMC (or off- and online) communications. We thus, in effect, address an oft-asked question: Can virtual communities be "real" and have the same basic qualities as f2f communities? The study is exploratory, because much of the necessary evidence has not yet been generated, and the relevant technologies are rapidly changing.

COMMUNITY DEFINED

The comparison proceeds by pointing out that to form and sustain communities, certain conditions must be met. We examine whether f2f and CMC satisfy these conditions and whether one of the two kinds of modes of communication is more effective in this regard.

One difficulty confronted in studying the questions at hand is that various researchers define the dependent variable — community — differently. Hence, when some show that CMC can provide for the formation and functioning of communities, and others demonstrate the opposite, they are not necessarily referring to the same phenomena. For instance, in writings about CMC systems, the term "community" is sometimes used to refer to tightly knit social groups, and in other occasions to signify aggregates of people who hardly know one another; sometimes it even is used to describe mere geographic places. For instance, Geocities (http://www.geocities.com) provides for "neighborhoods" purportedly designed to emulate real-world communities. The domain is divided into such areas as Hollywood for entertainment information, Rodeo Drive for shopping, and Wall Street for business. However, while Hollywood, Rodeo Drive, and Wall Street are places in which virtual communities may be formed, they cannot be assumed prima facie to exist.

This problem is not limited to the literature on CMC systems; it is also widely acknowledged in the writings about f2f communities. Robert Fowler dedicated an entire book to the different definitions thereof, and the confusion arising from the disparities.[1] Margaret Stacey even suggested that the term is so poorly defined it should be abandoned.[2]

For the purposes of this examination, we define "community" as having two attributes: first, a web of affect-laden relationships that encompasses a group of individuals — relationships that crisscross and reinforce one another, rather than simply a chain of one-on-one relationships. To save breath, this attribute will be referred to as bonding. Second, communities require a measure of commitment to a set of shared values, mores, meanings, and a shared historical identity—in short, a culture.

Community is defined as nonresidential because many social entities that are not residential have many of the attributes of residential ones. A case in point: many Jewish communities, whose members meet at a synagogue, Sunday school, festivities, etc., even though they live in different residential areas. The same can be seen in gay communities and even on those campuses in which the university becomes a community even though the faculty do not live next to one another.

If one follows the definition used here, one notes that there are many aggregations of people that do not qualify as communities. People who pass each other as strangers in bus terminals or railroad stations, or are all subject to an electronic broadcast, or "meet" for the first time in a chat room, are best referred to as aggregates or groups but not as communities, because they do not share social bonds and a culture. In any case, one should not conclude that because online *aggregates* lack attributes of offline *communities*, that virtual communities are not—let alone cannot—be "real," that is, meet the prerequisites that are needed to form full-fledged communities. In the following analysis we compare off- and online aggregates to one another, and off- and online communities to one another.

It should also be noted that the two key attributes used here to define community are continuous and not dichotomous variables. Thus, both on- and offline, a community may have either stronger or somewhat weaker bonds, and either an extensively shared culture or a less elaborate one. However, if both are low, no community will exist, but rather some other type of social entity will form. Some observers wonder if there are any examples of "real" communities on the Internet. There are reports of several such communities.[3] The extent to which they are full-fledged communities, and which steps might be taken to make them stronger communities, will become clear as our argument unfolds.

We turn now to spelling out the requirements of community

building and inquire to what extent f2f or CMC can meet these specifications, and whether one can meet them more effectively than the other.

ACCESS

Access is defined as the ability to communicate, not in the sense of articulating a message but in the sense of being able to reach others. (Access is a prerequisite for communication but not tantamount to it. Thus, phone lines provide access; they make this form of communication possible among those who have phones. They do not, however, determine who will call whom and to what extent they will be utilized.)

To form and sustain communities, members require access to one another. All other things being equal, people who have a higher amount of access, as well as modes of access that encompass more of the people in a given aggregate, are more likely to form communities than those who have a lower level of access.[4] Indirect evidence to this effect can be seen in areas in which the level of f2f communications is declining, or has been low for a while; in such cases, community members tend to seek to increase communication in order to sustain their communities. They use various means to this effect, among them enhancing the safety of public spaces, increasing walkways and front porches, and holding more "community" meetings (e.g., PTA or town meetings). (For the purposes at hand, we ignore the fact that at very high levels of access this proposition may not hold; furthermore, we recognize that the proposition holds only for populations that are not highly heterogeneous, as well as other qualifications irrelevant to the comparative task at hand.)

Face-to-face contact among people within a given area provides opportunities for access. However, merely being in the same space does not necessarily engender f2f communication or community building, as many have observed about contact avoidance on New York City subways and the anticommunication culture of many car pools. For f2f contacts to provide for communications requires mores that legitimate and value communications.

One further notes that f2f communications often are built into other social occasions or relationships, such as meeting at a country shop, strolling on a promenade, serving together in a voluntary association, or attending adult education classes. Hence, no special arrangements or investment of resources, energy, or time are needed to ensure that the needed communications will take place (as long as the culture legitimizes initiating contact).

Computer-mediated communications enable people to communicate regularly without significant economic or other costs and without being in close proximity either spatially or temporally (CMC can be asynchronous). These communications evolve across both geographic borders and time zones, and they encompass individuals who are home-bound because of illness, age, handicap, or lack of social skills. They provide safety for people who seek to communicate but fear leaving home, a major consideration in many cities. And they can encompass a very large number of individuals.

In short, both f2f and CMC can provide the needed access. Online communications seem to be superior in that they can reach more people, even those dispersed over large areas. Offline communications benefit from the fact that they are built into other social activities (for instance, having a drink in a neighborhood pub), and hence require fewer specific initiatives than online communications.

ENCOMPASSING INTERPERSONAL KNOWLEDGE: IDENTIFICATION, AUTHENTICATION, AND ACCOUNTABILITY

Bonding, one of the two core elements of community, requires a high level of encompassing (versus specific) knowledge of the others with whom one bonds.[5] Accordingly, one would expect a group of individuals who meet for the first time — for instance, at a scientific meeting — to share only technical communications (like their findings and methods), to bond much less than a similar group of scientists who also share personal information (a recent divorce, the serious illness of a child, etc.) and discuss their personal feelings, formative experiences, and life histories.

To gain encompassing knowledge of others, one needs (a) to anchor various different items of knowledge about those involved with specific identities and thus be able to compose broad and inclusive images of others; (b) to trust that the communications from others are crudely correct, which often entails finding some way to authenticate some of the messages; and (c) to develop a sense that one is able to hold others accountable, that the members of the group are reasonably responsible. Thus, for instance, if a person promises to send a draft resolution or a letter of recommendation and does not, one is in a position to know which party failed, avoid dealing with that person in the future, and as such have a deterrent effect on irresponsible conduct. For communities to evolve and be sustained, they must be able to either marginalize or de facto exclude people who are found to be frequently irresponsible or otherwise antisocial.

Face-to-face communication can meet these requirements with relatively few difficulties. Such communication relies on various personal identification markers, such as names, addresses, faces, and records. Thus, if one person protests strongly about the direction in which a town meeting is moving, most people present will know who that person is, an identity that often includes several relevant facts about that person. For instance, whether he or she is a major figure or a marginal one, whether he or she has good reasons to object or instead blows hot and cold over time, and so on. These factors are all taken into account in assessing this (and all other) responses.

While most offline communities have difficulties in maintaining close personal knowledge of all members, especially as they grow in size, there is usually not more than one degree of separation between any two members, allowing A to ask B about C, as well as preserving records one can draw upon. Also, because communities tend to be homogeneous, it is often easier to empathize with others even if one does not know them personally.

Novels, plays, and movies are based on the highly unusual circumstances that arise when a person is able to acquire membership in the community without disclosing themselves or presenting a false-self. *The Return of Martin Guerre* is a fine example of this phenomenon.

In CMC, "handles" or "log-in IDs" are generally used in lieu of proper identification; even when names are given, disclosure is often very limited, and identity is rarely authenticated. As a result, there is ample documentation of presentations of false-selves,[6] role playing, gender swapping, and so on.[7] In many chat rooms "membership" is open-ended and uncontrolled. People join and drop out at will. Members of groups that have been chastised, have been reported to drop out and return with other log-in IDs.

These CMC features may well be valuable for several purposes, such as to vent feelings one is inclined to expose only to strangers one is never expecting to encounter again. Moreover, these features enable people to experiment with selves (and identities) other than their "true" one. But these features, on the face of it, do not promote interpersonal knowledge.

To the extent that CMC systems provide participants with features that enable them to readily activate authentication procedures, the more amenable these systems are to community building. Note that supplying the features routinely available does not mean that participants will seek to use them and certainly not that they be *required* to do so by some external authority.

In short, f2f communication systems are significantly superior to most CMC systems as far as identification, accountability, and authorization are concerned. However, it should be noted that there are no design difficulties in providing a much stronger basis for interpersonal knowledge in CMC systems. In fact, several forums already demand that participants use their true names, and others verify such claims. For example, MediaMOO, a MUD (multi-user dungeon, basically a CMC) for professionals, requires participants to provide their actual names, e-mail addresses, and background on their area of research.[8] MediaMOO's administrator verifies this information. Participation is limited to members and controlled by passwords, and once a person's identity is known, over time a CMC group will learn to know its members by associating various attributes (e.g., a tendency to "flame") and viewpoints (e.g., she/he is the most liberal/informed/responsible member of the group) with various individual members.

Additional features that could be added would further enhance the ability of online groups to associate validated personal information with various log-ins, to be activated if the members so choose. For instance, CMC mechanisms could ensure that when a member has the floor, a recent picture of that person will be flashed on the screen.

INTERACTIVE BROADCASTING

To form and sustain shared bonds and values, communities need to be able to (a) broadcast, i.e., send messages that reach many people simultaneously rather than "pointcast" to one person at a time, as is done in typical f2f conversation. Communities also need to (b) provide for feedback from those who are addressed by the said broadcast, including that from many recipients of the broadcast to many other recipients (communal feedback) and not merely from one participant to another (as in telephone conversations). We refer to this combination of needs as "interactive broadcasting."

One reason community building requires interactive broadcasting is that if there are only point-to-point communications, interpersonal bonding may develop (e.g., friendships, romantic involvement), but the crisscross bonding that characterizes communities will not. The reason that broad-based feedback (that from many to many) is needed is to allow those who broadcast to take into account the reactions they engender in a summary and continuous manner. If those who broadcast are unable to take into account responses to their messages, even if not in real time, their ability to persuade their audiences will be hampered. And if the members of a group are addressed but unable to provide systematic feedback, they will tend to feel propagandized rather than persuaded. Mutual persuasion is needed for members of a community, who start from divergent viewpoints on a specific issue, to be able to develop a shared position.

Face-to-face communication generally provides rather limited opportunities for interactive broadcasting, especially if the number of people involved is large, or they are dispersed over a large area. The needs of interactive broadcasting are met to a considerable extent, but far from fully, in town meetings. When these take place, a person addresses all those present (meeting the first prerequisite), and it is possible for those present to respond in a way that both the original broadcaster(s), and all those who have been initially addressed, hear the responses (meeting the second prerequisite).

Note that in such town meetings[9] responses are not necessarily monolithic. For instance, some parts of the audience may applaud while others hiss, some may chuckle appreciatively while the rest frown, and some people may nod their heads approvingly while others look pained or even stream out of the room. All these cues allow those who broadcast to adjust the message, based on their "reading" of various segments of the audience, in a community-building manner. They may better explain their point, moderate it, even retract, and so on, all in response to the reactions they are receiving.

While town meetings might well be the closest a community can come to meeting the need for interactive broadcasting, opportunities for interactive broadcasting are limited even in town meetings by the fact that often only a fraction of the members of a community attend. Time limits on such meetings further restrict the potential for interactive broadcasting. Such meetings rarely last more than a few hours and cannot be reconvened too often.

Another form of f2f communication systems that communities rely upon is the cobbling together, over time, of various discussions of subgroups that may take place in pubs, country stores, PTA meetings, and over the back fence. This cobbling usually takes place informally, without any particular institutionalized arrangements. This informal piecing together is discussed below. It suffices to say here that it provides a measure of interactive broadcasting as people report to one subgroup what other subgroups were told and what their initial and closing reactions were. It is, though, a rather slow and somewhat cumbersome process whose results are difficult to predict.

Computer-mediated communications systems readily meet one of the interactive broadcasting requirements: they readily enable broadcasting messages to all members of a group simultaneously. However, so far most CMC have no features that allow meeting the other requirements. In most cases, a person "addressing" a CMC-based community will have no information while he or she "speaks" about the reaction of the members of the community (especially in real time), and the members who receive the broadcast will have no knowledge about how others react to the same broadcast. This defect can be remedied, however, and is not a congenital trait of CMC systems.

One of the authors of this essay conducted a lab experiment in which ten participants who were listening in ten isolated booths to a broadcast speaker could — while the person was speaking — tilt a lever to the left for agreement or to the right for disagreement. The more they tilted to the right, the stronger an amber light was shining, and each of the participants had such a light, so the speaker as well as all others could determine how members of the group were reacting while the broadcast was taking place.[10] These devices so far are available mainly in social science labs and in theaters that test audience reaction to commercials and movies, but not yet on CMC. Moreover, as long as such devices provide only a summary feedback, they do not allow reading of subaudiences and changes within them as well as changes in intensity of commitment. The light may shine equally brightly if some of the members are strongly won over, even if the number of supporters actually dwindles. In short, this mode of feedback is typically highly condensed and insufficient.

The ability to record and transmit audio and video across the Internet in real time could form one basis for much richer feedback transmission. A person broadcasting to a group could benefit from serial scanning of individual faces or view several simulations on a split screen, or even allow for a summary of noise feedback, while others in the audience may receive the same feedback (that is, they will be able to see and hear how others in the audience react).

A more serious design challenge for CMC is to provide for communal feedback that will be segmented rather than monolithic and will enable the separation of various subaudience responses. (For instance, a person who has the floor may seek to know how young people in the audience respond versus the older ones, or minorities versus whites, or those who have school-age children versus others and so on.) This might be relatively easy to do for survey responses but more difficult for rendering audio and video attachments to capture subgroup and not merely aggregate responses.

In short, CMC are much superior broadcasting systems to f2f systems. However, neither system satisfies the need for feedback, communal sharing of responses, and segmented signals. While f2f communications meet this requirement relatively well in town meetings, these are rare. While CMC can be adapted to meet this requirement, this has not been done so far on more than an experimental basis.

BREAKOUT AND REASSEMBLE (B & R)

Communities differ from intimate, close-knit groups of friends and families (including most extended families) in that they encompass a larger number of members. The larger the number, the more difficult it is for all members to participate actively in dialogues that maintain shared values or for members to bond with one another. For this reason, many Israeli kibbutzim strongly opposed increasing their membership beyond several hundred members. (They were horrified when, for the first time, one exceeded a thousand members.)

Large groups that seek to maintain a high level of dialogue provide structured opportunities for breakout groups, in which members meet in subgroups and then share their conclusions with the larger group by asking a representative of each breakout group to briefly address the reassembled plenary group. Such B & R systems are not considered as effective as scenarios in which all members participated in one small group (because then all those present could receive and respond to all communication), but are considered more effective than if all participate only in one large group and no breakout is provided.

Face-to-face communication systems sometimes provide for such B & R. This is the case, for instance, during conferences of members of large voluntary associations. Here, all those seated around a table are asked to discuss the issues at hand with one another before the discussion is returned to those who address the whole group. (Because of the resulting noise these sessions are sometimes referred to as "buzz" sessions.) In other conferences, the breakout groups retreat to separate meeting rooms before they reassemble. Much more informally, in many communities B & R occurs when subgroups of members meet in the country store, pubs, etc., and discuss subjects to be raised at a forthcoming town meeting or referendum, and then informally share with one another what they concluded in other such rump meetings.

While it seems that only very few CMC systems meet this requirement so far, they could readily provide for B & R sessions by adding this feature to the common chat room or newsgroup format. Many chat rooms already enable any two participants to break out, hold a private discussion and return to the larger group; however, these amount to point-to-point dialogues that lead to interpersonal relationships or business deals, but *not* to community building (which could occur if the breakout consisted of subgroups rather than pairs).

Group breakouts from chat groups do occur when sublists are created from a list and broadcasts are tailored to the sublists. Still, the prerequisites of a full-fledged B & R system are not met because those who engage in sublist dialogue do not "reassemble" the full group for reports or final community-wide deliberations.

There seem to be no insurmountable difficulties that would prevent one from designing a full-fledged B & R system online. All such a design would require is a predesignated schedule for breakout and reassembly. For example, if 120 people participate in a given chat room, they must be able to determine at the outset, perhaps by a vote based on preprogrammed options, that after a given time period, the group will break into 20 sublists for a given time period, at the end of which the full 120-member forum will reopen. Each of the smaller (20-member) groups would select a representative who would report each subgroup's deliberations after which general chat would resume.[11]

Variations on the system could include enabling the participants to choose which subgroup to join, to vote on the length of the total meeting, and to decide the proportion of time spent in breakouts versus the plenary.

In short, f2f allows B & R systems, needed to build consensus in a large group, to build this consensus into ongoing communal activities. They also do so in meetings of various voluntary associations and other social groups. There seem to be no great difficulties in allowing CMC systems to meet the same requirements, allowing large groups to communicate in subgroups and reassembling in larger ones to share the deliberations of the constituent subgroups. So far, however, B & R opportunities are not routinely provided.

COOLING-OFF MECHANISMS AND CIVILITY

Community dialogues, a major source of sharing a culture, seem to function most effectively when delay loops are built into the communication systems, and seem to function most poorly when they take place in real time. The designers of democracy, particularly the founding fathers of American democracy, were greatly concerned about the rule of the mob. They feared that demagogues would whip up irrational emotions and drive people to demand unreasonable policies and actions from their leaders. Democracy requires mechanisms for keeping passions in check and allowing reason to prevail; the House of Lords in the United Kingdom and the Senate in the United States are said to serve as such checks on the more populist lower houses. More recently, teledemocracy, in which the electorate is exposed to a message and asked to vote immediately, as suggested by Buckminster Fuller and Ross Perot, raises the same concerns regarding electronic voting and polling of public opinion.[12]

Most recently this issue has been faced when concerns have been expressed about the loss of civility and the rise in emotive tensions and polarization both in the public (especially under the influence of hosts of talk radio shows such as Rush Limbaugh and Howard Stern) and among elected officials. In short, constructive community dialogues and democratic government are believed to require cooling-off mechanisms. Effective cooling-off mechanisms provide delay loops — time intervals between receiving a message and sending a response — and use this lapsed time for dialogues that cross (and mute) previous divisions.

Face-to-face communication systems have built-in informal delay loops due to the constant nature of informal communication and gossip; furthermore, decisions often are deferred from one town meeting to another, or resolutions are reconsidered in subsequent meetings. Also, as townspeople meet, groups are regrouped so that dialogues occur among different combinations of people rather than only within one subgroup (to the exclusion of others). Both systems allow passions to cool as one learns about the objections and concerns of others, of people he or she is bonded with and of those whose views he or she therefore respects. The passions of the moment have a chance to cool off. While these informal mechanisms do not always suffice, especially when community bonds are weak or the community is in conflict with another, all f2f communities possess some cooling-off mechanisms.

Some CMC systems contain a modicum of cooling-off potential. When people compose a message on e-mail and order it to be sent, the program verifies with them if the command is definite. This allows for at least a short moment of reflection. America Online enables its users to compose mail and arrange for it to be mailed later, which allows one to reformulate messages composed in the heat of the moment.

Design changes could readily provide for much more effective cooling-off mechanisms. For instance, when one participates in certain community forums in which highly charged issues are deliberated, responses could be delayed automatically for 24 hours, during which one can pull them back before they can be retrieved by others, somewhat like being able to get a letter back from the post office after mailing it in a moment of impulse. (This design would differ from the America Online feature in that it would be an agreed communal feature rather than subject to individual impulse.) Most important, an agreed time interval could be set between the initial broadcasting of a message and the tallying of votes, rather than allowing instant responses.

In short, both f2f and CMC systems already have some built-in delay loops that enhance civility and provide time for cooling the emotions aroused by the initial messages, deliberation, and occasions for dialogues among members of the community before a final decision is rendered. However, the systems seem inadequate because currently they have, at best, rather meager delay loops. It seems that one could readily provide CMC systems with stronger civility options. (Measures that would enhance civility of f2f have not been discussed but are often explored when the need to promote a civil society is studied.)

MEMORY

The communal sharing of culture never starts from a tabula rasa. The process of sharing value draws on a prior sharing of history, communal identity, experiences, and rituals. Hence, the need for a communal memory.

Face-to-face communities use various devices for such memory, including elder talk, the town library, archives and records, minutes, monuments, and grave stones. These devices are much more effective in recalling and reconstructing a community's history, past normative commitments, shared tragedies, and celebrations than they are in recalling cognitive materials. These devices are often rather unreliable, which makes it easier to reconstruct the past in line with contemporary needs, but provides a poor foundation for logical and empirical endeavors.

Computer-mediated communications systems already provide for very powerful memory and retrieval systems. For instance, many representatives and senators maintain web sites in which constituents can access full archives of their speeches and voting records. CMC systems are much better at retrieving cognitive information, such as the text of resolutions previously passed by the town's council, past budgets, and earlier voting results, than at evoking the communal past.

In short, memories produced by f2f systems may be vague and unreliable, but they often are highly evocative and help forge a shared culture out of a varied past. Even without any additional increases in capacity and design modifications, CMC systems are vastly more effective than f2f systems in maintaining memory and retrieving it for communal purposes, as far as cognitive memories are concerned.

MIXED COMMUNICATION SYSTEMS

So far we have seen that when it comes to satisfying the communication needs of communities, it is a mistake to assume that f2f communications are greatly more effective than CMC systems or that it is difficult to form and sustain communities online. Thus, while f2f systems are better at providing encompassing knowledge and B & R systems than CMC systems, the opposite is true for retrieval of cognitive information that has been generated earlier. Moreover, in some areas, the differences are of degree rather than kind. For instance, both B & R systems are rather primitive, although those of f2f are somewhat more effective. When all is said and done, the specific profiles of CMC systems obviously differ from those of f2f ones, but this should not be taken to indicate that CMC are unable to meet the basic community criteria of bonding and sharing values. It follows that it is more productive to compare one type of community to another type and see their relative merits and demerits, than it is to ask what virtual communities lack compared to "real" ones.

Most important, we know from other comparative studies the faulty thinking that arises when one compares one type of system to another and overlooks the existence of hybrid systems. One case will stand for many other examples that could be given. Numerous studies originally compared traditional teaching to instruction on television (ITV). It was hypothesized that ITV would be superior to f2f teaching because ITV could use the best teachers, film lessons repeatedly until a very strong presentation was achieved, and allow the students to view the tape at their own pace (as many times as they liked, at the times most suitable to them, etc.). Others feared that the lack of personal involvement by the teachers on ITV would negatively effect the students' motivation to study, suppress their ability to absorb material, and prevent them from asking questions. It turned out that the best instructional systems are person-machine combinations in which teachers provide students with small discussion sessions that follow viewing of a teaching tape.

If one follows the same line of analysis, one would expect that communities that combine both f2f and CMC systems would be able to bond better and share values more effectively than communities that rely upon only one or the other mode of communication. While there is a very rich body of experience, experimentation, and literature on person-machine relations when it comes to computers, there is not much to draw on when one seeks to analyze mixed f2f–CMC systems in the practice of community building. Hence, one draws on informal observations and reports.

One kind of hybrid system known by many in professional or public life or in business is when groups of people meet in person and form some measure of shared understanding, then maintain bonding through CMC. There are also ample informal reports about people who bonded on a CMC and then met f2f, although these reports are largely about dyads rather than larger groups.[13]

Hybrids allow the special strengths of each system to make up for weaknesses of the other. Thus, hybrid systems — drawing on their CMC — have better memory capabilities than sheer f2f systems, and — drawing on their f2f links — a higher level of interpersonal knowledge than exclusive CMC systems.

One must expect that hybrid systems will not be all of one kind; a large number of different combinations can be readily conceived.

One variation stands out: the extent to which an f2f community is also "wired." For instance, f2f town meetings could not be followed with additional deliberations in a CMC forum if only half of the members had access to it. And bonding at PTA meetings would not benefit (and might even be set back) if only half of the parents (most likely the more affluent ones) had access to a CMC parent forum. Installing terminals in numerous public spaces, from the community library to shopping centers, may mitigate this problem, but will hardly overcome it.[14]

Another major consideration for a hybrid system is when its CMC component reaches people who are geographically dispersed; it is much more difficult for these people to develop f2f communications than when people are concentrated in a relatively small and contiguous area.

The various deficiencies of CMC and f2f systems stand as challenges to designers to create the kind of system that has the highest potential for bonding and evolving a shared culture, that best catalyzes the building of genuine communities. Far from finding that CMC systems cannot meet the needs of "real" communities, we find that there are no conceptual reasons or technical ones that CMC-based communities, especially given additional technical development, could not become full-fledged communities. Finally, we suggest that both f2f and CMC systems have strengths and weaknesses of their own, and that their proper combination promises to meet more of the prerequisites of community than either of them could separately.

VIRTUAL COMMUNITIES REVISITED[15]

When I revisited cyberspace communities a mere two years after the preceding portion of this chapter was initially written, I found that several important factors favorable to online communities, had been developed in the interval. Several more seem to be in the pipeline, especially audio and video feedback, which would significantly enhance community building for reasons explored in the above discussion. Several important studies of online communities have been published in the interval, as well.[16]

No subject lends itself to a false dichotomy like that of virtual and real communities. But the two are not opposites, not exclusionary, and not necessarily good for the same things.

For instance, the argument that virtual communities cannot do what real communities can, a common position, is analogous to the argument, when Model T cars rolled off assembly lines, that cars could not do what horses could: become your friends. Both modes of transportation, though, get you there, and cars command some obvious advantages of their own.

The current primitive virtual communities are stronger in several ways than the real thing: if you are lonely or down, you can go online any time, find out which of your buddies is around, and visit. (Try doing this at the neighborhood bar on Sunday at 7 A.M.)

If there is a snowstorm or you are sick with the flu, not very mobile or afraid of the streets, you may not make it to your local country store or senior center. But you can always log on.

When a car does something you thought only a horse could do, like inspire affection, for instance, it is surprising. So it is surprising that several important features of real communities are beginning to be provided online, albeit in different ways than offline — ways that have their own weaknesses and strengths.

One essential characteristic of communities is that they are largely self-policing. Real communities minimize the role of the state, the police, and the courts by relying on gossip. You know which store to avoid and who is likely to repair your roof on time because of a subtle system that rates and updates reputations through offline chatter.

Online communities also need to find ways to do this. In auctions, at least one side ends up taking a risk; it is often the buyer but occasionally it is the seller. So each party is keen to know the other's reputation. The huge auction site, eBay, (http://www.ebay.com), handles this problem through an ingenious system of rating reputations.

Similar systems are used by Amazon.com (http://www.amazon.com) and Auctions.com (http://www.auctions.com), among others.

After auctions or trades, both sellers and buyers are asked to rate one another. As a result, each participant acquires a score that reflects the number of positive and negative comments received. All are posted online.

Recently, I was considering bidding on a political science book by Harold Laski in an online eBay auction. To check out the seller's reputation, I looked at her feedback from other sellers and buyers. She had earned thirty positive comments and had drawn only one complaint. All the comments were listed; a typical positive comment was from a seller (whose own score was a high 1,502) who wrote: "Fast with payment, nice to deal with, AAAAAAA + + + + + + + + +." The negative comment did not impress me. The seller seemed reliable.

Digging further, I found that the eBay screen name and number appears above every negative or positive comment. Using that information, I could ascertain a complainer's reputation. The system seems to work like a charm: Fewer than one percent of eBay auctions involve fraud, said an eBay spokesman, Kevin Pursglove.[17]

There are no comparable statistics for satisfied customers in offline communities, which may not in fact do as well. Offline gossip is more nuanced. You would know, for instance, that a normally reliable person failed to fulfill an obligation because his wife had just discovered that she has breast cancer, and, as a result, you would give that person another chance. In an online community involving millions of people, such as eBay, though, this type of information would not be readily known. Offline gossip systems, on the other hand, rarely encompass any more than a thousand people, at the most.

Virtual communities cannot provide nearly as much subtle and encompassing knowledge of members as a real community. But they can include many more people. One's strong suit is depth, the other's is breadth.

Like reputation, trust is also important both online and off. For transactions to flow seamlessly, people must trust one another. In real communities, people's default is to do so. They are taught from childhood to presume that members of the community are good people. It is considered inappropriate to distrust any member, unless there is cause.

Most virtual communities start from the opposite assumption: I do not know you, other than your online alias, so how can I trust you?

But three developments allow for a measure of e-trust to develop. For low-value transactions (often up to $250), auction communities provide free insurance that covers any goods or payments that are not delivered.

For larger amounts, i-Escrow (http://www.iescrow.com) serves as an electronic form of trust for many sites, including GO.com (http://www.go.com), GimmeaBid.com (http://www.gimmeabid.com), and Mac4Sale.com (http://www.mac4sale.com). After an auction ends, the buyer deposits the money owed with i-Escrow. The seller is then told to ship the goods. Once the buyer verifies that the merchandise has been received, i-Escrow sends the money to the seller.

When quality makes a difference — such as when buying collectable stamps or Pokémon cards — quality can be determined by an appraiser, like those at the International Society of Appraisers (http://isa-appraisers.org). The seller can then post the information or send appraisal printouts to interested buyers. Or a buyer using i-Escrow can refer an item to appraisers before releasing payment. All that may sound a bit complex, but not for those who live by the mouse. And it does generate a trust level that allows the e-system to function despite some difficulties, for instance, shills placing bids during auctions.

Real communities foster intimacy as well as trust, as people get to know one another and form close, warm bonds. It is often argued that such closeness cannot be forged in cyberspace because people cherish their anonymity and hide their true selves behind handles and false presentations about who they are.

Actually, cyberspace has developed the tools that allow not only the fostering of intimacy in one-on-one relationships (such as e-dating) but also among members of groups. It is best to think about these tools as building blocks. Some virtual communities are based on only a few, while others accumulate a lot of them.

If a community is to be intimate, unfortunately, it must exclude some people. Real communities keep people out with high-entrance fees (e.g., condominiums, country clubs) and various admission criteria (e.g., no pets or children allowed). Communities can do this — as long as they do not violate laws concerning racial discrimination and a few other forms of bias. By keeping membership homogeneous and small — and if possible, stable — offline communities foster intimacy.

Numerous virtual communities work in similar ways, although they are much more upfront about their procedures than real ones. For instance, eCircles (http://www.ecircle.net) makes it easy for anyone to set up a closed community. Both Yahoo! (http://www.yahoo.com) and Excite (http://www.excite.com) run thousands of clubs. Some are not merely closed but invisible — they are unlisted. Others post the names of the administrators who handle requests for admission. And size is often limited; Excite's clubs, for example, can have no more than 2,000 members. The newest wrinkle is that Excite lets groups of up to ten members have an audible conversation online, in real time.

Much greater intimacy can be engendered if members of an e-community voluntarily surrender their anonymity and the community verifies identities. Some time ago, I joined one of the roughly eighty little-known H-nets run by the National Endowment for the Humanities. These are closed to the public and consist of groups of professors specializing in, say, French history and culture or, in my case, communitarian thinking. Participants must apply to be included, and many list their real names on the screen. Several H-nets — the one for people studying the Hapsburg empire, for example — verify these identities.

As a result, you can combine what you already know about Scholar X from University Y with what you hear from her on the H-net. Soon you feel as though you know one and all, as if you were in some kind of never-ending f2f meeting. You learn that Scholar A, whose writing you have long admired, is rather slow-witted and that

Scholar B, whom you have always suspected of not knowing what he is writing about, is rather sociable. Instead of small packets of personal information of dubious validity, you get a rather broad and reliable band, which is of great value for creating intimacy, maybe too much for your taste.

It seems that e-communities can reach the highest levels of intimacy only if all the building blocks are in place: the number of participants is kept relatively small, admission is controlled to foster affinity, and people drop their Internet masks. But even if one or two of these elements are missing, online communities can still allow people to build reputations and trust and foster intimacy, much like offline groups. However, they do so in different ways and, above all, can reach many more people, day or night, rain or shine.

V

Suffer the Children

Several leading civil libertarian groups and advocates (and libertarians) argue that minors of all ages are entitled to First Amendment rights. (To save breath, all will be referred to from here on as civil libertarians.) Reference is mainly not to "production" of speech but to "consumption," the unfettered access to cultural material. Basically, civil libertarians maintain that children should be treated the same as adults in this matter. After laying out the arguments advanced by civil libertarians in favor of this surprising position, I question the underlying reasons for these groups to embrace this position. I conclude by suggesting that civil libertarians can defend their liberty without hurting children.

CHILDREN'S FIRST AMENDMENT RIGHTS

Four Policies
Four recently contested issues show the way civil libertarians view minors' First Amendment rights. All concern the protection of chil-

dren from sexually explicit material and gratuitous violence in the media, from health hazards (specifically, luring cigarette ads), and from commercial exploitation.

One policy concerns the introduction of filters into computers used to access the Internet. Such software blocks access either to a given list of web sites or to messages that contain certain key words (e.g., bestiality). Brand names include X-Stop, Cyber Patrol, and Net Nanny. These filters are reported to be quite effective, although occasionally materials they seek to block out slip through,[1] and sometimes material that arguably should be allowed through (e.g., the Starr report?) is screened out.

The second policy at issue involves public efforts to persuade tobacco companies to stop placing the so-called "Joe Camel" type of ads. These ads reportedly target children and are believed to be particularly effective in enticing them to smoke.

A third policy concerns self-imposed limitations that several major corporations and industrial associations have adopted, which limit the information they collect about children who access their web sites or send them e-mail. These limitations apply especially to "cookies," devices installed by corporations in a person's computer, often unbeknownst to that person.[2] Cookies allow marketers to recognize an individual's computer when its operator approaches the web sites again, and to tailor advertising to that user.[3] In addition, information about users is often sold to other corporations. Responding to complaints that such profiling of clients violates their privacy, corporations such as Disney and Kellogg and associations such as the Direct Marketing Association and the Online Privacy Alliance announced that they would refrain from collecting information about children twelve years or younger unless the youths' parents consented.[4]

The fourth measure entails the introduction of V-chips in television sets, which enable parents to block their TV sets from screening programs that have more violent or vile content than they deem appropriate for their children to view. Federal law requires that V-chips be installed in all TV sets made after 1993. For the V-chip to differentiate between programs according to their violence rating or some other content attribute (e.g., offensive sexual material), the broad-casted programs must include ratings. For this to occur there must be an agreed-upon set of ratings, and a method for programs to include these ratings in a manner that the V-chip can recognize.[5] Most networks have reluctantly agreed to introduce a rating system.[6]

Civil Libertarian Objections

Civil libertarians argue that these policies limit the free flow of information and ideas and hence offend the First Amendment. The main parties challenging these policies are the American Civil Liberties Union (ACLU), the American Library Association (ALA), libertarians (specifically the Cato Institute), and the National Campaign for Freedom of Expression (NCFE). It is crucial for all that follows to note that these associations have demanded — and in some cases succeeded — that various protective devices be removed not simply for minors approaching maturity, but demand unencumbered access for children of all ages to all cultural materials. Indeed, public debates about the policies at issue center around the question of whether protecting children who are *twelve years old or younger* comports with the Constitution. (Both protection that may be provided by the state and allowing or enabling parents to act are at issue.)

A colleague who read a previous draft of this chapter wondered why the line was drawn at the age of twelve, and pointed out that older children require protection as well. This particular age is discussed not merely because it is at the focus of public attention (such as it is) on this matter, but also because children age twelve and younger serve as a sort of litmus test. If one cannot convince civil libertarians, judges, and policy makers about the need to protect infants, toddlers, and first graders — one can hardly expect these adults to shield adolescents.

Civil libertarians seem to realize the difficulty of convincing the public of the legitimacy of their position, hence, they often make their case indirectly. For instance, in objecting to limiting Joe Camel ads, the ACLU argues that it is unreasonable to suppress ads that target children because doing so also limits the information flow to adults. As the ACLU states, "Adults cannot be reduced to reading only what is fit for children."[7] And, "attempts to reduce the exposure of minors to tobacco advertisements cannot avoid restricting the same information for the adult population."[8] Thus, occasionally the ACLU avoids directly claiming that it favors exposing children to tobacco ads, but achieves the same goal by insisting that such curbs intrude on the First Amendment rights of adults.

Other times the ACLU simply states that *everyone* should have access to material considered damaging to children, but does not explicitly mention that children are to be included. Thus, the ACLU declares that, "We believe that the enactment of the proposed tobacco advertising restrictions would impose a drastic curtailment of commercial speech and could have a chilling effect on the right of the public and businesses to engage in free speech about controversial subjects."[9] Similarly, Steve Dasbach, the party chairman of the Libertarian Party, holds that, "if Congress ratifies this agreement, Americans will suffer from the second-hand smoke of the Bill of Rights being torched. . . . In their frenzy to control tobacco, politicians want the power to drastically restrict the First Amendment."[10]

In other situations, civil libertarians state their position quite explicitly. Thus, when a public library in Kern County, California allowed children free access to unfiltered computers after being threatened by an ACLU lawsuit,[11] Ann Beeson, an ACLU National Staff Attorney, wrote, "We applaud the Board of Supervisor's decision to honor the First Amendment rights of Kern County citizens by . . . allow[ing] all adult *and minor* patrons to decide for themselves whether to access the Internet with or without a filter."[12] Note that the term "minor" references children of all ages, and Beeson does not suggest protecting any of them or that there is any age at which they are unable to "decide for themselves." This is not a slip of a pen but a position consistently adopted. The same position was struck by the ACLU when it charged the Loudoun County Library Board of Trustees in Virginia, that has introduced filters, of "'removing books from the shelves' of the Internet with value to both adults *and minors* in violation of the Constitution."[13]

The American Library Association (ALA) makes the same case but more explicitly.[14] Its basic charter argues, with reference to Internet access, that "the rights of users who are minors shall in no way be abridged."[15] This position is based on the Library Bill of Rights, which holds that "A person's right to use a library should not be denied or abridged because of origin, age, background, or views." In the original 1948 version the document referred only to "origin, background, or views," as grounds which could not be used to deny service.[16] Age (any and all ages) was added in 1996.

Some tobacco industry advertisements have targeted young people, according to internal documents introduced in various trials.[17] In addition, some statistics indicate a strong correlation between certain tobacco advertisements and increasing numbers of teenage smokers. For example, "The largest increase in adolescent smoking initiation was in 1988, the year that the Joe Camel cartoon character was introduced nationally."[18] In response to government efforts restricting tobacco advertising, the ACLU has stated that "we [should] allow consumers to make decisions for themselves and stop government from deciding for us what speech we should be free to hear about legal products."[19]

The ACLU opposes the V-chip on the grounds[20] that children's access to television should not be curbed, because devices such as the V-chip screen out ideas, and because there is no evidence "that explicit sex information and even pornography . . . by themselves cause psychological harm to *minors of any age.*"[21]

In 1998, a group of representatives of privacy advocacy organizations met at the Electronic Privacy Information Center (EPIC) to prepare for a White House conference on ways to deal with privacy violations.[22] A representative from the Center for Media Education as well as one from the Communitarian Network favored the self-imposed, voluntary policies of corporations not to collect information from children age twelve or younger who visit their web sites, or to send them e-mail without their parents' consent. The ACLU's representative objected on the grounds that a young child may seek information about ways to deal with HIV or pregnancy and fear disclosing such a quest to his or her parents. EPIC's representative concurred.[23]

Similarly, the Cato Institute's reasoning is that "It makes little sense to morally condemn those who sell to children when we ourselves give children the means to buy. So regulation of marketing . . . that contain[s] information about children is *no more justified than regulation [that] contain[s] information about adults*."[24] The Cato Institute also points out that "the vulnerability of children is not a unique justification for restrictions on marketing, since myriad other speech activities may influence children."[25] And the Cato Institute wonders, "Do children face any real harm from marketing? The main risk seems to be that children might end up with a little more useless junk than they would otherwise."[26]

ARE CHILDREN "MINI-ADULTS" OR A DISTINCT SUBCATEGORY?

In evaluating the civil libertarian position one must consider whether children constitute a distinct category of persons. Obviously, suggestions that special measures should be introduced to protect children but not adults can be justified only if children are substantially different from adults in ways that are relevant to the exposure of minors to all elements of our culture. The answer to this question is not as self-evident as it might seem; the ways minors have been characterized and categorized have changed significantly over the ages and vary from one culture to another.[27]

In the Middle Ages, children often were treated as mini-adults, that is, were not considered a distinct category of people. For instance, when children misbehaved, they were considered to have acted out of ill will rather than from having not yet acquired societal mores. Punishment meted out did not differentiate between minors and majors. In contrast, in the modern era, especially in democratic societies, children often have been considered a distinct kind of people, especially vulnerable, incompetent, dependent, and in need of protection. Moreover, in these kinds of societies children are usually treated as members of a specific societal unit, the family, and parents have been charged with attending to their children and consequently accorded many rights of control over their offspring.

In recent decades, we have witnessed a retreat from regarding children as dependents and as family members. In an extension of various liberation movements, and the very legitimate rising concern for the human rights of minorities, women, gay and lesbian people, senior citizens, and disabled persons, we have also witnessed a new concern for the rights of children to make autonomous decisions — like adults.[28] This tendency has been further fueled by those who view the family as being phased out, hence requiring a new positioning of children.[29] While typically these observations have not led to arguments that there are no remaining differences between children and adults, when it comes to First Amendment issues, arguments move the social construction of children by civil libertarians as well as some liberals toward treating them as mini-adults rather than as substantially different. This is in sharp contrast to the position taken by the same group in opposition to treating children as adults in the court of law and in placing juveniles in adult correctional facilities and jails.

The treatment of children as mini-adults runs contrary to almost the total body of social science evidence, enormous bodies of law, and values embodied in the major institutions of democratic societies, all of which view children as *developmental creatures*. That is, children begin life as highly vulnerable and dependent persons, unable to make reasonable choices on their own, and gradually grow to become (as society hopes, and parents and educators labor to achieve) people able to make moral judgments, competent to act on their own, and ready to be autonomous persons.[30]

Stanford Law Professor Michael Wald makes this point as follows: "Younger children, generally those under 10–12 years old, do lack the cognitive abilities and judgmental skills necessary to make decisions about major events which could severely affect their lives. . . . Younger children are not able to think abstractly, have a limited future time sense, and are limited in their ability to generalize and predict from experience."[31] Yale Professor Joseph Goldstein adds, "To be a *child* is to be at risk, dependent, and without capacity to decide what is 'best' for oneself. . . . To be an *adult who is a parent* is to be presumed in law to have the capacity, authority, and responsibility to determine and to do what is good for one's children."[32]

John O'Neill puts it succinctly, when he writes, "Currently, there are attempts to define children's rights on the liberal model of individual rights exercised by potentially autonomous agents — despite the reality of children's dependency."[33]

Society's expectations from children, and the rights society accords them, reflect this developmental perspective. Society first requires children to be cared for by their parents and to heed them, as well as to attend school, while society allows children to leave both as they grow older. And society allows young people to consume alcohol, drive, marry, vote, serve in the armed forces, and sign contracts at different ages, but only rarely when they are very young. There seems to be no foundation in social science to assume that when it comes to exposure to information, children are initially less in need of adult protection and guidance than in other aspects of their lives.[34]

One may ask, as children grow to be independent individuals, won't each undergo a vulnerable trial period during which they will first be exposed to potentially harmful media images (e.g., cigarette ads, pornography, violence)? Might it not be more important for them to be exposed to this material at a younger age, when parents can more effectively provide a moral context for the incoming information? If the ultimate goal of a child's education is to have him/her making moral choices for him/herself, then shouldn't the child be confronted with both positive and negative images early on and guided to the correct choice, rather than initially robbed of the option to choose and have the "better" choice made for them?

Gradually exposing children to the violent and vile side of the adult world is indeed called for, but only commensurate with their ability to deal with the material. For instance, there is no reason to rush to expose preteens to sexually alluring material in order to teach them to deal with it. Moreover, for parents and educators to be able to help shape the children's responses, they must be aware of the specific inputs the children face and be able to arrange them in line with some kind of an educational agenda rather than allow them to be engulfed by violent video games and trash TV, and lost in the World Wide Web. Above all, for parents and educators to participate in developing judgment they must be given the tools that enable them to actively participate in the cultural choices their charges make and the ways they initially deal with them.

NOTCHING THE SLOPE

Why do leading civil libertarians ignore the significant differences between children and adults? One reason might be the tendency of strong advocates to push their thesis to its illogical conclusion. (Just as civil libertarians tend to treat children like adults, hard-core social conservatives often treat adults like children, for instance, by seeking to ban access to pornography to people of all ages.) In addition, civil libertarians fear the metaphorical slippery slope. For instance, the ACLU warns that "if this legislation [regarding tobacco ads] prevails, Congress could clearly impose similar restrictions on any commercial product."[35] If children are denied full court First Amendment rights in order to improve their character, could one not favor the same for adults?

This particular slippery slope, though, is clearly different from others in that clear markers can be set to prevent slippage. Unlike the difficulty in defining differences between fighting words (which, due to their dangerous effect, may be banned) and others, differences in age are rather easy to determine. Hence, public policies that prevent children from accessing certain materials, and above all policies enabling parents and educators to protect their wards, will not spill over to adults unless a more encompassing policy is deliberately embraced. Indeed, society expects parents and educators to actively participate in selecting the material to which their children are exposed. Civil libertarians should not hinder the development of the needed policies and tools merely for the sake of a paradigm that does not apply to children in the first place.

The attempt to extend First Amendment rights to protect children against their parents (rather than the government) is particularly puzzling and troubling. Such an extension is so farfetched that one may wonder whether it might be inadvertent. One may oppose a voluntary ban on Joe Camel ads because it was offered under pressure from Congress. Likewise, objection to the introduction of filters into public library computers may be justified. However, while the V-chip has been incorporated into TV sets by force of law, it is not activated unless parents so wish. And the refusal of libraries to inform parents of their children's choices in books has nothing to do with protecting them from Big Brother.

The notion that children should be treated as basically small adults is difficult to comprehend. The great classical liberal philosophers, who laid the foundations for our conception of individual rights, directly addressed this matter. John Stuart Mill, for instance, stated: "Children below a certain age cannot judge or act for themselves; up to a considerably greater age they are inevitably more or less disqualified from doing so."[36]

Our respect for people's choices rests on the assumption that their basic ability to render judgments has been formed and is intact. (This is the reason we, for instance, limit the choices of those whose mental capacity is significantly impaired.) Minors gradually develop the capacity to make choices, but are not born with it. For this reason when their age is tender, we are not charged with violating their right to free assembly when we prevent them from running into the street, or their privacy rights when we examine their homework, even without prior consent.

As I see it, parents not only have a right but a duty to help shape the educational environment of their children, help them choose which books they should read, which music they should listen to, which TV programs they should watch — and which to avoid. Of course, as children grow older such guidance is less necessary, but the debate swirls largely around those who are twelve or younger, who badly need their parents' counsel. This may include limiting the pornography they are exposed to, the games they may play, or even how many hours a day they may surf on the Internet—or watch TV—in the first place.

Even for teenagers, parents need to be involved rather than shut out. Thus, given the high suicide rate among teens, and the tendency for such acts to be emulated, if a child committed suicide in my son's school, and my son seems rather depressed and is spending long hours alone in the library, it is my duty to know if he merely reads Dostoyevsky or also the books of the Hemlock Society, which informs its readers how to best end their lives, with minimal discomfort. I also had better find out if one of my children is deep into *Mein Kampf*, the Unabomber Manifesto, or *The Anarchist's Cookbook*, so I can help him learn to properly deal with these poisonous works.

In effect, attending to the character development of children, so that when they grow up they will be equipped with the moral and intellectual faculties needed to make responsible choices, is to a large extent what parenting is all about. Anybody can provide room and board. Love comes naturally. But providing education—laying the foundations for adult choices—is the highest duty of parenting, which no civil libertarian should deny.

VI

Holidays: The Neglected Seedbeds of Virtue

Sociologists have long paid much attention to the family as the unit that initiates the socialization process and, in this context, to the effects that changes in family composition and structure and the rise of other child care institutions have had on the outcomes of socialization. Considerable attention has also been accorded to schools as agencies of socialization. In the last few decades, leaders and members of society at large have addressed these matters using code words such as "family values" and "character education." In contrast, little consideration has been given by sociologists and the public to the role of holidays and rituals as significant elements of the institutional foundations that undergird socialization and resocialization. I do not mean to suggest that holidays and rituals are as pivotal as families and other sources of child care including educational institutions, only that their role seems greater than the attention accorded to them in recent decades. For instance, the term "holiday" does not even appear in the index of the sixteen volumes of the otherwise rich and elaborate *International Encyclopedia of Social Sciences* (1968); it is not listed in the index of the *American Sociological Review* nor the *American Journal of Sociology* from 1975 to 1995, nor in the *Encyclopedia of Sociology* (1992). I am of course not arguing that there have been no sociological studies of holidays; indeed, several rather fine ones are cited at the end of this chapter.[1] I am only pointing out that they have been relatively few in number compared to those in other areas of study.

This chapter attempts to lay foundations for a sociological theory of holidays. Holidays are defined as days on which custom or the law dictates a halting of general business activity to commemorate or celebrate a particular event.[2] For the purposes of this study, the term "holidays" is used to encompass both rituals and holidays because rituals have the same basic role in society.

The chapter begins with an examination of Durkheim's well-known contributions[3] and suggests ways these may need to be modified to develop a theory of holidays. In addition, the chapter raises theoretical issues not directly addressed by Durkheim, particularly those that concern the prevalence of a holiday cycle (annual, repeated sequence) and holiday-engineering efforts by religious authorities and states that have sought to modify holidays to their purpose but without undermining their "sacred" legitimation. In the process, the essay draws on public accounts, personal observations, and findings culled from a few studies by contemporary social scientists.[4]

Because Durkheim's work has been systematically analyzed, well reviewed, and effectively summarized,[5] very little is to be gained by a reanalysis of Durkheim here. The main relevant points, following Durkheim's functional approach, are briefly:

1. Profane (secular), routine, daily life, the conduct of instrumental activities at work and carrying out household chores, tend to weaken shared commitments to shared beliefs and social bonds,

and enhance centrifugal individualism. For societies to survive these centrifugal, individualistic tendencies, they must continuously "recreate" themselves, by shoring up commitments to one shared ("common") set of beliefs and practices.

2. Rituals provide one major mechanism for the recreation of society, one in which the members of a society worship shared objects and in which they share experiences that help form and sustain deep emotional bonds among the members.

3. The specifics of the rituals, and the objects that are being worshiped or celebrated in these rituals, be they colored stones or woodcuts or practically anything else, have no intrinsic value or meaning. It is the society that imbues these objects with significance, and, thus endowed, they become the cornerstones of the integrative rituals built around them.

From this viewpoint, religious services during weekends serve to reinforce the commitments that have been diluted during weekdays. Holidays, in this context, are seen as "supra-weekends," as especially strong boosters of commitments and bonds.

To put it somewhat more formally, Durkheim hypothesizes that *rituals, holidays included, correlate negatively with societal disintegration* (defined as excessive individualism).[6]

Before I can both build on this theoretical starting point and seek to modify it, a methodological digression is needed.

HOLIDAYS AS "GLOBAL" INDICATORS

Holidays have a special methodological merit that makes them particularly attractive to students of societies: They provide indicators of the states and attributes of large collectivities. In studying societies, social scientists often rely on measurements based on aggregate data about myriad individuals, objects, or transactions such as public opinion polls, economic statistics, and census data.[7] For various reasons not explored here, such aggregated data are best supplemented with indicators that tap directly into collective attributes of the macro social system under study, sometimes referred to as "global" measurements.[8] For instance, to characterize a polity it is useful to determine not merely the voting and alienation rates of millions of citizens, but also to establish whether there are two dominant political parties or numerous small ones and whether there is a written constitution. These are significant macro (or "system") attributes not derivable from data about the attributes of citizens or from other aggregates.

In studying the belief systems of a society by using global indicators, researchers have drawn on various cultural products to "typify" a particular group, such as books (e.g., novels by William Faulkner as reflecting the "mind" of the South), select movies (e.g., A Clockwork Orange), or major speeches by public leaders (e.g., Martin Luther King, Jr. and Louis Farrakhan). Using such cultural products as indicators seems unavoidable when one deals with earlier periods such as ninth century feudalism in France, from which only a very limited amount of such material is available. However, for contemporary societies such cultural products are available in huge quantities and their content varies greatly. Hence, choosing a particular book, movie, or speech as indicative of a period and system of beliefs is often difficult to justify, and analyzing all of them (or even a random sample) is an onerous task (even when setting aside problems that arise from questions regarding the proper universe to be sampled, for example, whether one should include imported books and movies). In contrast, the ways holidays are celebrated — whether their focus is nationalist, militarist, or religious, whether they are dominated by merchandising and conspicuous consumption or dedicated to public service, whether they take place in people's homes or in public spaces, and so on — provide relatively telescoped and, hence, economic global indicators. Moreover, data about the ways holidays are celebrated in a particular society are often available about countries in which one cannot conduct reliable public opinion polls nor gain many other kinds of aggregate data, for instance, Tibet.

Such usages of holidays as indicators might be rather misleading if the focus is only on the content of the occasions, for instance how religious versus secular they are. To the extent possible, it is very desirable to determine the rough number of the participants, the extent of their involvement, and any specific attributes that distinguish them from other members of the society. For instance, observation of a Promise Keepers' ritual revealed that most who attended were male and white.[9]

To point to the merits of observing holidays as a source of data and insight into the belief systems of a society is not to argue that such data are fully accurate or can be relied upon as the sole source of evidence. Holidays, like other cultural products, tend to offer a somewhat refractory reading of society.[10] Thus, one cannot rely on the finding that many in India watch MTV to conclude that they are becoming Americanized. Indeed, studies show that when members of different ethnic groups watch the same TV program, they see rather different things.[11] Nor can one necessarily conclude that because Times Square in New York City, and several other such sites in major cities, are crowded with jubilant people on New Year's Eve, that the entire country is in a happy mood. I merely suggest that observations about holidays provide one major and relatively accessible source of global data about the beliefs and other attributes of a given society. The resulting readings, like those of other indicators, need to be compared with other sources of data.

Finally, it should be noted that, unlike many other measurements (GDP levels, for instance), which are social science constructs or artifacts, holidays are both a social phenomenon of considerable sociological interest in their own right as well as a source of data on a society at large. Hence, those who study holidays reap a double benefit: They advance our understanding of a set of specific social phenomena, and they cast light on the community or society of which they are a part. All this comes to support the suggestion that holidays deserve more sociological attention than they have received in recent decades, and point to the merit as well as the limits of using holidays as macro sociological indicators.

HOLIDAYS AS SOCIALIZATION AGENTS

To move beyond the Durkheimian starting point, one must recognize that Durkheim basically treats all rituals—holidays included—as if they were of one kind, in the sense that they all fulfill one societal "function"; they all foster integration by reinforcing shared beliefs.[12] To put the same proposition in somewhat different sociological terms, *holidays serve to socialize members of a society as well as to reaffirm their commitments to values, and as such serve to sustain the integration of society.* (Socialization, it is widely recognized, is not limited to the young; adults are continuously socialized in the sense that social processes and resources are dedicated to recommit adults to existing beliefs or introduce them to new ones.)

While it may be true that all holidays serve a socializing function to one extent or another, I suggest that (a) *different holidays play different societal roles; indeed no two holidays serve the same societal role,* and (b) *not all holidays are integrative.* (The last proposition assumes that one holds constant one's frame of reference; a holiday may be integrative for one group or another, but not all holidays are integrative for the society at large, as Durkheim suggested.)

To proceed, one must first note that there is no agreed upon typology of holidays to draw on, let alone one based on the societal roles fulfilled by various holidays. Some scholars have arranged holidays by the seasons they mark;[13] others have called attention to the holiday's role in the lives of the individuals involved (rather than to the societal roles of holidays);[14] still others see holidays as largely historically shaped. I attempt here to provide a typology based on the varying societal roles fulfilled by different holidays.

Probably the most important distinction among holidays from this viewpoint is those that use narratives, drama, and ceremonies to directly enforce commitments to shared beliefs (which I shall refer to as *recommitment holidays*), and those that fulfill this role indirectly, by releasing tensions that result from the close adherence to beliefs (which I term *tension management holidays*).[15] One and the same holiday may serve in both ways, but according to a very preliminary and informal survey of the societies that I am familiar with, each holiday serves in one way more than in the other. (However, such a primacy is changeable over time, as we shall see below.)

Recommitment holidays are most familiar; they are the ones Durkheim had in mind and are commonly associated with his integration thesis. Easter and Passover are typical holidays of recommitment. Easter dramatizes and extols the essential message of Christianity: the resurrection of Christ, the joy and fulfillment of redemption, and rebirth and reaffirmation of faith. The holiday is marked by specific and elaborate rituals, such as services at sunrise and rousing music to celebrate the Resurrection. Passover is built around the reading of the Haggadah, a narrative openly dedicated to socialization with special focus on children. The associated seder ritual is rich with symbols that entail reaffirmation of one's commitment to the beliefs of political liberty, deliverance by a supernatural force, and the importance of a distinct cultural identity and tradition. The implied sociological-Durkheimian hypothesis is that those who share the particular Christian or Jewish beliefs at issue and *who participate in these holidays, will be more committed to the shared beliefs and institutions of their respective communities after such participation than they were before*. (To test this proposition by comparisons of intensity of commitments to beliefs of those who participate in the said rituals to those who did not is somewhat more difficult because of the effects of self-selection.)

While holidays of recommitment are expected to directly serve the socialization and hence societal integration, *holidays of tension management are expected to serve societal integration indirectly and pose a higher risk of malfunction*. Holidays of tension management include New Year's Eve, Mardi Gras, Purim, Oktoberfest, and their equivalents in other cultures. (Whether or not Halloween belongs in this category is a matter of considerable conjecture, which cannot be resolved here.[16] April Fools' Day also belongs in this category although it is hardly a holiday.) During these holidays, mores that are upheld during the rest of the year are suspended to allow for indulgence, and some forms of behavior usually considered asocial and hence *disin-*

tegrative are temporarily adopted. Anthropologists report that in some societies, there are holidays in which daughters-in-law are permitted to insult their mothers-in-law. New Year's office and other parties are known for suspending mores against excessive consumption of alcohol and sexual infidelity.[17] During Mardi Gras in New Orleans, thousands of students expose themselves on the balconies in the French Quarter. Orthodox Jews, usually warned against interrupting their studies of scriptures for idle chatter and even appreciation of aesthetic beauty, are allowed to play games on Purim.

Tension management holidays are expected to contribute to reinforcement of shared beliefs and institutions indirectly, by releasing tension that results from conformity to societal beliefs and the behavioral prescriptions they entail. The underlying theoretical assumption is that people cannot be fully socialized and that sublimation is not fully successful, and that hence there will be a significant and accumulative residue of alienation from all commitments, even if they are not imposed by some foreign power or cultural or political elite.[18] Occasional release of this tension is expected to enhance socialization (including resocialization).

The extent to which a tension-release holiday, which occurs every few months, actually serves to vent alienation, or at least keep it at a low level, has, as far as I can establish, not been a subject of empirical study. Thus, there seems to be no systematic evidence that people who return to work after New Year's Day have a stronger commitment to their duties than before, though Jack Santino suggests that people do return to work "psychologically refreshed" after the holidays.[19] (He does not suggest how long such "refreshment" lasts.) The proposition that holidays fulfill such a role, therefore, should be treated largely as a hypothesis rather than as a finding.

Tension management holidays that set clear time limits are expected to be more integrative than those that do not set such limits. Time limits refer to points in time after which participants are expected to return to the conformist modes of behavior that reflect shared societal beliefs. It is as if society fears that once its members experience the raw satisfaction that results from suspended mores, members might be reluctant to return to the tighter restraints entailed in social roles. (A similar point has been made about people recovering from an illness who are reluctant to return to work because of the "secondary gains" of being sick, being legitimately exempted from numerous duties from working to attending to household chores. Physicians — and work rules about sick pay — are used to curb such tendencies.) Thus, Mardi Gras is followed by a recommitment on Ash Wednesday. New Year's Eve is followed in the United States by one day of vacation (New Year's Day), but there is a rather clear expectation that on the following day people must return to work. Several religions set a clear time limit on mourning and for the conclusion of other rituals, as Judaism does at the end of the Sabbath. In contrast, for secular mourning there is no clear time limit.

In testing the preceding hypothesis and others that follow, one must take into account that while holidays are largely of one kind or the other, they are not pure types. A recommitment holiday may include some opportunities for indulgence and suspension of mores (for instance, those entailed in work) and tension management holidays may include some recommitment (for instance, prayers), but the dominant activities tend to be of one kind or the other.

Critics may question whether a functional analysis of holidays biases the analysis in a conservative direction. Indeed, the analysis so far has focused on one societal role, that of evolving and sustaining commitments to prevailing societal beliefs and the behavioral expectations they contain. We shall see in the following paragraphs that holidays also serve as opportunities for societal change by providing occasions to symbolize and embody new conceptions of social relations and entities. This is illustrated later in the development of new roles for women in religious holidays, especially for rituals in the home.

I turn next to show that holidays can and are employed to strengthen the commitments to a great variety of societal entities rather than to uphold the dominant society; these entities include social movements, ethnic or racial groups, deviant religious denominations, and still other societal entities that challenge established regimes or seek to form new societies. Like pipelines, holidays are largely indifferent to the content of the normative "flows" they facilitate.

UNITY, DIVERSITY, AND RELATIONS AMONG THE PARTS

While as a preliminary approximation it might suffice to propose that various attributes of holidays (such as their prevalence, number of participants, the strength of recommitment they evoke) correlate negatively with societal disintegration, this proposition must be further specified. Because many, if not all, holidays may have some kind of an integrative function, I hypothesize *that numerous holidays that help integrate some societal entities have the opposite effect on others.* Returning to my starting point, to the work of Durkheim, one notes that he focused on the integrative function of holidays for whole *societies* and for societies that did not have significant internal divisions, at least none that he recognized. This approach is best understood if one takes into account not only the utilitarian and individualistic bodies of thought Durkheim was challenging, but also that his empirical base observations were drawn from studying Australian totemism. That is, he was dealing with a very small society with a rather high level of homogeneity and integration.

A theory of holidays applicable to complex societies needs to abandon the assumption that holidays are necessarily unifiers of societies and specify which social entity they are serving. Instead, it should be assumed that: (a) while holidays do provide an integrative mechanism, this mechanism *may work to solidify member groups and not necessarily a whole society* (indeed, an examination of the holidays of a given society can serve as an indicator of the level of unity of that society); (b) the integrative *effects of holidays on the society will depend on the relationships among such groups and the society-at-large,* which can vary from confrontational to complementary, and that (c) these relationships can in turn be *changed, and tensions "worked through" during holidays.*[20] Some illustrative observations follow which give some preliminary and limited support for the preceding propositions.

An example of a holiday that encompasses and unifies most members of a community is provided by observations of the celebrations of Passover in early, small and homogenous Israeli kibbutzim. In contrast, in contemporary American society, one finds, in addition to some holidays that are widely, although not universally, shared on a national level (for instance, Memorial Day), numerous holidays that are specific to one religious group or another (e.g., Christmas and Hanukkah),[21] or to one ethnic group or another (e.g., St. Patrick's Day, Kwanza, Cinco de Mayo, Chinese New Year), and—much less often—to one class (May Day).

If there were systematic evidence indicating whether or not all these various differences in the ways holidays are practiced by various social entities have increased or decreased over a given period (for instance, during the second half of the twentieth century) in a given society, this would provide a global indicator of the extent to which that society, in that period, had become more fractionated or more unified. For instance, one would expect that the rising diversity and intergroup tensions in American society between 1960 and 1990 would be reflected in a rising diversity in the way holidays are celebrated by various ethnic and racial groups. Lacking systematic evidence to this effect, one must either rely on rather casual and informal observations to this effect, or regard the preceding statements as strictly theoretical propositions.

Holidays can serve to modify the relationships between societal parts and the whole, to the extent that such a whole exists and is recognized. In some ceremonies, conscious and systematic efforts are made to ensure that a particular group holiday (one observed only by a given group) does not undermine the commitment to the whole. One symbolic expression of the commitment to the whole is displaying flags during parades, ceremonial speeches, and prayers. When a group in the United States seeks to reinforce its members' commitments not only to the group but also to the society at large,[22] the celebrants often display both ethnic flags (e.g., Italian) and the Stars and Stripes. Most speakers, religious functionaries, and community leaders — if the said disposition is sought — are careful to include "God bless America" or some other such expression, to indicate their loyalty to the whole, stressing that their group upholds dual loyalties, and hence, its particularistic commitments do not conflict with its commitment to the national society.

Clearly, not all particularistic holidays are celebrated in such a dual (group *and* society building) way. Some group celebrations are disintegrative for the society as a whole, are openly oppositional, and challenge the societal mores and symbols. They can even be outright expressions of a breakaway from the societal whole or from some other group. Native Americans, especially the Wampanoag, use Thanksgiving as a protest holiday, a day of fasting and mourning.[23] Several New York City schools have also adopted this protest perspective, teaching children that Thanksgiving marks a day on which "'strange looking' people . . . landed in the family's backyard and proceeded to ransack their homes, cut down their trees, kill their pets, and take tomatoes from their gardens."[24] Intense debates about Columbus Day mark similar societal divisions, with some seeing the day as a recognition of a great discovery by the man who opened the door for the creation of the American society, while others view the day as celebration of a brutal killer and conqueror who should not be lionized.[25]

Finally, *holidays can be used to work out a new relationship between society and a member group, and in the process advance and ritualize a change in the beliefs of those involved.* That is, integration is achieved as Durkheim would expect, but in a way he did not expect: by changing the beliefs around which society congeals. (The point is not that Durkheim did not recognize changes in symbols and rituals, but that his theory did not allow for changes in the level of societal integration that are achieved, in part, by changing the content of holidays, as is hypothesized here.)

Some illustrative examples follow. Initially, the idea that there should be a holiday marking Martin Luther King, Jr.'s birthday met with considerable opposition, especially from conservative Americans, including President Ronald Reagan. After fifteen years of considerable lobbying by civil rights groups, a federal holiday was finally declared in 1986. Several states continued to oppose the declaration of this new national holiday, and were only gradually won over. Conservative Arizona was particularly slow to join the other states in this regard. New Hampshire chose to follow its individualistic streak and instead declared a Civil Rights Day.

A much more successful working through of an intergroup difference helped by and reflected in a holiday, can be seen in the participation of Vietnam veterans in parades and other activities on Veterans Day. Initially, the refusal of large segments of society to treat Vietnam vets as returning heroes, as individuals who served their country on par with those who fought in the first and second World Wars, caused many to be reluctant to participate in these parades. Nor could they expect a warm welcome from other veterans who did march.[26] However, as the rift over Vietnam gradually healed in the early 1990s, Vietnam veterans participated much more often in these parades, were more warmly received by the public at large and by other veterans, and felt more positive about participating in these national ceremonial occasions.[27] In Chicago in 1994, Mayor Richard Daley conducted a ceremony that officially honored Vietnam veterans.[28] In 1995, the city council of Berkeley, California, once a center of anti-Vietnam War protests, held a commemoration on Veterans Day honoring those who fought in the Vietnam War.[29]

All this suggests that, to advance a theory of holidays, one must strongly modify Durkheim's notion that holidays serve to integrate a *society* and recognize that, while they may solidify member groups, the relationships of these groups to the whole may vary from being highly complementary and hence integrative to rather conflictive and disintegrative. The relationship may range from one of a group that is self-aware and well-defined yet deeply integrated into a more encompassing whole, to hostile relations or even civil war (Kurds in Turkey, for instance). Additionally, groups that started as conformist may draw on reinterpretation of holidays to aggrandize their distinctiveness, while hostile subgroups — and the societies in which they are situated — may reformulate holidays as part of the reconstruction of society, its core beliefs, and its relations to the member groups.

In short, (a) whether or not a given holiday is integrative cannot be assumed by merely observing that a holiday is celebrated, even if it is well attended and celebrants are deeply involved. In addition, one needs to specify the reference unit: Which entity is being integrated, the society as a whole or some other social entity, or both; (b) the nature of the relationship between this entity and the society needs to be examined, as reflected in the given holiday and otherwise; and (c) one needs to introduce a dynamic perspective that calls attention to the fact that holidays that originally integrated a group into society as a whole may change to undermine that bond, or — that holidays that originally served to divide, may help work through differences to enhance not only the internal integration of a particular group but also of the society as a whole. For instance to illustrate the latter point, before 1917 Christmas seems to have been, relatively speaking, an integrated holiday for Russian society. It ceased to be so after the Soviet Revolution, although it has clearly far from vanished.

PUBLIC VERSUS PRIVATE HOLIDAYS

Durkheim assumes that *holidays are public events*, in the sense that members of tribes assemble as one group in one space, and the rituals involved are shared by and visible to one and all. It follows therefore that *this integrative function cannot be served, at least not as well, if holidays are celebrated privately by individuals* (or their families) in their huts, shanties, or suburban homes rather than in public squares, parade grounds, or other points of assembly. Parsons suggested a different interpretation of Durkheim in this regard, suggesting that holidays can be integrative even if celebrated privately as long as the commitment to the society at large is recognized, a point discussed later.[30]

Durkheim's hypothesis finds some initial support in numerous reports of communal rather than individualized celebration of holidays in nonliterate tribes as well as in Western societies, at least in the preindustrial eras. For instance, in eighteenth century rural America, when society was more homogenous and most communities were much smaller than contemporary ones, holidays were often celebrated in public spaces. For example, a typical Fourth of July celebration centered around a parade that ended up in a church, in which the crowd was blessed and shared a communal meal.[31]

In contrast, in recent decades, many holidays have been celebrated in private homes, by families or other small groups.[32] The Fourth of July is now often played out at private picnics, outings with friends or coworkers, or in backyard barbecues. And it has become less committing. It is popularly reported that Thanksgiving initially was a communal holiday in which Pilgrims and Native Americans celebrated together, but long ago became mainly a family holiday. "By the mid 19th-century, Thanksgiving had become associated with homecoming. . . . Returning home for Thanksgiving was both a metaphor and a ritual performance of solidarity, renewing or validating family ties."[33]

Still, it is far from established that the privatization of holidays is necessarily disintegrative. There seems to be some evidence to suggest that *private rituals can engender recommitment to the society at large as do public, shared rituals*. Religions, for instance, differ in the extent to which they rely on rituals that take place in shared and public spaces, such as Sunday rituals in churches, as compared to those that build on family-based rituals that take place in private homes, such as the kind that play a major role in Judaism. There is, however, no immediate evidence that Jewish holidays are less integrative than other ones, although to the extent that I could determine, this topic has not been subjected to empirical research.

True, holidays are rarely, if ever, completely private. One tends to mention to coworkers and friends, even shopkeepers, about the occasion and its special meaning. But this of course cannot make up for the decline in participation in shared communal events.

A related question is *whether the increased privatization of holidays reflects an adaptation of holidays to a decline in the level of inte-*

gration of society or vice versa, whether a privatization of holidays helped cause a decline in societal integration as Durkheim would have it.[34] So far, most observers have depicted the increase in privatization as driven by societal factors, as opposed to the other way around. Among the factors cited are a decline in public safety and an increase in the level of heterogeneity[35] and the decline of close (or "primary") relations in growing cities.[36] That is, the increase in private holiday celebrations are said to reflect a general decline in bonding that ties small social entities into a society and in the level of individual commitments to this society. As well, they reflect a growing loyalty to particularistic groups (ethnic, religious, etc.), small, intimate social circles, and emphasis on personal achievement and interests. While there is little solid evidence to support these hypotheses, it should be noted that according to several accounts, individualism rose between 1960 and 1990 in American society, the same years holidays have become less public.

It should also be noted that since 1990, following increased concern about the rising level of individualism and the decline of public spaces, limited attempts have been made to restore the public nature of holidays. For instance, a community in Ontario, California annually sets up a two-mile long table, around which many members of the community, from divergent social backgrounds, are reported to picnic together on the Fourth of July.[37] Furthermore, there are some reports about a rise in efforts to celebrate holidays in "artificial" extended families for single parents, other singles, gays and lesbians, and still others who seek communities that are more extensive than their households, especially to share holidays.[38] All this provides some very tentative support for the hypothesis that societal changes drive holiday changes rather than holidays changing society.

THE SIGNIFICANCE OF THE HOLIDAY CYCLE

To advance the sociological theory beyond Durkheim's work, one must determine the sociological significance of the fact that in most, if not all, societies holidays are repeated over time and in the same sequence. While I was unable to find a comparative study directly focused on this point, an informal survey of numerous cultures suggests that a fixed and annual sequence of holidays is one of the most robust observations one can make based on cross-cultural comparisons, in the sense that it can be seen in societies that differ a great deal on numerous other accounts.[39]

The question for the sociologist is: What is the societal significance of the particular sequence in which holidays are arranged? To suggest that holidays follow the climatic seasons per se may be true, but casts little sociological light on the matter, unless one uncovers the social reasons some seasons are ritualized while others are ignored.

One interesting sociological hypothesis that has been advanced in this context deals with what might be called holiday subcycles. For instance, Williamson noted that holidays focused on children — Christmas for instance — are preceded and followed by festivities that are built around aggressive, sexual, adult themes (e.g., Christmas is preceded by the Christmas office party and followed by New Year's Eve).[40] We have already noted the difference between recommitment and tension management holidays; the hypothesis should be added here that these *two kinds of holidays will "alternate," rather than holidays of one kind being followed by more of the same kind.*

The underlying assumption of both Williamson's observation and our hypothesis is that the serving of various societal needs is arranged in a sequence so that after one need is attended to, attention to the other gains predominance. The question of this hypothesis, developed on the basis of informally observing a few holidays, can be extended to all holidays, requiring a macro analysis of societal needs to determine if they are all served by one holiday or another. This is a task that remains to be faced. Only after this is completed can one seek to determine whether societies whose holidays are "properly" sequenced show a lower level of social tension, a higher level of integration, and a greater commitment to their shared values than societies whose holidays are out of sequence for one reason or another, perhaps as a result of the attempts at social engineering introduced by totalitarian governments and more recently by religious fundamentalist ones.

DESIGN AND TRADITION: HOLY DAYS
COMPARED TO CIVIC CELEBRATIONS

Durkheim often treated societies and their holidays as given or as evolving under the impact of unfolding historical and social forces, rather than as subject to deliberate societal change.[41] Modern societies, though, are engineered to some extent, and are subject to public policies that attempt to change the relations among racial, ethnic, and economic groups. As holidays serve to solidify the society at large, the member groups, or both, attempts to change these entities, and above all the values around which they congeal, have led numerous public authorities to deliberately recast holidays in order to change the beliefs of one or more member groups and their orientation to the encompassing society. Given, however, that holidays must build on the legitimation of tradition and affective attachment founded on shared memories and histories,[42] the question faced by public authorities, and of much interest to the sociological study of change, is whether holidays lose some or all of their power to reinforce commitments to values once they have been openly redesigned. As religions are typically more traditional than secular ideologies (if only because the latter tend to have significantly shorter histories), one promising place to start the examination of the limit and opportunities of social reengineering of holidays is to ask whether secular holidays are less degraded by being recast than religious ones.

While Durkheim recognized the difference between religious rituals carried out by nonliterate tribes and those national holidays that Robert Bellah analyzed as examples of "civil" religion, to Durkheim these were but two forms of religion, fulfilling the same essential integrative function. For Durkheim, while a society could replace God as the source of sacredness, this did not secularize the icons, cults, and rituals the society endowed in this peculiar manner. They were all sacred.[43]

Contemporary sociologists might well find it necessary to draw a distinction between holidays that are built around sacred religious objects and those that surround revered secular objects, including days that mark national liberations, independence, armistices, or civic occasions such as New Year's Eve. Like many other typologies, reference here is not to pure types but to the dominant elements. Thus, a secular holiday may include some prayers, but the main focus of the objects held in special awe, the values dramatized and ritualized, are secular. In the same vein, a largely religious holiday may include some secular elements. Once this is taken into account, one can formulate the hypothesis that, counter to common sense, *religious holidays can be more readily redesigned, without losing their legitimacy, than secular ones.*

In the Soviet Union, continuous, systematic, and deliberate efforts were made to secularize holidays. Christmas and Easter were abolished in 1920, and November 7th (the anniversary of the founding of the Bolshevik government) and May 1st (the day celebrating the unity of labor) were introduced as holidays. In 1929, Sunday was abolished to make for a six-day work week. Gift exchanging was moved to New Year's Eve, and a secular "Father Frost" replaced Santa Claus.[44] These efforts were widely resisted. Religious holidays continued to be observed by millions, often, although not always, in secrecy. Sunday was restored in 1940. And while the Soviet regime did not survive, the celebration of religious holidays did.[45]

A case in point would be the Catholic Church's shift from the use of Latin to the use of the vernacular, symbolizing a move from strong universalism to greater openness to local cultural differences, as a part of a much larger attempt to downgrade the central role of authority and place greater emphasis on communal elements of the church.

Traditional Jewish holidays were profoundly changed by Conservative and Reform Jews attempting to make the religious rituals more accessible to congregations whose members by and large do not understand Hebrew, have been less willing to participate in prolonged rituals, insist on some measures of gender equality, and otherwise seek to reconcile their Jewish commitments with other normative ones, including feminist and gay agendas.[46] (Also, most modern versions of the Haggadah drop or reinterpret a line that calls on God to wreak his vengeance on "other" people.)

While debates continue within these and other religious groups about the appropriateness of deliberate efforts to redesign holidays, and there have been some efforts to restore traditional features in recent years, many of the new modes of celebrations are very widely followed. And, while there has been a loss in the intensity of commitment, it is far from clear that the changes in the way holidays are celebrated contributed to, rather than helped stem, this loss.

Establishing the extent to which holidays can be deliberately recast, and the comparative effectiveness of various ways and means of such endeavors, is particularly significant in light of a challenge posed by John R. Gillis.[47] He argues that American holidays, rituals, and myths are lagging behind reality: that they represent a distorted view of a society that is long gone, especially the notion that there was and ought to be one "traditional" kind of family. He argues — drawing on Marxist and Freudian ideas about the possibility of developing a higher level of consciousness — for a profound change of our core myth (and hence holidays and rituals), toward a formulation that provides a higher level of reality-testing and a more genuine expression of our true feelings and psychic needs. One may argue that this is what is taking place, under the influence of various consciousness-raising and reeducation drives, despite opposition by traditional groups. However, until more research is conducted on these questions, such a conclusion is at best tentative.

RESTRUCTURING OF GENDER AND KINSHIP ROLES: A LAGGING SECTOR

Durkheim, dealing with small homogeneous societies, assumed that they were rather monolithic; he characterized whole societies either as well integrated or as suffering from lack of integration. However, it should be hypothesized for complex societies that change in some sectors will lag after developments in others. And, based on some very preliminary and informal observations to follow immediately, a plausible hypothesis is that *holidays tend to lag rather than lead societal change, and the more they lag, the more they hinder rather than enhance societal integration.* The reason is that some members of society are likely to be more involved in the leading segment of society (for instance, those younger than 50) while others might be more involved in the lagging segments (those 65 or older). Hence, the greater the sectorial lag, the more tensions one would expect between the social groups involved.

This hypothesis can be illustrated by changes in women's roles in the preparation for and celebration of holidays. Women's roles in holidays seem to have been akin to their roles in other parts of the socialization infrastructure. Thus, it is hardly surprising to learn that in traditional American society, for instance in the 1950s, women were charged with preparing the celebratory meals, shopping for gifts, promoting the holiday spirit, and so on.[48] Similar accounts are available from some earlier periods; for example, the Pilgrim dinner, to which native Americans were invited and which laid the foundation for the first Thanksgiving in 1623, is reported to have been prepared exclusively by women.[49]

As the feminist movement started to challenge women's roles in the 1960s, their holiday roles were also recast, but these changes seem to have lagged behind other changes in society, and/or there has been a significant measure of *regression toward traditional mores during holidays.* While there seems to be no systematic evidence to support the preceding statements, informal observations suggest that even in those households where women work outside the home and husbands assume some household and child care responsibilities, women still seem to do a disproportionate share of the inviting, planning and preparing, cooking and serving of holiday meals, and above all are expected to be the ones to ensure the warm glow of the holiday spirit.[50]

All this is not to suggest that changes in women's societal roles have not been reflected in the internal structure of holidays. Some women lead religious services in both communal and home-based rituals in several religious denominations and some have been ordained for posts from which they previously had been excluded: a fair number of Jews have added Bat Mitzvah (for girls) to Bar Mitzvah, and rituals for naming girls to parallel the Bris; there have been several attempts to edit sexist language out of traditional texts, for instance by reading "she" (or alternating between "she" and "he") whenever the Lord is referred to as masculine. But these changes often followed rather than led role changes in other societal areas and seem less extensive than changes in work roles, for instance.

One of the least noted but rather indicative changes in the ways holidays are celebrated and rituals are performed is the splitting of traditional gender roles, reflecting changes in the structures of the nuclear family and more widely, in the kinship structures. Where formerly only one father role and one mother role existed, there are now several versions of each, variously referred to as "natural" versus "social" fathers, parents versus stepparents, "biological grandparents" versus step-grandparents, and so on. The increasing complexity of roles and relations is reflected in the inclusion in family holidays of a large number of people who are related neither by blood nor marriage, but by former marriages, what one sociologist half-jokingly calls the "x-kinship structure." The parents of former spouses (if they are grandparents of one or more of the stepchildren) are sometimes included. (One student reported that his Christmas celebration as a child included both his divorced parents and his father's "new wife".) A considerable etiquette has been developed about who "gives away" the bride (e.g., the natural father or the stepfather?) and the place of the natural mother during the wedding ceremony and in other rituals when a stepmother is present. These examples indicate role changes, as the society is struggling to come to terms with new gender and related family structures. But again, these changes are not widely recognized, codified, or institutionalized, lending further support to the hypothesis that the *internal restructuring of holidays lags after major societal changes,* and hence in this regard hinders rather than serves integration, as the adaptation of one part of the society — holidays — lags behind the others.

CYBERSPACE — BEREFT OF HOLIDAYS?

The clash between the modernistic forces of globalization and the conservative forces of tradition came face to face on May 27, 1999. On this day, the board of the National Association of Securities Dealers (the parent organization of Nasdaq) announced that it planned to open an evening trading session for stocks between 5:30 P.M. and 9:00 or 10:00 P.M.. Nasdaq president, Richard Ketchum added, "there may come a day when we trade 24 hours."[51] Actually a "24/7 week," was already at hand. People can trade stocks and much else twenty-four hours a day, seven days a week (including holidays), on the Internet.

One day earlier, the Central Conference of American Rabbis, the board that guides Reform Jews, voted to call on its members to return to the observance of traditional rituals such as observing the Sabbath, wearing a skullcap, and keeping kosher.[52] Numerous other religious groups, including practically all Christian denominations, already have in place drives to renew their religious commitments.

At first it may seem that there is no conflict between trading stocks around the clock and religious renewal. Theoretically, people could wheel and deal five days and nights (even six) and rest on the seventh day, as the Lord prescribes. Nor is the conflict between commerce and family, community and religion, a new one. At the very onset of industrialization, concerns were already raised that having looms at home might entice people to work "after hours." That conflict between work and home intensified as many mothers followed most fathers to labor outside the household. Cyberspace, however, presents a qualitative jump in the scope of opportunities and temptations offered, because it knows no clock or calendar.

For those who seek to trade or labor within the Internet's rapidly expanding confines, any time is as good as any other. While in the "old" pre-Internet world, banks still closed at some hours and days, rapidly rising e-banks are operational at all times. And while some shops stay open late nights and weekends, only on the Internet can one safely assume that it matters not what time it is or day or date. Nobody needs to ask about the Internet mail carrier's rest day; e-mail flows into one's PC seamlessly, nonstop. In short, cyberspace has neither Sabbath nor holidays, not even Christmas or Yom Kippur. It stands to eradicate whatever is left from "institutionalized" barriers, those that are used to separate and protect, at least to some extent, the sacred from the secular, the social and spiritual from the economic.

All these new opportunities to trade, bank, and shop have risen so quickly that the engulfed societies have barely had a chance to examine their full significance. Most new books exploring cyberspace and globalization (including those by Thomas Friedman[53] and Benjamin Barber[54]) proceed in ways that are open to challenge. These books associate the onrush of enriching choice with the West, and suggest that other parts of the world resist the spread of the Internet, and more generally, of globalization, out of traditionalism and parochialism. In short, those not enamored with cyber-possibilities are viewed as parochial if not worse. Viewed in this way, it is a small wonder the Nasdaq move was greeted with so little fanfare. In contrast, the rabbis' call was greeted with the mix of consternation and criticism that is rained on those who try to roll the clock back in the name of tradition.

One may however look at the renewed call to increase social efforts to secure more room for family, community, and religious life, as not simply traditional and certainly not "backward." It is not a simple call to return to the past, to observe rituals and tenets "because that is the way we have always done things" or "because that is the way the Lord or the scripture commands." Instead, society faces still *more* choice; its members are challenged to examine which rituals they will adapt and which new rituals they will develop — to protect life beyond commerce and work in cyberspace. This effort could include defining turfs where cell phones will be turned off, and bringing laptops will be considered inappropriate (e.g., places of worship).

In seeking such places away from the glare of computer screens, society is not limited to the shade of old olive trees, but is choosing what to plant and cultivate to replace them.

If one needs a symbol for the new world of chosen rituals it may be the lowly dinner. Unless Nasdaq traders plan to have dinner at 11:00 P.M. or so, they are extremely unlikely to share a meal with their families on weekdays—unless they choose to miss the evening session. Most other members of society have long faced the decision of whether, given their busy households and conflicting schedules, they plan to have shared dinners—at least on some agreed days of the week. (Such meals these days rarely just happen because food is always served at a given time and everybody knows they are expected at the dinner table.) Indeed, additional deliberate choices are involved: those who seek dinners that are occasions where family members can truly communicate with one another must formulate "policies" on matters such as turning off the TV, not answering the phone, and staying at the table until an agreed time.

The same now increasingly holds for weekends and holidays. Cyberspace makes it even more necessary than in the past to decide where to draw the line. While it has long been possible to bring home briefcases bulging with work, the Internet makes it much easier and hence more tempting to trade stocks from home or the beach, to call up the office, or to exchange work-related e-mail messages.

The fact that selection, rather than a simple return to tradition, is what we now face is evident when we compare those rituals we seek to uphold or adapt versus those we choose to ignore. These are decisions we increasingly make on the basis of what seems meaningful to us rather than what is handed down to us from earlier generations. Observing the Sabbath thus may well be one of those rituals that is meaningful to many because they see the virtue of securing time away from economic activities. At the same time, following the Jewish tradition of purification in a public bathhouse for women after they have their menstrual period may well be one of those rituals that may lack the same contemporary conviction for most—to put it mildly.

I am not suggesting that tradition will play no role. It is one major source of options people consider, rather than *the* depository of the answer. In effect, religion may be viewed as a place where earlier approaches were preserved so that members of contemporary societies can reembrace them. They do so not merely because that is the way they are commanded by religious authorities or that is what they have learned from their forefathers and mothers — but because they find elements of these traditions compelling and meaningful. The way people plan weddings today is a case in point. Various alternative rituals are considered, from traditional nuptials to newly composed vows, tailored to the particular couple.

Some of these decisions people are able to render as individuals and as families. For instance, whether or not — and when — to attend church. Other choices, though, require communal dialogues and shared decisions; for instance, whether committee and board meetings, which are increasingly conducted on listservs, will be conducted only on work days and during "regular" hours (whatever that means) or if they will go the way of round-the-clock stock trading.

The conflict is not between choice and tradition. Rather, cyberspace poses a new opportunity for society to choose how much space it is willing to dedicate to spiritual, cultural, and social activities in cyberspace and elsewhere.

CONCLUSION

Holidays provide a valuable tool for a sociological analysis of societies because they both reflect various attributes of societies and their major constituting social entities (i.e., are effective macro indicators), as well as serve to modify these attributes (i.e., constitute forces of societal change). To develop such an analysis suggestions are provided for the sociological theory of holidays that, in several instances, significantly modify Durkheim's hypotheses, and add factors he has not considered.

The main propositions that arise from the discussion are:

1. If one uses the society as the frame of reference, tension management holidays are expected to be less integrative than holidays of recommitment. While both might contribute to the integrative state of a societal entity, tension management holidays are more prone than others to foster antisocial behavior.

2. A theory of holidays will benefit from taking into account that one and the same holiday may have differential effects on the integration of the society at large as compared to that of some member units. For instance, some ethnic holidays strengthen the communal bonds of members units but undermine the societal integration, while other holidays help to reinforce not merely the integration of the member units but also their relations to the society at large. Moreover, a holiday that started as fragmenting may serve as a societal process that helps work through conflicts among the member units and the society at large.

3. The extent to which holidays that have been previously celebrated in public are privatized is expected to correlate with the rise of diversity in society. Moreover, the privatization of holidays that used to be public will undermine societal integration, in conflict with Durkheim's expectation that all holidays will serve to enhance this kind of integration.

4. The particular reasons holidays are arranged in a given repeated sequence (or cycle) in a given society are not known. A preliminary hypothesis suggests that holidays follow the sequences observed in order to change the societal needs different holidays serve, so that sooner or later most or all needs are covered. For this reason, tension management holidays and holidays of recommitment tend to alternate rather than a set of one kind being followed by a group of the other.

5. In contrast to common sense intuition, religious authorities seem to be more effective at deliberately changing holidays without alienating large numbers of their followers than civic authorities.

6. Changes in gender and kinship roles during holidays are ex-

pected to lag behind changes in these roles in other institutional sectors, undermining the integrative role of holidays.

In short, once we abandon Durkheim's assumption of a close, positive correlation between the occurrence and participation in holidays and societal integration, we are on our way to laying the foundations for a richer and more realistic sociological theory of holidays.

VII

Salem without Witches

Utopias often serve as a screen on which to project our values. Erik Olin Wright, for instance, highlights the value of a world in which there is radical equality although he knows of "no institutional design that could implement this value without major negative effects."[1] My attempt at outlining a utopia differs in that it envisions a good society, but not one that is exempt from the basic sociological laws of gravity. It concerns itself with the fact that we are compelled by values and needs that cannot be made fully compatible with one another and hence force us to make tough choices. Philosophers and ideologues often try to derive their utopias from one moral principle or overarching value; libertarians, for instance, from liberty, and social conservatives from social order. As I see it, a sociological treatment of utopia should include a recognition that both of these values cannot be ignored and that while up to a point they can be reconciled, to some extent they are contradictory. So are community and individuality, and community and modernity.

Two fair warnings: Before I proceed to outline the design of a good society, I should note that this chapter is not a review of the enormous existing literature on the subject. Instead, this chapter is dedicated to an exploration of select relevant issues. By necessity, the discussion is both empirical and normative. Finally, I choose to introduce several matters that I consider of sociological importance rather than analyze in detail any particular one of them.

COMMUNITIES DEFINED

A key concept I draw upon in the following characterization of a good society is the term "community." Given that it has been repeatedly argued that such a social entity cannot be defined, this matter is first addressed. Several critics have argued that the concept of community is so ill-defined that it has no identifiable designation. Robert Booth Fowler, in his book, *The Dance with Community*, shows that the term is used in six different and rather incompatible ways.[2] Colin Bell and Howard Newby write, "There has never been a theory of community, nor even a satisfactory definition of what community is."[3] In another text, Bell and Newby write, "But what is community? . . . It will be seen that over ninety definitions of community have been analyzed and that the one common element in them all was man!"[4] Margaret Stacey argues that the solution to this problem is to avoid the term altogether.[5]

As I see it, this "cannot be defined" is a tired gambit. We have difficulties in precisely defining even such a simple concept as a chair. Something to sit on? One can sit on a bench or bed. Something to sit on with four legs? Many chairs have three, or even just one, and so on. The same criticism has been leveled against rationality, democracy, and class, and yet nobody seriously suggests we stop using these concepts.

The following definition seems to me quite workable: "Community is a combination of two elements: (a) A web of affect-laden relationships among a group of individuals, relationships that often criss-cross and reinforce one another (rather than merely one-on-one or chainlike individual relationships). (b) A measure of commitment to a set of shared values, norms, and meanings, and a shared history and identity — in short, to a particular culture."[6]

The definition leaves open the amount of conflict that occurs within a given community, but does define it as a social entity that has the elements necessary (bonds and shared values) to contain conflict within sustainable boundaries. Moreover, the definition indicates that communities need not be territorial. Indeed, there are many ethnic, professional, gay, and other communities that are geographically dispersed; that is, the members of these communities reside among people who are not members. (Often, these communities are centered around particular institutions, such as places of worship, hiring halls, bars, or social clubs.)

The observation that social entities that meet the above two defining criteria can be identified, and that they resemble those entities most people informally refer to as "communities," does not claim that such social units are good in the normative sense. The discussion next examines the normative standing of one element of communities, bonding; the standing of a common moral culture is explored later. However, to reiterate, no a priori assumption is made here that communities are necessarily socially desirable.

THE VALUE OF BONDS, AND THEIR LIMITS

The idea that people ought to be related to one another by bonds of affection rather than merely treat each other as instrumental means is so widely established that it barely needs discussing. From Kant to Marx, many consider the dominance of the instrumental orientation a major threat to human well-being. Others have drawn on empirical research to document that people are social creatures and require bonding with others for their mental and physical well-being. It would thus first seem that bonds are good per se.

Actually, the said view reflects the fact that these matters are often discussed within a Western context, in which bonding is believed to have declined over the last centuries. More attention should be paid to the opposite condition, in which bonding is excessive. The reference here is not to hierarchy, power relations, or oppressive legal or moral codes, all of which are distinct negatives. Reference is instead to communities in which bonds, even those among peers, are very restrictive, preventing proper development of self, cramping individuality, spontaneity, and creativity, a condition many associate with the Japanese society, at least until recently.

Novelists have been more effective than social psychologists in describing the loss of self-identity and autonomy of those slavishly in love; of women who lose their self-identity when defined merely as mothers and wives; of teenagers and gang members who are lost in their peer groups.

It follows that both frayed bonds and tightly knit ones are incompatible with basic human needs,[7] that social bonds are essential for human well-being but only if they remain rather slack; it follows that one attribute of a good society is that it is one in which strong communal bonds are balanced by similarly powerful protections of self. Such a society is not communal, period, but—like two taut and tensed stays of a mast which keep it erect—firmly upholds both social ties and autonomy, at the foundation of social order and liberty. It further follows that societies may need to move in opposite directions in order to approach the same good point of balance—Some to shore up their weakened social bonds; others, to loosen them. (In Buberian terms the needed movement is not from an I-focused society to a We-focused society, as some have suggested, but rather from either an I- or the We-dominated one to the I & We.)

EXCLUSIVITY LIMITED BY LAWS

This discussion has already established that communities are not good per se; only communities that exhibit certain attributes, a balance between bonds and protection of the self, might qualify as good. I move next to further specify what makes a good community.

Given the realities of social life, all communities have built into them by their very nature a serious normative defect: they exclude. All communities draw distinctions between members and nonmembers, and most times treat nonmembers less well than members. (Exceptions include some religious orders and secular voluntary associations that sacrifice their members' well-being as they administer to the sick and poor.) Exclusivity arises out of one of the two defining elements of community, that of bonding. There are severe limits to the number of people any one person can bond with. Moreover, bonding is much more achievable with people who are similar in social background and perspective than with those whose social attributes are different. Finally, turnover must be limited if bonds are to solidify.

The fact that communities exclude is normatively troubling to the point that several critics regard communities negatively merely on this ground alone and prefer to limit social relations to those based on universal criteria, especially individual achievements. Indeed, if we treat one and all as unique persons, we avoid community-based exclusivity. (Consistent champions of this approach reject treating legal and illegal immigrants differently, or members of our national community from that of others.) However, a society that seeks complete elimination of exclusivity will grossly neglect the profound human need for social bonds.

Given this background, utopian writing that is concerned with a modicum of institutional design, of the kind practiced here, points to a society that allows communities to maintain some limitations on membership, but at the same time greatly restricts the criteria that communities may use to enforce such exclusivity. The criteria for exclusion cannot be race, ethnic origins, religion, sexual orientation, and a whole host of other criteria based on ascribed statuses. The bonds of good communities, it follows, are based on affinity whose nature remains to be defined.

CONFLICT WITHIN CONSENSUS

The very notion of society (and it as a community) is Durkheimian in the sense that it presupposes one societal entity, and asks if the conditions that its continued integrity requires, are met. Critics, from Spencer to Mrs. Thatcher, have argued that the very concept of society is a fiction; there are only aggregates of individuals. And left-leaning scholars, especially Lewis Coser, have maintained that the concept conceals that society is an arena of conflict, not one of unity. Indeed, social conservatives historically used to call for national unity, to urge people to refrain from fighting for that which is due them in the name of preserving the organic whole. For a more recent and much more nuanced discussion of the point, see Elizabeth Frazer's *The Problems of Communitarian Politics.*[8]

Nevertheless, the concept of society as a community is viable, especially if one treats it not as a given but as a variable (that is, some societies are much more of a community than others, and their communal quality changes over time). Most important, there is nothing inherent in the concept of society or community to exclude conflict. The only assumption that these concepts entail is that these conflicts be contained by an overarching commitment to the bonds and values that define the whole. If this is not the case, we do not have one community or society. It might therefore be most productive to stop viewing consensus and conflict models as strictly alternatives and see them as combinable. There is room for conflict within consensus, as long as such clashes do not break out of the containing bonds and culture. One may well wish to study the conditions under which conflicts are sustained within communal boundaries as opposed to outside the community, but such an approach merely further highlights the value of the basic concept, community, rather than being found invalid or biased on the face of it.

A good society, it follows, is one that keeps conflicts within bounds, of the shared bonds and culture. However, there is nothing in the definition of community (and hence society) that requires that the said bonds themselves will not be changed, and quite thoroughly.

Along the same lines, one notes that while communities in earlier ages and in other cultures often have been authoritarian and oppressive, contemporary communities are often much more democratic and moderate. That is, to respond to Amy Gutmann's challenge to communitarians, yes, communities that do not witch-hunt are not merely conceivable but rather common.[9]

COMMUNITY AND INEQUALITY

Another normative issue raised when one seeks to assess the value of communities, their goodness, is the relationship between the close social bonds communities entail, and the allocation of all that there is to be allotted, a huge subject. So much has been written about it by ideologues, economists, and sociologists that it is hazardous to one's societal designing to even broach this subject. Hence, merely a few brief observations.

Most readily agree that equality among members as a general attribute is neither possible nor desirable. For instance, there are considerable limits on the extent to which beauty and musical talents can be equalized, nor is it immediately obvious that all these kinds of equalities would be good. Even achieving "merely" equality of economic assets, power, and social status — if by that one means every community member receives the same share, or even from each according to one's ability, to each according to one's needs — is both extremely elusive and not necessarily good (given, for instance, that these entities are believed to grossly undermine efficiency and productivity, a fact that no community can completely ignore). Utopian writing of the kind practiced, therefore, is concerned with greatly reduced inequality, rather than with equality as the end state.

As I see it, a good society can reduce inequality to a larger extent than the one provided by the Rawlsian rule of approving of increased inequality as long as the have-nots benefit from the increased resources that result from the growing share of the haves — even if the haves' share increases much more than that of the have-nots. This formula (which the American society seems to have to a certain extent approximated between 1997 and 2000) puts no upper limits on how much more the haves may gain, and on the growing disparity between them and the have-nots. While there are of course all kinds of statistics that tell different stories, the following might serve to illustrate the point: In 1990, CEOs were paid 85 times more than the average blue-collar worker. In 1999, CEOs were paid 475 times more than the average blue-collar worker.[10] Such high and rising levels of inequality threaten to split society into two separate camps, one highly affluent and gaining, the other a bit better off but falling ever further behind the first camp. Given that control of economic resources is correlated with political power, growing inequality must be expected to undermine not merely the societal bonds but also the democratic elements of society. It follows that a good society would not only secure, as Stephen Nathanson says, a "rich minimum" for all its members,[11] but also labor to cap inequality by slowing down increases in the slices of the total resources gained by the higher strata. These rules would apply to each community.

In moving the discussion from the level of communities to that of societies one notes that in many discussions the latter is often depicted as if it were an aggregate of individuals. Thus, typical discussions of American consumers, voters, even citizens evokes the image of millions of individual actors, acting on their own, and in accumulation affecting the direction of the economy, polity, and society. Actually, even in the most modernized societies many individuals are members of communities. Indeed, it is best to think about societies as communities of communities, which also contain a fair number of unaffiliated individuals.

It follows that in seeking to characterize a good society, inequalities in allocation of resources *among* communities (and not just among individuals) must also be taken into account. The issue can be highlighted quickly by an actual case. A school district in New York City was about to fire a teacher considered a fine instructor by her school because of budget pressures. Concerned parents raised funds allowing the district to keep the teacher on its payroll. However, the chancellor of the citywide school system objected on the grounds that these parents were giving something "extra" to the children of their community rather than to all of the city's children. (Similarly, some state courts have ruled that all the school districts in a state must spend equal amounts on each child, rather than affluent districts spending more than poor ones.) However, the sociological rules of gravity again assert themselves. In thousands of school districts across the country, parents do extra things for "their" school and the court rulings calling for interdistrict equality have been largely ignored.

Ergo, however one may cherish equality, the quest for a good society must recognize that equality among communities has never existed, or been approximated, even during the heyday of the Soviet regime, Cuban socialism, or even among kibbutzim. A good society instead applies to intercommunity allocation of assets the same rules already outlined for members of any one community. No community should be left without a rich (and rising) minimum, and the allocations attained by any one community must be capped. (To achieve these desiderata, of course, entails evolving mechanisms for transferring some wealth and power from affluent communities to others, mechanisms not explored here.)

In short, a good society is one in which inequality within each community and among them is being significantly reduced. Equality per se is not under consideration.

MORAL DIALOGUES AND THEIR LIMITATIONS

The second element of community is much more difficult to evaluate and raises numerous taxing questions. A community, as defined here, is not merely a social entity whose members are bound by a web of crisscrossing affective bonds but also one in which members share a set of core values, a moral culture. A good society, rich in communities, is hence by definition also one governed not merely by contracts, voluntary arrangements, and laws freely enacted, but also by a thick layer of mores that are in turn derived from values. This raises the question: where do these values emanate from? And are they justifiable? Are they good?

A common sociological answer is that values are handed down from generation to generation, via socialization, and in this sense are traditional. However, tradition is clearly not the only source of values. What are the major other sources of values, and how is one to determine the moral standing of values, whatever their source?

In addressing this question it is important to distinguish between the initiation of values and their gaining social roles. New value formulations are often the work of one person, such as a rebelling clergy member (Luther?), public leader (Rachel Carlson?), or social philosopher (Martin Buber?). However, for values to acquire social significance, they must be embraced by a considerable number of people. For members of a community to integrate new values into their moral culture, these values must undergo a process I refer to as a moral dialogue.[12]

Moral dialogues are social processes by which people take part in deliberations that involve not merely facts and logic, reasoning, and rational exchanges, but also include intensive discussions in which their normative commitments are engaged. To illustrate, over recent decades, the American society has had such dialogues on such matters as our obligations to the environment, to marriage partners, and to children. There have also been moral dialogues about proper race relations, relations between men and women, between heterosexual and homosexual people, and numerous others. Dialogues such as these are often complex, massive, and seem disorderly. However, several of these did advance to a point that resulted in extensive (although never universal) changes in the values endorsed by members of the society. Thus, the American society's values regarding many of the subjects listed above, from commitments to the environment to relationships among people of different social categories, have changed significantly over the last decades.

A good society greatly relies on such moral dialogues to determine the values that will constitute the shared cultures of its communities rather than merely base these on tradition.

The literature that explores the manners in which communities formulate their course is deeply influenced by the liberal way of thinking. Liberal thought maintains that typically the way people ought to proceed (and/or do proceed) is for them to assemble and dispassionately discuss the facts of the situation, explore their logical implications, examine the alternative responses that might be undertaken, and choose the one that is the most appropriate as determined on the basis of empirical evidence and logical conclusions. The process is often referred to as one of *deliberation*.[13] The overarching image that is reflected in this concept is that of a New England town meeting or of the ancient Greek polis.[14]

James Kuklinski and his associates describe it well: "From Kant to Rawls, intellectuals have unabashedly placed a high premium on deliberative, rational thought and by implication, rejected emotions and feelings as legitimate (although unavoidable) elements of politics."[15] Jack Knight and James Johnson write, "Democratic legitimacy accrues to political outcomes insofar as they survive a process of reasoned debate sustained by fair procedures."[16] They elaborate,

> Deliberation involves reasoned argument. Proposals must be defended or criticized with reasons. The objective is to frame pressing problems, to identify attractive, feasible solutions to them, and to persuade rather than compel those who may be otherwise inclined to recognize their attractiveness and feasibility. Here the crucial point is that parties to deliberation rely only on what Habermas calls the 'force of the better argument'; other forms of influence are explicitly excluded so that interlocutors are free to remain unconvinced so long as they withhold agreement with reasons.[17]

Deliberation and civility (or democratic polity) are often closely associated. A civil society is one that deals with its problems in a deliberative manner. James Kuklinski and his associates sum up this view:

> In a democratic society, reasonable decisions are preferable to unreasonable ones; considered thought leads to the former,

emotions to the latter; therefore deliberation is preferable to visceral reaction as a basis for democratic decision making. The preceding words summarize a normative view that has dominated thinking at least since the Enlightenment. It prescribes that citizens are to approach the subject of politics with temperate consideration and objective analysis, that is, to use their heads when making judgement about public affairs. Conversely, people are not to react emotionally to political phenomena. A democracy in which citizens evaluate politics affectively, to use the current language of social psychology, presumably leaves much to be desired.[18]

To round off the picture, deliberations are contrasted with an irrational, harmful, if not dangerous, way of attempting to chart a new course. As James Q. Wilson writes, "The belief in deliberation is implied not only by the argument for an extended republic but also by the contrast Madison draws between opinions and passion, since opinion implies a belief amenable to reason whereas passion implies a disposition beyond reason's reach."[19]

Indeed, deliberations are often implicitly, if not explicitly, contrasted with "culture wars;" a term used to suggest that the people are profoundly divided in their commitments to basic values, and that segments of the public confront one another in unproductive manners instead of dealing with the issues at hand.[20] In culture wars, two or more groups of members of the same community or society confront one another in a highly charged way, demonizing one another, turning differences into total opposition.[21] Such culture wars tend to make reaching a shared course more difficult and they often invite violence (from bombing of abortion clinics to outright civil war). James Hunter writes that: "Culture wars always precede shooting wars. . . . Indeed, the last time this country "debated" the issues of human life, personhood, liberty, and the rights of citizenship all together, the result was the bloodiest war ever to take place on this continent, the Civil War."[22]

Given such sharp contrast between deliberations and culture

wars, reason and passion, amicable resolutions versus emotional dead-lock (or war), it stands to reason that many political scientists strongly favor the deliberative model. To argue, in contrast, that deliberations of the relatively pure kind are almost impossible to achieve, or even to approximate under most circumstances, invites the response that they are still normatively superior to culture wars, and that they provide a positive normative model to which one ought to aspire even if it is not attainable. The question remains if one can find a model that is more realistic than deliberations *and* morally much more compelling than culture wars.

I suggest that an examination of the actual processes of sorting out values that take place in well-functioning societies, shows that rather different processes are taking place, which neither qualify as rational deliberations nor constitute culture wars.[23] Furthermore, that these "other" processes are fully legitimate — at least in the eyes of those who approve of social formulations of the good. I refer to these processes as moral dialogues. In these, the participants combine work-ing out normative differences among themselves, in a nonconfronta-tional manner, with limited but not insignificant use of facts and logic, of rational reasoning but largely by engaging their values. (If reasoned deliberations smack somewhat of scientific processes, moral dialogues are more akin to ethical thinking.)

There are two reasons the purely deliberative model needs to be replaced with one that includes moral dialogues. First, in charting a shared communal course, participants are not two-legged computers stuffed with information and analytic software; they are members of the community who must earn a living, attend to their children, and so on. Hence, unlike privileged males in ancient Athens, these citi-zens must study matters of public policy in their rather limited spare time. Moreover, even if each deliberant did come equipped with a mind full of information and statistical techniques, and a supercom-puter, they still would not be able rationally to complete the analysis of the kind of issues they typically face — a problem widely recognized by the champions of artificial intelligence, not to mention of the hu-man kind. It is common to point out that it is impossible to decide in a chess game what the optimal (most rational) move is because the permutations are too numerous. But compared to real-life decisions, chess is a very simple choice space. In chess, there are only two players, immutable rules, all the necessary information is right in front of the actors, power relations among the pieces are fixed, and the rules of engagement are fully established. In communities and societies, the number of players is large and changing, rules are modified as the action unfolds, information is always much more meager than what is needed, the relative power of those involved and those affected changes frequently, and the rules of engagement are in flux. As a result, participating in all decision making must rely on much humbler processes than the rational decision-making school, at the heart of the deliberation model, assumes.[24]

Second, the issues that are subjects of discussion are to a significant extent normative and not empirical or logical matters. Even considerations of many issues that seem technical are often deeply influenced by normative factors. For instance, the question of whether or not to put fluoride into a town's water system brings into play values of those who oppose government "paternalism";[25] the importation of tomatoes from Mexico evokes values associated with questions such as the extent to which we should absorb real or imaginary health risks for the sake of free trade and better neighbor relations; and questions concerning the best way to teach English to immigrant children raise value questions concerning the commitment to one's heritage versus that to one's new nation. There seem to be few, if any, norm-free decisions of any significance. And hence most, if not all, communal conclusions require processes through which shared normative foundations can be found or at least normative differences can be narrowed.

I am not arguing that when public policies are examined by communities and societies, information and reason play no role. Rather, I am pointing out that they play a much smaller role than the deliberation model assumes, and that other factors play a much larger role. I turn now to explore these "other" processes that are not deliberative in the usual sense this term is used.

Moral dialogues occur when a group of people engage in a process of sorting the values that will guide their lives. For example, in the United States there is an intense dialogue over the question of whether or not the virtue of a color-blind (nondiscriminating) society or of affirmative action (to correct for past and current injustices) should guide employment and college admission policies. And, there was a moral dialogue over the extent to which we should curtail public expenditures in order not to burden future generations with the debt we have been accumulating. More recently, there has been a dialogue about the proper uses of our budgetary surplus.

Such dialogues take place constantly in well-formed societies — which most democracies are — and they frequently result in the affirmation of a new direction for the respective societies (albeit sometimes only after prolonged and messy discourse). For instance, moral dialogues led in the 1960s to shared normative understanding that legal segregation had to be abolished, and in the 1970s, that as a society, we must be much more responsible in our conduct toward the environment than we had been in the past.

Moral Voices and the Law

To ensure broad and genuine adherence to values, a good society relies on the moral voice — the informal controls members of communities exert on one another — rather than law. The law has often been viewed as the tool of society to ensure that millions of its members will live up to the prescriptions contained in the society's values. Indeed, one obvious sociological function of the law is to prescribe how people are expected to behave (from paying taxes to meeting obligations to caring for children) and to proscribe what people should refrain from doing (from smoking in defined public spaces to selling, buying, or consuming crack cocaine). Usually, laws also contain penalties to be meted out (and sometimes rewards to be accorded) for those who ignore (or live up to) these normative prescriptions.

When values are less and less heeded, it is often argued that the society requires more laws, more regulations, stronger sanctions, more law enforcement resources and powers, and more severe punishments for those who violate the laws. Indeed, in most Western societies one can observe over the last decades that as social order has deteriorated, there has been a constant demand for more and harsher punishments, more police, and more powers to the various public authorities. However, as the rising economic and social cost of this approach to value-enforcement shows, and as indicated by the failing war against controlled substances, and the fact that while crime declined in the United States recently it is still at much higher levels than it was a generation ago, the high reliance on law enforcement for value fortification does not make for a good society.

In contrast, for a society to be good, much of the social conduct must be "regulated" by reliance on the moral voice rather than on the law, and the scope of the law itself must be limited largely to that which is supported by the moral voice. This is the case because the moral voice can be made much more compatible with a high level of respect for self, with autonomy, and hence with a good society. (Here again the good society is defined as one that triangulates two values, social order and autonomy, rather than maximizes one.[26])

The main point is that if people ignore the law, their wages are garnished, mortgages are foreclosed, and their homes sold out from under them; they can be jailed or even executed. (The notion advanced by some philosophers that the actor always has a choice, even if he or she has to choose to die, is belied by those who are forced to change course by being restrained, jailed, or forcibly evicted from protest sites, like the Greenpeace people who were removed from nuclear testing sites by French authorities — i.e., their choices are curtailed, if not preempted.) In contrast, when one disregards the moral voice one can proceed, although some social costs may be attached. That is, the person's basic autonomy is maintained. Therefore, *law in a good society is first and foremost the continuation of morality by other means.*

The limited ability to rely on introducing social changes through law that is not backed up by values truly accepted by the members of the community, and the severe distorting effects that result if this is tried, are highlighted by the failure of many prison authorities to prevent inmates from dealing drugs in jails. If authorities cannot enforce a law here, when they have the perpetrators locked up twenty-four hours a day, seven days a week, under constant and close supervision, with next to no autonomy, how can one expect to enforce a law this way in a free society?

Often, when one points to the merits of greater reliance on the moral voice and less on law enforcement (an approach that assumes that one seeks to mainly sustain values that are supported by the moral dialogues of the communities), one is asked which public policies would serve this purpose. What public policies, regulations, and administrative acts should be introduced?

The answer, that is compatible with the vision of a good society spelled out here, is that the best way to change the direction of a society is to have "megalogues" about the substance of members' values and the intensity of their commitments to values they affirm. By megalogue I mean a societywide dialogue, one that links many community dialogues into one often nationwide give-and-take. While at first it may seem that it is impossible to have a societywide dialogue, the fact is that such megalogues occur almost incessantly about one topic or another, often triggered by some dramatic event or deliberately staged drama. Oil spills served to trigger megalogues about the environment; the Thomas-Hill hearings, about sexual harassment; and the Clinton impeachment hearings, about what constitutes offenses that will drive an elected official out of office.

It is true that megalogues are fuzzy in the sense that one cannot determine a priori with any precision when the process will be completed, which values will prevail, or which new public policies will be endorsed. In effect, one can only predict that the process often will be disjointed, emotive, repetitive, and meandering. But these are all earmarks of processes that truly engage a mass of people in examining, redefining, and redirecting their values and moral commitments — earmarks of moral dialogues, essential for truly endorsed social change.

All this is not to deny that laws and public policies have a place in societal change, including moral regeneration, but rather to stress that they are not the main factor. Most important, for a good society to evolve, the laws and public policies themselves must reflect the change in values rather than significantly diverge from them. This is the case because the more a society relies on members' convictions that the societal demands on them are just, and the more they conduct themselves voluntarily in line with these values because they themselves subscribe to them, the better the society. To put it more sharply, the good society is not first and foremost one of law-and-order, but one based on shared moral values that the members affirm.

A main criticism of the position advanced here is that the outcomes of megalogues reflect not the true preferences of the members of the society but those fostered by the media and those who control it, the power structure of the society, given that the media is an essential tool of megalogues. This is a subject that cannot be properly treated as an aside in a discussion of this scope. Briefly, it should be stated that to the extent the power structure of a society prevents authentic megalogues from encompassing most members of the society, it cannot be a good society. One step toward a good society would be for large segments of the media to be owned by the public, somewhat the way the BBC and NPR are. Social restructuring and public education would have to ensure that people have the basic economic, social, and intellectual conditions that enable them to participate in the megalogues. For instance, to the extent that these take place on the Internet, would need to all have access to it, and not be burdened by economic concerns to the point they could not find the time and energy to participate. At the same time, it should be noted that while all media — even small town gossip — have some distorting effects, the magnitude of such distortion seems to have been vastly exaggerated. The Soviet experience shows that even when a state has near total control of the media as well as the educational systems, it still cannot control public opinion. And the results of American megalogues are often not in line with that which one would assume those who own or control the media would prefer. Most important, to return one more time to sociological realism rather than utopian writing: the media can be much improved but not circumvented if societywide megalogues are to take place, and their pivotal role has already been established.

GOOD AND ERRANT VALUES

While sharing values is a defining attribute of communities, to reiterate: it is not assumed here that all communities (or community per se) are good. An essential part of their evaluation entails determining not merely whether they share values, but the moral standing of the values they do share.

Some have argued that if shared values arise out of moral dialogues, whether limited to communities or extended to societywide megalogues, the resulting consensus legitimates the outcome. Others have posited (especially Jürgen Habermas), that if certain procedures are followed, a sort of Robert's Rules of Ethics, the results will be morally sound. However, a simple mental experiment raises rather troubling questions about consensus (and other, procedure-based) criteria: If the members of a given community agree, all of them, unanimously, to lynch strangers who stray onto their turf, burn books, or treat women as second-class citizens, obviously this consensus will not make these agreements morally good ones. That is, we are drawing on external and substantive criteria to evaluate the values communities come to share as a result of dialogues judging the moral standing of values handed down from previous generations.

One should note that at first blush a sociologist might find the wording of the previous sentence strange given that many sociologists use the term "value" in a value-neutral manner, referring to democratic as well as Nazi values, to humanitarian and Afrikaner values by the same term. However, if one is to engage openly in normative assessments, as any discussion of the good society requires, one cannot avoid evaluating the comparative moral standing of various values.

Ethicists have developed some criteria employed to determine which values are morally superior to others, for instance those that are symmetrical (applying to ego the same way they apply to alter) are deemed superior than those that are not. But the quest for the values defining the good society may well not be satisfied by such formal criteria. Several attempts have been made to find the other criteria. Some recently have turned to biology; we are all said to be hard-wired one way or the other. Even if this were true, one wonders whether such wiring serves merely as a constraint on what a community can do, or also provides opportunities on which it can build. In either case biological factors do not define that which is good. Others have tried to base their ethical systems on those values all societies share, that every human society endorses.[27] While there are disagreements over how encompassing this list is, it seems rather meager. Thus, many societies consider killing a nonmember quite legitimate. And according to one study, the scope of such worldwide consensus does not reach beyond mores such as that in revenge killing — killing more than eight people is not acceptable.[28] Still others have developed a calculus of harm according to which acts that cause less harm than others are deemed moral, a criterion that is extremely situational. Moreover, it hides the implicit value judgments evident in decisions such as how far into the future consequences are taken into account, as well as the weight one assigns to various affected groups.

A possible source for overarching criteria are those values that, to use the language of the founding fathers of the republic, are "self-evident." (In ethics one refers to deontology, a system based on the values that convey compelling moral causes to us.) A case in point is the observation that when one considers whether truth telling is morally superior to lying (under most conditions, excluding such limiting conditions as, say, if one were hiding Jews and a Nazi asked of their whereabouts), one response is that truth telling is on the face of it morally superior. Analysis, for instance along the Kantian line, that if one person lies, soon others will follow and then the liar will suffer (which sociologically by the way is far from obvious) follows and might cement or undermine the initial judgment, but its original and basic source is the fact that certain moral truths speak to us in compelling terms.

Ultimately, the quest for the values of the good society may require combining all these sources: local consensus, worldwide parallelism, formal and procedural criteria, as well as the sense that certain values are self-evident. One may follow different considerations, but without some such combination of ethics and sociology a good society cannot be characterized.

Throughout this chapter I use terms such as ethical and moral, without indicating that the values or attributes that are so characterized refer to a particular culture or society, as if these were universally valid. A commentator on a draft of this chapter fairly asked me to clarify whether these are not merely "Western" concepts. As I see it, there are *some nontrivial, indeed important* universal values, that are self-evident to all people once they are exposed to free dialogue liberating them from the false consciousness their culture may have fostered. Dignity of the person and the value of affective particularistic social bonds are two cases in point. I cannot provide within the confines of this chapter the empirical evidence (such as it is)[29] nor the debate over the question of whether such values are "hard-wired" (biologically anchored) in all human beings or other reasons to support my deontological universalist position. At the same time there are, *in addition*, very important cultural differences in the values a particular society upholds, reflecting a mixture of tradition restructured via megalogues (and dissemination from other cultures). However, I did not draw on such values in this chapter.

Relativism is the curse of a good society, because when driven to its logical conclusion it in effect says, if you believe in concentration camps, gulags, ethnic cleansing, sex slaves, homophobia, sexism, racism, or whatever — that is your good society; I have my own definition of mine. To be able to conduct a moral discussion, which the very concept of a good society entails, we require a foundation that is postrelativistic, as increasingly even diehard relativists recognize. In effect, when we learn about the behavior of other communities, and they of ours, we do not refrain from passing moral judgment. The only difference is that if we refuse to recognize cross-cultural criteria, such judgments are either arbitrary or unaccounted for. I urge that we make such judgments and submit to them, but openly recognize their foundations, and where they are obscure, work to uncover them through worldwide megalogues. In effect, they have already been initiated on issues such as the treatment of ethnic and racial minorities, women and children, the environment, and numerous other issues from land mines to whales. Sociologists can do much to enrich and advance these megalogues as long as they overcome obsolescent views of cultural relativism or scientific objectivism.

VIII

Social Norms: The Rubicon of Social Science

THE REDISCOVERY OF NORMS

Legal scholars have rediscovered social norms. For decades, the insights and findings of law and society[1] were largely ignored, and law and economics — which mostly ignores social norms — was all the rage. In the past few years, however, new powerful essays about social norms have begun appearing in law reviews.[2] As Richard Epstein noted, "the subject of social norms is once again hot."[3]

Some of the scholars at the forefront of this revival attempt to integrate social norms into the law and economics paradigm,[4] which in turn is based on what might be called neoclassical assumptions,[5] while others may fit better under the emerging "law and socio-economics" model, which combines the law and economics and law and society perspectives into a single discipline.[6] Much more is at stake than the division of labor among academic disciplines; at issue are different conceptions of human nature and the social order, of the ways people behave, and of the ways laws can both modify and be modified by social conduct.

To highlight the alternative approaches to the study of social norms, I examine three pairs of opposing concepts central to a full exploration of the subject: (a) whether social norms affect individual behavior merely as environmental/external factors or whether they also shape people's intrinsic predispositions; (b) the specific processes by which norms influence people (i.e., whether preferences are considered predetermined or assumed to be modifiable as a result of internalization and persuasion); and (c) the ways social norms themselves are formed (whether merely via rational choice or also through historical transmissions). Law and economics scholars tend to use the first elements of each of these pairs (environmental factors, predetermination, and intentional choice) to integrate social norms into their models, to depict the actor as a free agent, and to portray the social order as based on aggregations of voluntary agreements. The law and society approach is based upon the opposite elements of the pairs: intrinsic predisposition, internalization and persuasion, and history. Law and socio-economics combine these two sets of elements in ways to be discussed.

All the legal scholars who study social norms stand out compared to the much larger number of colleagues who have yet to include this important concept in their scholarly paradigm. These same pioneering legal scholars differ, though, in terms of the concepts they draw on to conceptualize social norms. Only some deal with internalization, still fewer with persuasion, and next to none with the role of history. This essay argues that a full analysis of social norms requires the inclusion of all three conceptions. One can view the three concepts as the building blocks of a pyramid whose foundation is secure, while the other tiers are best shored up—or, in some cases, constructed.

After briefly highlighting the importance of social norms for legal scholarship, this chapter examines the core concepts of law and socio-economics and the importance of these for the understanding of social norms in general.

SOCIAL NORMS: A MAJOR FOUNDATION OF SOCIAL ORDER

Social scientists define norms as rules for conduct, the standards by which behavior is judged and approved or disapproved of.[7] They are specifications of values, their concrete manifestation. For example, one of the norms of the value that one ought to care for one's children, is that one ought to be at home when young children return from primary school.

Both social norms and laws serve as foundations of social order, helping to ensure that people will act in ways considered prosocial by their society, from taking care of their children to paying their taxes. The relationship between social norms and laws is complex, and not the subject of this chapter. It suffices to note for present purposes that it is widely held that strong social norms reduce the burden on law enforcement, that laws supported by social norms are likely to be significantly more enforceable, and that laws that are formulated in ways that are congruent with social norms are much more likely to be enacted than laws that offend such norms.

Robert Ellickson points out that social norms theory fills a significant lacuna in traditional law and economics models through its assertion that decentralized mechanisms also have an important role to play in maintaining social order:

> Oliver Williamson has used the phrase *legal centralism* to describe the belief that governments are the chief sources of rules and enforcement efforts. The quintessential legal centralist was Thomas Hobbes, who thought that in a society without a sovereign, all would be chaos. . . Hobbes apparently saw no possibility that some nonlegal system of social control — such as the decentralized enforcement of norms — might bring at least a modicum of order even under conditions of anarchy. . . . The

seminal works in law and economics hew to the Hobbesian tradition of legal centralism.[8]

Epstein captures the importance of social norms, in a few well-chosen phrases:

> Even persons whose own world views are widely divergent often share one common belief about their preferred norms: they all believe the norms should be legally enforced. The set of purely social norms is often regarded as falling in an awkward no-man's land between the world of purely subjective preferences (vanilla against chocolate ice cream) and the law of fully enforceable legal norms. The older term, "imperfect obligation," refers to obligations enforced by conscience and social pressures but not law, and was thought in classical natural law theory to represent the *correct* way for society to implement norms of benevolence.[9]

Tracey Meares puts it succinctly: "It is time for us to take seriously the notion that social norms are better and more effective constraints on behavior than law could ever be. It is time to give norms a chance."[10]

In short, the study of social norms is of considerable importance for full study of the law.

A METHODOLOGICAL ASIDE

Recognizing the very existence and importance of social norms is an important step in constructing a more encompassing and sounder analysis of the law than law and economics has traditionally provided. Seeking such a construction is clearly one goal that compels at least some members of this new scholarship.[11]

There is no need to list again the various limitations of the law and economics model,[12] save for two, because they are directly relevant to the steps next undertaken. Law and economics proponents argue that while their paradigm may be unrealistic, it is highly parsimonious (or "simple") and thus generates valid predictions even if based on false models.[13] Actually, while it is true that neoclassical economics[14] (the foundation of law and economics) starts from a few basic axioms, numerous ad hoc assumptions are added before most empirical observations can be made. For instance, in his attempt to explain addiction, Gary Becker uses eighteen pages of ad hoc assumptions and mathematical equations.[15] The same holds true for many other economic theorists.[16] And neoclassical economics, unlike practically all other sciences, very often "fits" mathematical formulas or conceptual exercises to previously collected data, rather than first formulating hypotheses and then collecting new data to test them.[17] But the record of predictions made based on these models is far from compelling.[18] It seems reasonable, therefore, to seek to establish whether a paradigm whose basic assumptions are somewhat less parsimonious, but which uses fewer ad hoc assumptions, might provide better understanding and predictions of economic and especially social behavior, including of course those generated by laws. Three elements of a such paradigm, that of law and socio-economics, are explored next.

SOCIAL NORMS: ENVIRONMENTAL AND INTRINSIC

A socio-economic paradigm draws on the observation that social norms are not merely a part of the actors' environment but also affect their intrinsic predispositions. "Intrinsic predispositions" refers to the directions in which an actor would channel his or her efforts if left to his or her own devices. They reflect a combination of biological urges and cultural imprinting. Such predispositions can be rather open-ended (for instance, the quest for food), somewhat specified (the quest for healthy food), or even highly so (the quest for a particular kind of healthy food). Specified predispositions often are referred to as preferences. That is, intrinsic predispositions include preferences but encompass other concepts as well.

Not all of the new studies of social norms have incorporated into their paradigm the observation that social norms help shape intrinsic predispositions. Some legal scholars treat social norms basically as one more factor in the environment that the actor faces, an assumption that enables these scholars to incorporate social norms into law and economics without modifying the paradigm's neoclassical tenets. In such treatments, social norms are treated as one more source of costs the actor considers (e.g., would it annoy my neighbors if I were to operate my chain saw late at night, and would the gains from doing so exceed the costs of my neighbors' censure?), as one more constraint under which an actor labors, or as one more resource the actor can draw on. Thus, Eric A. Posner writes: "A norm constrains attempts by people to satisfy their preferences."[19]

In the same vein, Lawrence Lessig notes that social norms do not merely impose a cost but also serve like economic resources — for instance, when norms motivate people to work — but he still treats norms basically as external, environmental factors. Lessig uses the term "social meanings" to describe the shared cultural understandings of concepts like right and wrong that norms rely upon. He then observes that "these social meanings impose costs, and supply benefits to, individuals and groups."[20] In such a treatment norms are akin to droughts or rain, interruptions of supplies, or new roads — that is, changes that take place outside the actor, which the actor includes in his or her calculations and choices.

Along the same line, Cass Sunstein writes, "We can understand a norm — with respect to choices — as a subsidy or a tax."[21] Sunstein elaborates:

> Hence an emphasis on social norms should not be seen as an attack on rational choice approaches to social and political problems. From the standpoint of an individual agent, norms provide a part of the background against which costs and benefits are assessed; more specifically, they help identify some of the costs and benefits of action. From the standpoint of the individual agent, this is hardly irrational, and it is hardly inconsistent with self-interest. (Whether certain norms are rational for society as a whole is a different question. Undoubtedly some of them are not.)[22]

I have no quarrel with these statements about the environmental roles of social norms, and the recognition of the importance of social norms in this external capacity clearly advances the study of law. However, these statements do not encompass a major way in which social norms affect behavior in general, and the law specifically. An example might help introduce the point. I start by examining the environmental factors and move to the intrinsic ones: if a Jewish butcher in an Orthodox Jewish community is unwise enough to try to sell pork, he will soon learn the full constraining power of social norms. He will lose his customers overnight and be ostracized by members of his community. Moreover, the community is likely to draw on public authorities to prevent him from acting in a way that violates the community's very strongly held norm against consuming pork. Norms clearly *do* constrain behavior, externally.

However, social norms have yet another important effect on human behavior: they are a major factor among those that shape predispositions, the wants of people, and the bases of individual choices.[23] Beyond affecting the content and intensity of numerous particular predispositions, social norms help form (and reform) the self, by profoundly influencing people's identities, their world views, their views of themselves, the projects they undertake, and thus the people they seek to become.[24]

To return for a moment to our butcher, the notion that he might sell pork would seem such a gross violation of his values and preferences that he would likely dismiss the notion without any serious consideration, were it to ever cross his mind in the first place. To sell pork would be profoundly incompatible with who he is, the way he perceives himself, and who he seeks to become. This aversion to pork reflects no constraint on his choices in the way this term is typically used, because the actor in this case never was inclined to act in this way in the first place. One cannot constrain or suppress (and hardly needs) a nonexistent urge, want, or preference. In short, this example serves to illustrate that social norms, aside from their environmental role, also play a key role in ensuring that certain preferences will never be formed in the first place, while others will be strongly held.

The significance of the distinction between treating social norms as part of the actor's environment — affecting costs and constraints — and treating them as factors that shape the actor's predispositions, stands out in several important respects. First of all, the contrast is apparent in the levels of compliance with social norms achieved, the level of social order sustained, and the relative costs of enforcing norms. If people follow their community's social do's and don'ts because they see the social norms as costs or constraints, they will tend to violate the norms when the benefits of abiding by them are lower than the gains of violating them and the risks of detection are low (e.g., dumping garbage at the side of the road if the town dump has been moved to a far away place). If norms shape their preferences, people will tend to abide by these norms because such adherence is a source of intrinsic affirmation.[25] They will pray not out of fear that they will otherwise be beaten (as people are in some fundamentalist countries) or end up in hell, but rather because they find the activity itself to be an expression of their inner self.

A related systematic difference between the compliance of those adhering to norms because of environmental considerations versus intrinsic ones is noted by several of the social norms scholars, such as Richard McAdams and Robert Cooter, when discussing the difference between shame, which is externally generated, and guilt, which is internally generated.[26] Individuals motivated by the former will tend to resent the socially imposed costs of the norms, the "tax" they contain, and hence endeavor to evade or to change them. In contrast, if people accept the expected behavior as largely in line with their predispositions, they will be likely to blame themselves if they fail to live up to expectations and seek to change their behavior rather than the norms. As a result, compliance based on intrinsic forces such as guilt is less costly and more stable than that based on extrinsic forces such as shame.[27]

Neoclassical economists, law and economics scholars, and even some students of social norms try to obviate the need to modify their basic paradigms by arguing that when people abide by norms for what seems like intrinsic predispositions, they actually have extrinsic motivations, such as aiming to please their friends or acquiring prestige. To the extent that this can actually be proven, rather than merely presumed, environmental explanations prevail. However, a socio-economic view suggests that there are numerous forms of behavior (such as voting or work done out of enjoyment of one's scholarly, professional, or artistic role) that cannot be empirically shown to be motivated by external considerations and do correlate with indepen-dent measurements of internal commitments.

Moreover, the different sources of compliance produce expected consequences: studies of taxpayers, for instance, show that they are much more compliant with the law and much less resentful when they feel that tax laws are square with prevailing social norms of fair-ness (e.g., a fair sharing of the burden) and that the funds are being used for what they consider to be legitimate goals, than if taxpayers comply merely because they fear being caught if they cheat.[28]

The implications of such findings for the law are enormous. Given the billions of transactions people engage in each day, a social order based on laws can be maintained without massive coercion only if most people most of the time abide, as a result of supportive social norms, by the social tenets embedded in the law, and only if the majority of transactions are sufficiently undergirded by social norms, and thus do not require constant intervention by public authorities. Above all, laws work best and are needed least when social norms are intrinsically followed. For example, the failure of Prohibition is often attributed to the populace's unwillingness to accept temperance as a norm. Finally, those social norms that shape actors' intrinsic predis-positions are less likely to be subjected to attempts by members of the community to change them (e.g., not only was Prohibition not abided by, but lacking political support, it was repealed) or weaken their force (e.g., calling for decriminalizing rather than repealing laws pro-hibiting the use of marijuana).[29]

A reviewer of a draft of this chapter argued at this point that the distinction made here may be of interest to those concerned about the "truth," but that "a pragmatic law and norms scholar might not much care" because whether or not norms are driven by the environment or internalized, they will still serve to curb criminal behavior. As I see it, not only would there be significant differences in the costs and stability of law enforcement backed by the two different sources of social norms, but understanding the different sources (or causes) leads to rather different pragmatic public policies. For instance, the more one is blind to the importance of internalization, the more one would be inclined to increase fines and jail sentences to curtail crime, but if one understands internalization and the ways it can be enhanced, one would rely more on character education, shaming, and peer groups.[30] Moreover, to rely on enhanced internalization, one must have an understanding of the ways it works. To put it in more general terms, the quest for truth and pragmatic measures, while far from identical, tend to enrich one another.

ADHERENCE TO SOCIAL NORMS: FIXED VERSUS SHAPED BY INTERNALIZATION AND PERSUASION

Given the importance of intrinsic adherence to social norms, the question arises whether one can convert compliance that relies largely on environmental factors into compliance that relies mainly on intrinsic forces. Such a change would be reflected in a change of preferences to modify either what the actor actually prefers (e.g., increasing desire to attend church rather than play golf) or the intensity with which the actor prefers one activity or object over others (e.g., engendering support for the purchase of recycled paper).

Most neoclassicists tend to assume that preferences are given and fixed.[31] Ellickson notes, "One of the [rational actor] model's most serious limitations is its failure to explain how people come to hold particular preferences."[32] As Cooter observes, "Internalization of norms changes preferences and decisively affects behavior. However, economic theory cannot explain internalization or predict its occurrence. Filling this gap requires a theory of endogenous preferences linking economics and developmental psychology."[33]

Assuming that people's inner predispositions and selves are immutable allowed law and economics scholars to focus on environmental factors. Indeed, the assumption of predetermined preferences is crucial for the neoclassical paradigm. It is profoundly related to the core assumption that people are free and rational agents. These assumptions can be sustained only if the actor's preferences are given, and he or she selects the most suitable means for realization of these goals. If the preferences themselves are changeable by social and historical factors and processes the actor is neither aware of nor controls, the actor's behavior may be nonrational and is not free.[34] To some extent this is true by definition: without drawing on information and deliberation, the actor is not acting rationally. (The possibility that the norms themselves will lead to rational behavior, even without deliberations by the actor, is discussed below.) And to the extent that the actor's choices are set by others, he or she is not a free agent.

Socio-economics, in contrast, assumes that people's predispositions (including preferences) are formed in part by social norms, and thus can change over time as social norms are changed, as well as that these changes can take place through nonrational processes. (The differences between nonrational and irrational are discussed below.) A particularly cogent essay on this subject, by Tracey Meares and Dan Kahan, pays special attention to "social influence." The authors stress that what is at issue is not merely value consensus but the extent to which the community is willing to foster the values at issue. The article then analyzes various crime-fighting strategies from this viewpoint.[35]

The new field of socio-economics and the older one of law and society have paid much attention to the processes involved in numerous studies of value socialization, character education, and, above all, internalization.[36]

Internalization is an element of socialization whereby the actor learns to follow rules of behavior in situations that arouse impulses to transgress, and there is no external surveillance or sanction.[37] This is accomplished through such nonrational processes as identification with authority figures and affective attachments.[38]

Dennis Wrong has pointed out that while internalization is not coercive in the physical sense of the term, he agrees with Freud that the fear of losing the love of a parent is quite threatening for a child.[39] I simply agree. I am not suggesting that socialization is free of tension or conflict; I merely note that these are fundamentally different from those involved when a person is subject to coercion. Both may be alienating, but—as I have shown elsewhere—the use of force is more alienating than other applications of power or influence.[40] And the use of force obliterates autonomy rather than merely curbing or offending it.

Several of the legal scholars who study social norms have recognized the importance of socialization. Cooter, for instance, observes that "internalization of obligations is pivotal in a theory of decentralized law: after internalizing an obligation, the net benefit from cheating becomes a new cost to the actor. This sign reversal dramatically lowers the costs of enforcing norms."[41] One should disregard Cooter's economist-like wording and focus on the pivotal observation: internalization is a remarkable process through which imposed obligations (compliance with which must be forced or paid for) become desires. Sign reversal is not a phenomenon that is often observed in the social sciences; the mathematical metaphor effectively captures the magnitude and importance of the difference between externally enforced norms and norms that have been internalized.

Similarly, McAdams notes that internalization of norms refers to the process by which "an individual acquires a preference for conformity to a behavioral standard and suffers some psychological cost— guilt is an appropriate term—when she fails to conform, whether or not others are aware of her violation."[42]

McAdams points out that although norms initially elicit compliance through external reinforcement, they often are subsequently internalized by individuals: "Without internalization, one obeys the norm to avoid external sanctions made possible by the desire for esteem, though the sanctions may in fact include material punishments. After internalization, there is yet another cost to violating a norm: guilt. The individual feels psychological discomfort whether or not others detect her violation."[43] Lawrence Lessig also agrees that internalization plays a key role in generating compliance with norms.[44]

Cooter suggests that preferences can be changed not only through nonrational internalization but also through another process, which he also calls internalization and which is compatible with the rational assumptions of law and economics. He describes this process as "acceptance of a new reason."[45] According to this view, which Cooter associates with Jean Piaget and Lawrence Kohlberg, "A child perfects the ability to internalize norms as he or she acquires a capacity for general reasoning."[46] Writes Cooter:

> Piaget's and Kohlberg's research, like my characterization of internalization as acceptance of a new reason for acting, makes the process sound cool and rational. In contrast, "depth psychology" often traces the internalization of morality to processes that are hot and inchoate. According to these theories, internalization of morality ingrains new impulses in a child through emotional experiences. An example is Freud's theory that morality is the "ghost in the nursery," meaning the repressed memory of parental punishments. Repression transmutes fear into guilt, which changes behavior.[47]

Upon closer examination, however, one notes that Piaget's and Kohlberg's research actually deals with cognitive development and not with changes of preferences. Kohlberg posits that all human beings pass through several stages of development of their moral judgment as they mature intellectually. There are six stages, grouped into three major levels. In the preconventional level (Stages 1 and 2), individuals obey rules out of fear of punishment or some similar self-interest. In the conventional level (Stages 3 and 4), individuals are able to grasp basic ethical concepts like the Golden Rule. In the postconventional level (Stages 5 and 6), individuals reason in terms of abstract notions like individual rights, utilitarianism, and the social contract.[48]

Thus, while individuals who have progressed through Kohlberg's stages may well be capable of complex ethical reasoning, this does not necessarily mean that they will have stronger moral commitments or act more virtuously.[49] Kohlberg himself is quite explicit in his belief that it is possible to "reason in terms of such [high level] principles and not live up to them."[50] Unfortunately, to know the good cannot be equated with doing the good; one can be rather conversant with Kant and Rawls and still act immorally. To put it in the terminology followed here, knowledge affects behavior by affecting considerations of costs and benefits but, as a rule, does not shape preferences. Internalization clearly does.

A major goal of education (as distinct from teaching) is to foster internalization of social norms by children and thus to affect their preferences. Children are born with broad, vague predispositions. For instance, they are predisposed to food over hunger, but these general predispositions are translated into specific preferences in line with the particular social norms they internalize. Thus, while children have an inborn need for food and perhaps even for variation in food and combinations (e.g., proteins and carbohydrates), the specific foods they consider desirable — kosher, soul, those their parental or peer subcultures cherish — are a function of acquired tastes. Moreover, the acquisition is often not the result of any conscious reasoning. Teenagers do not prefer Cokes and french fries because they have calculated that such consumption will enhance their peer standing; they *feel* that these are the right foods to consume and typically are unaware how they gained such tastes.

Once children become adults, their preferences do not suddenly become immutable (like the "Rocky Mountains," as Stigler and Becker put it),[51] independent, or hermetically sealed. Nonrational processes continue to affect them. Persuasion is the term often used to refer to the nonrational processes through which adult preferences are changed.[52] Persuasion works by nonrational means, such as identification with authority figures (like Minister Louis Farrakhan); group enthusiasm generated through rituals and appeals (e.g., Ku Klux Klan leaders' calls for a cross burning); and relating new forms of behavior to values that the person already holds in high regard (e.g., convincing a nonactivist to join a political demonstration on the grounds that the person already believes in the ideals of political activism and in the cause the demonstration seeks to advance). Persuasion is also part of processes such as acculturation (especially of immigrants from other countries or of people moving within the same society from one area to another where the subculture is different), religious conversions, joining social movements, or joining a cult. Leadership, mass hysteria, mob rule, and propaganda are all forms of persuasion.

The issue at hand is highlighted by the debate over the role of advertising. Neoclassical economists tend to insist that advertising is strictly informational rather than a means of subconsciously affecting people's preferences, and thus a form of persuasion.[53] Becker writes of his disagreement with thinkers like John Kenneth Galbraith, who claim that "the advertising 'persuades' the consumer to prefer his product, and often a distinction is drawn between 'persuasive' and 'informative' advertising. . . . We shall argue in direct opposition to this view, that it is neither necessary nor useful to attribute to advertising the function of changing tastes."[54] The underlying reason that neoclassicists must deny the existence of manipulative ads is that if people purchase an item which does not serve their preferences, but rather those that some Madison Avenue firm has implanted in them without their knowledge, people could no longer be considered logical–empirical (rational) actors. Furthermore, they could not be the free agents the neoclassical paradigm assumes them to be.[55]

In contrast, a socioeconomic paradigm has no reason to deny that many ads contain information about changes in costs and constraints (e.g., flight schedules and fares), but it also pays attention to the persuasive element of much advertising; for example, ads that appeal to people's subconscious motives ranging from guilt to sexual desire.

It should be noted in passing that to argue that preferences are initially set by internalization and thereafter subject to persuasion is not to deny that the actors have several degrees of freedom. They can become more aware of the forces that shape them, including social norms, and they can work with others to change these forces. There are, though, considerable limits to their ability to liberate themselves from the constitutive influence of social norms. And the extent of freedom they possess is significantly less than the neoclassical paradigm posits, although smaller than some law and society paradigms assume, the Marxist's for instance. A wit expressed the difference by suggesting that in economics everything has a price; in sociology — nothing. Socio-economics builds on the notion that some transactions are highly affected by prices, while other relations are not transactions at all, and not affected by prices except under unrealistic, limited conditions. (One might note in addition that the desire to gain insight into self and enhance one's independence, for instance through psychoanalysis, is itself, in part, a reflection of social norms. A comparison of the relevant social norms of Westerners to those of Asians, of this generation's to those of earlier ones, and of people on liberal campuses to those in traditional small towns, further highlights this point.)

Recognizing that social norms can affect compliance with mores and laws by forming preferences and by changing those that have been formed, through internalization and persuasion, is an important element of the law and socio-economics paradigm. Several legal scholars have adopted these ideas. Others have kept one foot in the law and economics camp and planted the other in law and society, while still others have yet to add these core conceptions to their evolving paradigm.

SOURCES OF SOCIAL NORMS:
RATIONAL CHOICE VERSUS HISTORY

The more one recognizes the importance of social norms, the more one is drawn to the question of where these norms come from and what forces influence their development. The new social norms scholarship has yet to reach definitive conclusions on this subject. Some of the discussion reflects law and economics responses; some, law and society; and some, a synthesis of the two much like the socio-economic approach.

The law and economics position is that norms themselves are "rational" and thus can make actors act rationally, without having to deliberate before each action — or even at all. Norms are said to either reflect previous deliberations or, while not traceable to any actual deliberations, seem "as if" they were the outcome of rational choice. That is, the specific norms adopted "fit" the assumption of rationality as if rationality was some kind of a mathematical formula that best fits the patterns of the evidence at hand.

A simple example of a rational rule is that of an actor who follows a rule of carrying an umbrella every day, rain or shine. His rule is considered to be rational because he is portrayed as having assumed to have calculated that the costs of checking weather forecasts every day (and their reliability) are higher than those of carrying the umbrella on rain-free days. No evidence is provided that anyone ever made such calculations; however, such assumptions allow law and economics to reconcile certain seemingly irrational behaviors with the presumption of rationality.[56]

McAdams provides one of the many highly theoretical models of how norms may arise rationally:

> Under the right conditions, the desire for esteem produces a norm. For some behavior X in some population of individuals, a norm may arise if (1) there is a consensus about the positive or negative esteem worthiness of engaging in X (that is, either most individuals in the relevant population grant, or most withhold, esteem from those who engage in X); (2) there is some risk that others will detect whether one engages in X; and (3) the existence of this consensus and risk of detection is well-known within the relevant population. When these conditions exist, the desire for esteem necessarily creates costs of or benefits from engaging in X. If the consensus is that X deserves esteem, a norm will arise if the esteem benefits exceed, for most people, the costs of engaging in X. Conversely, if the consensus condemns X, a norm will arise if, for most people, the esteem costs exceed the benefits of engaging in X.[57]

Ellickson's pioneering study of the matter stands out precisely because he examined the matter empirically. He concludes:

> In uncovering the various Shasta County norms, I was struck that they seemed consistently utilitarian. Each appeared likely to enhance the aggregate welfare of rural residents. This inductive observation, coupled with supportive data from elsewhere, inspired the hypothesis that *members of a close-knit group develop and maintain norms whose content serves to maximize the aggregate welfare that members obtain in their workaday affairs with one another*. . . Stated more simply, the hypothesis predicts that members of tight social groups will informally encourage each other to engage in cooperative behavior. It should be stressed that this proposition was *induced*, rather than deduced from an explicit model of social interactions.[58]

Others, following Axelrod's work,[59] have argued that rational norms arise out of experience. Cooter writes:

> The economic analysis of social norms draws upon a fundamental result in game theory: One shot games with inefficient solutions . . . often have efficient solutions when repeated between the same players. This generalization grounds the "utilitarianism of small groups," by which I mean the tendency of small groups to develop efficient rules for cooperation among members."
>
> The utilitarianism of small groups has been demonstrated for cattle ranchers, Chinese traders, medieval merchants, and modern merchant associations. Research on property rights has revealed variety and detail in the political arrangements by which small groups manage their assets. Utilitarianism applies to social groups whose members repeatedly interact with each other, such as the Berkeley Chess Club, but not to social categories of people who seldom interact, such as chess players in California.[60]

Other mechanisms that lead to rational norms are said to include rational elites who cause rational selection of rules even if most people do not deliberate.[61] Still others assume that history is rational, as if God were a utility maximizer who guided history through all its gruesome developments, an assumption initially embraced (though later abandoned) by Nobel laureate Douglas North.[62]

The new scholars of social norms have increasingly recognized that while some social norms are certainly rational, others are clearly affected by the force law and society focus on: history, broadly understood, including tradition, institutions,[63] customs, and habits. ("History" refers here not merely to past events but also to the narratives about such events, which are interpreted in ways that help transmit social norms.) According to this approach, the sources of norms are remote in time (e.g., Moses brought the Ten Commandments down Mount Sinai); they are passed from one generation to the next; and they derive authority by virtue of their being a part of tradition rather than reflecting deliberations.

To return to the umbrella example for a moment, law and society students would argue that taking an umbrella on sunny days in the dry season is irrational (say, obsessive) or nonrational, or that if a person does so, somebody must have persuaded him that carrying it is the right thing to do, perhaps because it is a status symbol. (British citizens used Bowler hats and rolled up umbrellas in this way.) Cooter makes this point as follows: "Someone subsequently convinces me, contrary to my previous beliefs, that smoking is morally wrong ('God forbids us to harm ourselves for pleasure's sake,' 'You risk orphaning your child,' etc.). After my conversation, I have an additional reason for not smoking; smoking violates a moral rule I now hold."[64]

Some of these norms are irrational; many others, nonrational. For example, most people who pay their brokers for stock selection act irrationally, and so do most of those millions who put money into their IRA accounts toward the end rather than beginning of the year.

Much more often, social norms are nonrational as they govern behavior dealing with matters that Talcott Parsons called "other worldly" and hence do not implicate empirical–logical matters.[65] These include whether or not one believes in God, spirituality, the idea of progress, and many other such beliefs. Each of these are not merely abstract values but also the source of numerous norms.

Many of these values, and the norms that govern the behavior associated with them, are transmitted from generation to generation, through communal processes such as rituals, holidays, and identification with older authority figures. These norms are commonly legitimated on such grounds as tradition, superstition, nationalism, or some other such cultural factors. While people often also offer valid consequentialist-utilitarian instrumental arguments to explain why they heed the norms under discussion, these explanations are secondary to ritualistic invocations of the past.[66] Thus, many New Age gurus recommend meditation as a way to reduce stress. However, should social science tests show that meditation has no such effects, most followers of these gurus would probably not stop meditating. Religious people speak of the benefits to mental hygiene of being devout, but this obviously is not the leading reason they are religious.

Socio-economics can accommodate both cultural and cost considerations. Social norms are often heeded because they are viewed as "how things are done here." Norms, however, are more likely to be modified when costs they inflict are high than when they are low.

Dennis Chong recognizes this dual position of norms, although at times he slips into a law and economics line of thinking:

> Although some group norms appear calculated to further the interests of group members, many group norms seem to be adopted without reflection and appear instead to be driven mainly by imitation and group identification. . . .
>
> Although much cultural transmission has this inertial quality, it does not always violate the process of rational decision making. No individual has the resources to evaluate thoroughly all of the choices he must make, so by conforming to the status quo he takes advantage of the cumulative wisdom of the community. In effect, he operates on the assumption that existing practices have survived the trial and error test.[67]

Chong adds: "Even if people act primarily in response to the advantages and disadvantages of the options presented to them, they still economize in their decisions by developing and relying on rules and information embodied in their attitudes, beliefs, and values."[68] At another point he concludes: "The economic model . . . underestimates the extent to which motivation from enduring group loyalties and values can override changes in the opportunity costs of available choices. People sometimes resist cultural changes even when environmental changes undermine the original rationale for their values and actions. Also, much value formation and transmission occurs through limitation and conformity without involving explicit instrumental calculation."[69]

This point is also recognized by Lessig, who writes: "For even if an institution arises in response to demands of efficiency, it does not follow that the institution survives if and only if it continues to advance efficiency. 'At a particular time in a particular economy, there may exist lots of institutions which serve no social purpose and which though once valuable to society, may now actually be harmful.'"[70]

THE SOCIO-ECONOMICS OF SOCIAL NORMS: THE ART OF COMBINATIONS

Once one fully accepts that human behavior is deeply affected both by social norms imbedded in the actor's environment and by their embodiment in the self, that the actor's predispositions are formed and modified in part by processes of internalization and persuasion, and that social norms themselves are in part the fruits of rational choice and in part reflect historical processes, one can explore the ways in which the factors modeled by law and economics and law and society may be effectively combined into a socio-economic perspective. This is a huge, complex, and new subject that is only briefly illustrated here.

Social factors often play a larger role in setting "priors" than in determining the considerations that follow. Thus, social factors (especially psychological and cultural ones) may largely determine the extent to which a given actor (or actors in a given culture) is risk-averse. Economic factors may play a larger role in determining which specific low-risk investment an actor will choose, given his or her particular predispositions.

Another form of combination of the two kinds of considerations can be observed in well-functioning economies, where social factors play a significant role in setting the limits on the reign of market forces, but leave it largely to economic forces to form the processes that take place within the market.[71] For instance, the government sets the limits of acceptable pollution but leaves it to the industry to choose the most efficient way to reduce pollution rather than requiring that smoke stacks be equipped with government-approved scrubbers.

Another way to think about socio-economic combinations is to view them as defining a two-dimensional space. Behavior that is both endorsed by social norms and also rewarding in narrow economic terms, is likely to be the most stable. Conversely, behavior that is censured by social norms and economically unrewarding is most likely to be abandoned. The differences between the stability of behavior that is highly normative but not rewarding, and behavior that is considered a violation of norms but still rewarding remains to be studied. The particular response is, of course, affected by the respective magnitude of the two key factors. For instance, acts that are considered minor violations of norms but are highly rewarding are much more likely to occur than acts that are considered serious violations of norms and are not highly rewarding.

To reiterate, these very preliminary illustrations are intended solely to call attention to work that largely remains to be done.

An important subject not explored in this essay is the question how is one to determine which norms are "good" versus "bad." While both kinds of norms can be internalized, promoted through persuasion, and institutionalized, we shall obviously seek to nurture those that meet our moral standards and oppose the others. A brief discussion of my views of this subject is provided elsewhere in this volume (see Chapter XII), and more extensively elsewhere.[72]

CONCLUSION

The observation that human nature allows elders and peers to constitute and reconstitute our preferences, points to a much less sanguine view of the individual and society than the image of a group of free and rational citizens, of people who convene to deliberately, voluntarily, and reasonably form (or reform) the social norms they seek to live by. However, socio-economics does not assume that people are fully determined. It builds on the observation that we are both persuadable and deliberative creatures, that social norms both affect our predispositions and reflect our choices.

It encompasses both facets of the self, recognizing our more vulnerable side. While not ignoring our deliberative capacity, it takes into account that we are susceptible to persuasion. Indeed, it suggests that such an understanding of the self will enhance the reach of our choice and reduce the scope of those forces we neither understand nor control.

The focus of this chapter's discussion was the concepts needed for a fuller understanding of the role of social norms. The complex relations between social norms and the law have not been explored here,[73] other than to briefly note that strong social norms allow for less reliance on the coercive power of the state, make for better law enforcement of enacted laws, and make it less likely that laws will be repealed, and hence are more compatible with liberty.

IX

Why the Civil Society Is Not Good Enough

A very tempered debate between William A. Galston and Robert P. George brought into relief the importance of a concept neither one employed, that of the good society.[1] Galston argued, drawing on Aristotle, that we ought to differentiate between the good *citizen* and the good *person*. The preliberal state, he added, was concerned with the good person; the liberal state is one that limits itself to the cultivation of the good citizen. George, true to his social conservative position, countered that he does not see a great need or compelling merit in drawing a sharp distinction between the good citizen and the good person. Before I suggest a third position, a few more words of background.

Galston is representative of a communitarian variation of classical liberal thinking. Liberals limit themselves to ensuring that individuals develop those *personal* virtues that they need to be good citizens of the liberal state, for instance the ability to think critically.[2] In contrast, social conservatives maintain that it is the role of the state to promote not merely citizenship but also the good person, not only skills needed to participate in the polity but also *social* virtues — those that make the society a good one.

George Will champions this position, arguing that people are self-indulgent by nature: left to their own devices, they will abuse their liberties, becoming profligate and indolent as a result. People need a "strong national government" that will be a "shaper" of citizens and help them cope with the weaker angels of their nature.[3] William Kristol and David Brooks argue that antigovernment themes provide too narrow a base for constructing a winning ideological political agenda. Conservatives, they conclude, need to build on the virtue of America, on the ideal of national greatness.[4]

Religious social conservatives have long been willing to rely on the powers of the state to foster behavior they consider virtuous. The measures they favor include banning abortion, most kinds of pornography, making divorce more difficult, curbing homosexual activities, and institutionalizing prayers in public schools. Additionally, both religious and secular social conservatives have strongly advocated longer, more arduous prison terms for more individuals, for more kinds of crime, favoring especially life sentences without the possibility of parole and death sentences. These penalties often are applied to people of whose business and consumption the state disapproves (a large proportion of those in jail are there for nonviolent, drug-related crimes) rather than for failing to discharge their citizen duties or actually endangering public safety. These are, on the face of it, not citizen issues but good-person issues.

The term "good state" appropriately summarizes this position because far from being viewed as an institution that if extended inevitably would diminish or corrupt people, the state is treated as an institution that can be entrusted with the task of making people good. That is, while it is not at all suggested that the state is good in itself, it is indicated that the state can be good — provided it acts to foster virtue.

Before moving on, it should be noted that among social conservatives, as among all such large and encompassing schools of thought and belief, there are important differences of opinion. It is relevant for the discussion at hand to note that there are many social conservatives who are less state- and more society-minded, such as Michael Oakeshott and a group associated with the Heritage Foundation called the National Foundation for Civic Renewal. That there are strong and less-strong social conservatives does not, however, invalidate their defining characteristic. To put it differently, thinkers who would rely mainly on the society and on persuasion to promote virtue by my definition are not social conservatives, but rather have one of the defining attributes of communitarians.

Both the liberal and social conservative positions have rich, well-known histories, and profound roots in social philosophy and political theory. While I will not retrace their often-reviewed intellectual foundations here,[5] I refer to one item of the sociology of knowledge: Each of these two positions can be viewed as addressing a particular historical constellation. The liberal position speaks to both the authoritarian and dogmatic environments in which it was first formulated by Locke, Smith, and Mill, as well as the totalitarian experiences of the twentieth century. At its core is a profound concern with the overpowering state and established church, especially if these institutions muster not merely superior and encompassing force but also actually succeed in acquiring an ideological mantle of virtue. The liberal position, which arose as a rejection of the good state, tended to reject all social formulations of the good.

Contemporary social conservative positions, by contrast, address the loss of virtue that modernization and populism have engendered, and reflect a profound concern with rising moral anarchy. While such concerns have been raised since the beginning of industrialization (if not before), they have particularly reintensified since the 1970s. It is this condition that religious fundamentalism seeks to correct, whether the fundamentalists in question are Muslims, Orthodox Jews, or some members of the religious right in the United States.

The third position, the communitarian one, which focuses on the good society, addresses the same socio-historical conditions that motivate contemporary social conservatives, but provides a fundamentally different response. Much like its liberal cousin, the communitarian position rejects state regulation of moral behavior. Liberals, however, typically take this position because they favor moral pluralism; that is, they hold a broad conception of tolerance that includes the "right to do wrong." In the words of Michael Sandel, they "take pride in defending what they oppose."[6] Communitarians, by contrast, advocate state restraint because they believe that the society should be the agent responsible for promoting moral behavior. Thus, while the communitarian alternative I outline here may seem similar in certain limited respects to both social conservative and liberal positions, it nonetheless should be clear that its focus on the good society is conceptually distinct from both of these.

THE CORE, NOT THE WHOLE

A good society formulates and promotes shared moral understanding rather then merely pluralism; hence it is far from value-neutral. This does not mean, however, that a good society sets an all-encompassing or even "thick" moral agenda. I discuss first the special nature of the formulation of the good by a communitarian society and then its limited scope.

Much has been written about whether or not there are sociological needs and moral justifications for social formulations of the good. The discussion, it has been stressed, concerns the public realm, namely the formulations that guide the state, which in turn may impose them on those who do not see the goodness of these formulations.[7] I refer here to shared formulations that arise out of moral dialogues among the members of the society, initiated by secular and religious intellectuals and moral authorities, community leaders, other opinion makers, and nourished by the media.[8]

Developing and sustaining a good society does require reaching into what is considered the private realm, the realm of the person. (Indeed, it might be said, that this "is" where the society is in the first place.) A good society, for instance, fosters trust among its members not solely or even primarily to enhance their trust in the government or to reduce burdens on the general public (for example, the problem of litigiousness), but rather to foster what is considered a *better* society.[9] (What is "better" can be accounted for in utilitarian terms — for instance, by observing that in a society with a higher level of trust among its members there will be less white-collar crime — as well as in deontological ones, a notion I do not pursue further here.)[10] Other examples: a good society may extol substantive values such as stewardship toward the environment, charity for those who are vulnerable, marriage over singlehood, having children, and showing special consideration to the young and elderly. These are all specific goods with regard to which the society, through its various social mechanisms, prefers *one* basic form of conduct over all others. For instance, contemporary American society considers commitment to the well-being of the environment a significant good. While differences regarding what exactly this commitment entails are considered legitimate, this is not the case for normative positions that are neglectful of, not to mention hostile to, the needs of the environment.

To suggest that conduct in the private realm needs to be guided by shared values, however, does not mean that all or even most private matters need to be subject to societal scrutiny or control. Indeed, one major way the communitarian position differs from its totalitarian, authoritarian, theocratic, and social conservative counterparts (referred to from here on as holistic governments) is that while the good society reaches the person, it seeks to cultivate only a limited set of *core* virtues rather than to be more expansive or holistic. A good society does not seek to ban moral pluralism on many secondary matters. For example, American society favors being religious over being atheist, but is rather "neutral" with regard to what religion a person follows. Similarly, American society expects that its members will show a measure of commitment to the American creed, but is quite accepting of people who cherish their divergent ethnic heritages, as long as such appreciation does not conflict with national loyalties. Unlike totalitarian regimes, American society does not foster one kind of music over others (both Nazis and Communists tried to suppress jazz). There are no prescribed dress codes (e.g., no spartan Mao shirts), correct number of children to have, places one is expected to live, and so forth. In short, one key defining characteristic of the good society is that it defines shared formulations of the good, in contrast to the liberal state, while the scope of the good is much smaller than that advanced by holistic governments.

DRAWING ON CULTURE

Aside from limiting the scope of its moral agenda, the good society differs from its alternatives in the principal means by which it nurtures virtue. The basic dilemma that the concept of the good society seeks to resolve is how to cultivate virtue if one views the state as an essentially inappropriate and coercive entity.

In addressing this question it is important to note that reference is not merely or even mainly to obeying the relevant laws, but rather to those large areas of personal and social conduct that are not governed by law, as well as to those that must be largely voluntarily carried out even if covered by laws, if law enforcement is not to be overwhelmed. At issue are such questions as what obligations parents owe to their children, children to their elderly parents, neighbors to one another, and members of communities to other members and to other communities.[11]

The means of nurturing virtue that good societies chiefly rely upon often are subsumed under the term "culture." Specifically, these means include: (a) agencies of *socialization* (family, schools, some peer groups, places of worship, and some voluntary associations) that instill values into new members of the society, resulting in an internal moral voice (or conscience) that guides people toward goodness; (b) *agencies of social reinforcement* that support, in the social psychosocial sense of the term, the values members already have acquired (especially interpersonal bonds, peer relations, communal bonds, public visibility, and leadership) — these provide an external moral voice; and (c) values fostered because they are built into *societal institutions* (for instance, into marriage). I explore first the moral voice (internal and external) and ask whether it is compatible with liberty, and then the question of how the role societal institutions play in the good society differs from that which they play in the civil society.

THE MORAL VOICE AND LIBERTY

One main instrument of the good society, the mainstay of "culture," is the moral voice, which urges people to behave in prosocial ways. While there is a tendency to stress the importance of the inner voice, and hence good parenting and moral or character education, communitarians recognize the basic fact that without continual external reinforcement, the conscience tends to deteriorate. The opinions of fellow human beings, especially those to whom a person is attached through familial or communal bonds, carry a considerable weight because of a profound human need to win and sustain the approval of others.[12]

The question has arisen whether compliance with the moral voice is compatible with free choice, whether one's right to be let (or left) alone includes a right to be free not only from state controls but also social pressure. This issue is highlighted by different interpretations assigned to an often-cited line by John Stuart Mill. In *On Liberty*, Mill writes, "The object of this Essay is to assert one very simple principle, as entitled to govern absolutely the dealings of society with the individual in the way of compulsion and control, whether the means used be physical force in the form of legal penalties, or the moral coercion of public opinion."[13] Some have interpreted this statement to suggest on its face that the moral voice is just as coercive as the government. Similarly, Alexis de Tocqueville, years earlier, wrote that "the multitude require no laws to coerce those who do not think like themselves: public disapprobation is enough; a sense of their loneliness and impotence overtakes them and drives them to despair."[14] If one takes these lines as written, the difference between reinforcement by the community and that by the state becomes a distinction without a difference. One notes, though, that de Tocqueville is also known for having highlighted the importance of communal associations in holding the state at bay. As I see it, it is essential to recognize not only that there is a profound difference between the moral voice of the community and coercion, but also that up to a point, the moral voice is the best antidote to an oppressive state.

At the heart of the matter are the assumptions one makes about human nature.[15] If one believes that people are good by nature, and external forces merely serve to pervert them, one correctly rejects all social input. It follows that the freer people are from all pressures, the better their individual and collective condition. If one assumes that people possess frailties that lead to behavior that is damaging not only to self but also others, the question arises of how to foster prosocial behavior (or the "social order"). Classical liberals tend to solve this tension between liberty and order by assuming that rational individuals whose interests are mutually complimentary will voluntarily agree to arrangements that provide for the needed order. Communitarians suggest that reasonable individuals cannot be conceived of outside a social order; that the ability to make rational choices, to be free, presumes that the person is embedded in a social fabric. Moreover, communitarians posit that there is an inverse relation between the social order and state coercion: tyrannies arise when the social fabric frays. The moral voice speaks for the social fabric, thereby helping to keep it in good order.

Aside from being an essential prerequisite of social order and hence liberty, the moral voice is much more compatible with free choice than state coercion. The internal moral voice is as much a part of the person's self as the other parts of the self that drive his or her choices, the various tastes that specify the person's pleasures. The external moral voice, that of the community, leaves the final judgment and determination of how to proceed to the acting person — an element that is notably absent when coercion is applied. The society persuades, cajoles, censures, and educates, but that final decision remains the actor's. The state may also persuade, cajole, and censure, but actors realize a priori that when the state is not heeded, it will seek to force the actors to comply.

Some have questioned whether the moral voice is never coercive. In part, this is a definitional matter. When the moral voice is backed up by legal or economic sanctions, one must take care to note that it is not the moral voice per se, but rather these added elements that are coercive. Also, it is true in the West that in earlier historical periods, when people were confined to a single village and the community voice was all-powerful, a unified chorus of moral voices could be quite overwhelming even if it was not technically coercive, as physical force was not used or threatened. (This clearly can still be so in some limited parts of the West, and most assuredly in other parts of the world.) However, most people in contemporary free societies are able to choose, to a significant extent, the communities to which they are psychologically committed, and can often draw on one to limit the persuasive power of another. The voices are far from monolithic. Indeed, it is a principal communitarian thesis that, in Western societies, moral voices often are, by and large, far from overwhelming. In fact, more often than not, they are too conflicted, hesitant, and weak to provide for a good society.[16] In short, highly powerful moral voices exist(ed) largely in other places and eras.

A comparison of the way the United States government fights the use of controlled substances and the way American society fosters parents' responsibilities for their children highlights this issue. The war against drugs depends heavily upon coercive agents; the treatment of children, by contrast, relies primarily upon the moral voice of members of the immediate and extended family, friends, neighbors, and others in the community. Admittedly, the state occasionally steps in. Yet most parents discharge their responsibilities not because they fear jail, but rather because they believe that this is the right way to conduct themselves, notions that are reinforced by the social fabric of their lives.

The difference between the ways societies and states foster values is further highlighted by comparing transferring wealth via charity to taxes; between volunteering to serve one's country and being drafted; and between attending Alcoholics Anonymous meetings and being jailed for alcohol abuse.

The basically voluntaristic nature of the moral voice is the pro-found reason the good society can, to a large extent, be reconciled with liberty, while a state that fosters good persons cannot. It is the reason the good society requires a clear moral voice, speaking for a set of shared core values, which a civic society and a liberal state do not.

VIRTUES IN SOCIAL INSTITUTIONS

The other main instrument of the good society is social institutions. While the moral voice often is correctly referred to as "informal," because it is not encoded in law, and is integrated into one's person-ality and interactions with others,[17] societal institutions are formal and structured. Institutions are societal patterns that embody the values of the particular society or community.[18] A large volume of interactions and transactions are greatly facilitated in that they are predated by social forms upon which actors draw. Contracts are a case in point. Not only can actors often build in whole or in part on texts of con-tracts prepared by others, but the actors find the very concept of a contract and what this entails in terms of mutual obligations and the moral notion that "contracts ought to be observed" ready-made in their culture. While these institutions change over time, at any one point in time many of them stand by to guide social life, especially in well-functioning societies.[19]

Social institutions are important for the characterization of the difference between the good society and others, because most institu-tions are neither merely procedural nor value-neutral; in effect, most are the embodiment of particular values. For instance, the family, a major societal institution, is never value-neutral, but always reflects a particular set of values. This reality is highlighted by the reluctance of the Catholic Church to marry divorced people, attempts by several organized religions to encourage people to prepare better for their marriage (e.g., through premarital counseling), and to strengthen their marriages (e.g., by means of counseling, retreats, and renewal of vows). All these institutionalized endeavors reflect the value of marriage — and a particular kind of marriage — that society seeks to uphold.

Similarly, societies do not merely provide public schools as neutral agencies for the purpose of imparting knowledge and skills. Public schools typically foster, despite recent tendencies to deny this fact, a long list of values, including empathy for the poor, interracial, inter-ethnic, and other forms of mutual respect (beyond merely tolerance), and high regard for science, secularism, patriotism, and stewardship toward the environment. That societies foster specific values, through their institutions, is crucial for the understanding of the limits of conceptions of the civic society.

A CIVIL AND GOOD SOCIETY

A comparison of the good society with the civil society provides a clearer delineation of both concepts. It should be noted at the outset that these terms are by no means oppositional. The good society is merely a more expansive concept. Thus, far from being uncivil, it fosters additional virtues beyond the merely civil. To put it differently, the two concepts are like concentric circles, with the smaller circle representing the domain of civil society, and the larger that of the good society.[20]

While there is no single, agreed-upon, definition of civil society, most usages of the term reflect two institutional features and the values they embody. One is a rich array of voluntary associations that countervails the state and that provides the citizens with the skills and practices that democratic government requires. Another is holding of passions at bay and enhancing deliberative, reasoned democracy by maintaining the civility of discourse.

In a special issue of the *Brookings Review* dedicated to the civil society, editor E. J. Dionne, Jr., characterizes the civil society as (a) "a society where people treat each other with kindness and respect, avoiding the nastiness we have come to associate with 30-second political ads and a certain kind of televised brawl." And (b) a collection of voluntary associations that includes Boy and Girl Scouts, Little League, veterans groups, book clubs, Lions and Elks, churches, and neighborhood crime watch groups.[21] Most discussions stress the second feature. "Bowling alone" has become somewhat of a symbol for this line of thinking. Robert Putnam argues that bowling with one's friends (which he terms alone) is less sustaining of civil society than bowling as members of a bowling league because such leagues are part and parcel of the voluntary associations that civil society requires.[22]

From the viewpoint of the discussion at hand, the most important aspect of these characterizations of civil society is that they draw *no difference among voluntary associations with regard to any substantive values* that are fostered by bowling leagues, book clubs, Little Leagues, or any other such voluntary associations. I am not suggesting that these associations are actually without specific normative dispositions. Little Leagues, for instance, may cherish a healthy body and sporting behavior (or — winning at all costs); book clubs foster respect for learning and culture, and so on. But from the viewpoint of their contribution to civil society they all are treated by champions of civil society as basically equivalent; none is, normatively speaking, inherently morally superior to the other. In this particular sense, they are treated as normatively neutral.

Certainly champions of civil society do recognize some differences among voluntary associations, but these are limited to their functions as elements of the civil society rather than their normative content. For instance, voluntary associations that are more effective in developing citizen skills are preferred over those that are less so. But the actual values to which these people apply their skills is not under review nor are other substantive values the associations embody. Thus, the civil society does affirm some values, but only a thin layer of procedural and/or tautological ones; it basically affirms itself. Hence, the civil society (and the associations that constitute its backbone) cherishes reasoned (rather then value-laden) discourse, mutual tolerance, participatory skills, and, of course, volunteerism. Yet these values, upon closer examination, do not entail any particular social formulations of the good. They do not suggest what one best participates in or for, what one should volunteer to support, or which normative conclusions of a public discourse one ought to promote or find troubling.

Particularly telling are recent calls to find a common ground and to deliberate in a civil manner—two contentless elements of civility often evoked whenever civil society is discussed. Commonality is celebrated on any grounds as long as it is common. And the proponents of civility seem satisfied as long as one adheres to the rules of engagements (not to demonize the other side, not raise one's voice, etc.), and as long as the dialogue itself is civil, regardless of what actually is being discussed.[23]

For the civil society, an association that facilitates people joining to play bridge has the same basic standing as NARAL (a political reproductive rights organization) or Operation Rescue; members of the Elks share the same status as those of the Promise Keepers; and bowling leagues are indistinguishable from NAMBLA, whose members meet to exchange tips on how to seduce boys who are younger than eight years of age. Indeed, beyond league bowling (and bridge playing), other mainstays of "social capital" that Putnam found in those parts of Italy that are more soundly civil and democratic than others were bird-watching groups and choral societies.[24] Bird-watching groups may enhance respect for nature and choirs may cherish culture (or certain kinds of culture over others), but this is not the reason Putnam praises them. As Putnam puts it, he extols them because "taking part in a choral society or a bird-watching club can teach self-discipline and an appreciation for the joys of successful collaboration."[25] So could most, if not all, other voluntary associations.

In short, from the basic standpoint of the civil society, one voluntary association is, in principle, as good as any other.[26] They differ greatly, however, from the perspective of the good society, precisely because they embody different values. Thus, to the extent that American society cherishes the notion of interracial integration, it views the Urban League and NAACP as much more in line with its values than the Nation of Islam, and the Ripon Society more so than the Aryan groups—all voluntary associations.[27]

The concept of the good society differs from that of the civil one in that while the former also strongly favors voluntary associations — a rich and strong social fabric, and civility of discourse — it formulates and seeks to uphold some *particular* social conceptions of the good. The good society is, as I have already suggested, centered around a core of substantive, particularistic values. For instance, different societies foster different values, or at least give much more normative weight to some values than other societies that exhibit a commitment to the same values. Thus, Austria, Holland, and Switzerland place special value on social harmony, acting only after profound and encompassing shared understandings are achieved. Many continental societies value the welfare state, lower inequality, and social amenities more than American and British societies do, and also put less emphasis upon economic achievements.

Similarly, the question of whether or not religion is disestablished is far from a procedural matter. Many democratic societies that establish one church (e.g., Anglican in the United Kingdom, Lutheran in Scandinavia) also allow much greater and more open inclusion of a specific religion into their institutionalized life than does American society. The routine of praying in British state-run schools further illustrates this point. Promoting these religious values is deemed an integral part of what is considered a good society.

I digress to note that none of the societies mentioned are "good" in some perfected sense; they are societies that aspire to promote specific social virtues, and in this sense aspire to be good societies. The extent to which they are successful, and the normative evaluation of the specific virtues one society promotes as compared to others, are subjects not studied here because this would require an extensive treatment that I have provided elsewhere.[28] All that I argue here is that good societies promote particularistic, substantive formations of the good; that these are limited sets of core values that are promoted largely by the moral voice and not by state coercion. The conditions under which the particular values fostered earn our acclaim is not studied here.

To summarize the difference between a good and a civil society regarding the core institution of voluntary association, one notes that while both kinds of society draw on these associations, these play different roles within these two societies. In civil societies, voluntary associations serve as mediating institutions between the citizen and the state, and help cultivate citizen skills (ways to gain knowledge about public affairs, form associations, gain a political voice, and so on); they develop and exercise the democratic muscles, so to speak. In the good society, voluntary associations *also* serve to introduce members to particularistic values, and to reinforce individuals' normative commitments. Thus, while from the perspective of a civil society a voluntary association is a voluntary association, from the view of a good society, *no two voluntary associations are equivalent*. The regard in which voluntary associations are held ranges from those that are celebrated (because they foster the social virtues the good society seeks to cultivate), to those that are neutral, to those that — while voluntary — sustain values divergent from or even contradictory to those the society seeks to foster.

Hillel Steiner argued that only "some particularly crass *cultural liberals*" would take the position that one voluntary association is as functional as another, from the viewpoint of a civil society.[29] But many of my examples are taken from Robert Putnam who is surely far from being crass and is highly regarded by liberals, including those who question his statistics. Moreover, while liberals — if asked — might well concede that they favor some voluntary associations over others, most do not raise this issue, for good reason. The civil society way of thinking is neutral on this issue and hence does not bring it to mind. Moreover, liberals have no systematic way to justify their preference as long as they rely on the civil society construct.

Soon after Steiner finished questioning my argument that liberals are neutral, he complained that communitarians oppose same-sex marriages. I am not aware that any of my political theory colleagues (Charles Taylor, Michael Sandel, and Michael Walzer) or sociological ones (e.g., Phillip Selznick or Robert Bellah) have taken this position. From Steiner's viewpoint one kind of marriage is as good as another, which of course is a neutral position. (And, I assume, he would take the same position about being married and not marrying.) His comments lead me to suggest that from a communitarian viewpoint, from a good society perspective, no two institutions (not merely voluntary associations) are morally equivalent. This does not mean that some institutions need to be condemned while others are to be considered virtuous. Some may be merely a second best, but no two have the same standing. A good society may well, for instance, prefer marriages that produce children (especially when it is rapidly aging) over *all* marriages that do not. (This preference is reflected in the tax policies and provisions for parental leaves ofmany societies.) It may prefer stable marriages over serial ones, especially when children are involved (as reflected in the laws governing divorce); marriage over cohabitation (as reflected in laws concerning palimony);[30] and marriages that unite a society over those that lead it into cultural wars. (The same point might also be made regarding the presence of crucifixes in Bavarian schools.) Steven Macedo makes the point that a democratic society lets some differences ride in order to curb conflict.[31] (As I see it, domestic partnerships do not provide gay men and lesbians all the justice they seek, and do not satisfy the religious right, but they are close enough to a compromise both sides can live with — the kind a democratic society thrives on.) To reiterate, preference should not be equated with condemnation.

To put it differently, communitarians may tolerate various lifestyles, that is they may well refuse to condemn or outlaw some, but this does not mean that they must treat them all as equally compatible with the society's values. Indeed the term tolerance implies that I will live with your preference although it is not mine. Liberals, in contrast, often show their preference for a pluralism of equal positions by suggesting that they equally *respect* various normative and social position.

Steiner further argues that communitarians disregard that liberals do share a definition of a good — they all respect liberty.[32] This is indeed a failing not of communitarians but a major sign of inconsistency of the liberal position. While liberals oppose shared social characterizations of the good, the value that undergirds their position is exempt from this ban.

THE IMPLICATIONS OF VARYING DEFINITIONS

I now consider briefly the various definitions of civil society offered by particular scholars to further highlight the differentiation between the civil and the good societies.

Michael Novak provides a straightforward, value-neutral definition of the civil society. He writes: "The term for all these nonstatist forms of social life — those rooted in human social nature, under the sway of reason — is *civil society*. That term includes natural associations such as the family, as well as the churches, and private associations of many sorts; fraternal, ethnic, and patriotic societies; voluntary organizations such as the Boy Scouts, the Red Cross, and Save the Whales; and committees for the arts, the sciences, sports and education."[33]

In a book often cited in this context, Berger and Neuhaus view mediating structures as a key element of the civil society and define mediating structures as:

> Those institutions that stand between the private world of individuals and the large impersonal structures of modern society. They "mediated'" by constituting a vehicle by which personal beliefs and values could be transmitted into the mega-institutions. They were thus "Janus-faced" institutions, facing both "upward" and "downward." Their meditations were then of benefit to both levels of social life: the individual was protected from the alienations and "anomie" of modern life, while the large institutions, including the state, gained legitimacy by being related to values that governed the actual lives of ordinary people.[34]

This definition is essentially value-free. It does not distinguish between different mediating structures according to the specific normative foundations or values they extol. A federation of labor unions might fulfill the mediating function as well as one of industrialists; a group of churches as well as a league of atheists; an association of stamp collectors as well as the Sierra Club. At one point, Berger and Neuhaus address this issue of value-neutrality with more directness and candor than any of the other sources examined. The two clearly state that a mediating structure is a mediating structure regardless of its values, even if these might be nefarious, criminal, or otherwise wholly objectionable. Indeed, in the revised edition of their book, Berger and Neuhaus fully concede the limitations of their concept:

> Possibly, though, we were a bit carried away in our enthusiasm for these institutions, overlooking the fact that some of them definitely play nefarious roles in society. Thus, strictly speaking in terms of our definition, the Mafia, the Ku Klux Klan, and the social branch of an organization seeking to get the government to negotiate with visiting aliens in UFOs could also be described as mediating structures. They do, indeed, mediate between individuals and the larger society. It just happens that the beliefs and values thus mediated are criminal, immoral, or just plain crazy. We would suggest now that there are (to put it plainly) both good and bad mediating structures and that social policy will have to make this differentiation in terms of the values being mediated.[35]

While Berger and Neuhaus are best characterized as social conservatives, John Rawls is considered by most to be a liberal. Regarding the issue at hand, however, he seems to hold a compatible view. Indeed, Rawls even seems to go a step further, not only implying that the various mediating institutions are morally equivalent, but also suggesting that the entirety of civil society — not merely the liberal state! — is little more than a neutral zone in which various virtues compete, and in which none is prescribed or even preferred as a matter of societal policy. (I write "seems" to indicate that I do not join here the very elaborate debate concerning what Rawls says, really meant to say, and how he changed his mind from one volume to the next.) The following quote seems to me to speak quite directly to the issue at hand, and it is this Rawls I address here:

> All discussions are from the point of view of citizens in the culture of civil society, which Habermas calls the *public sphere*.

There, we as citizens discuss how justice as fairness is to be formulated, and whether this or that aspect of it seems acceptable. . . . In the same way, the claims of the ideal of discourse and of its procedural conception of democratic institutions are considered. Keep in mind that this background culture contains comprehensive doctrines of all kinds that are taught, explained, debated against one another, and argued about—indefinitely without end as long as society has vitality and spirit. It is the culture of daily life with its many associations: its universities and churches, learned and scientific societies; endless political discussions of ideas and doctrines are commonplace everywhere.[36]

This text is compatible with the notion that a civil society is not a good society because it does not promote one "comprehensive doctrine," but rather provides simply the forum in which a plurality of such doctrines can be debated "indefinitely without end," within the numerous voluntary associations. Civil society is thus desirable because it affords and sustains endless debate, thereby precluding any general consensus on the good to which society at large can subscribe and attempt to foster in its members. In that sense, the "endless" element is not merely dismissive but actually essential.

Michael Walzer, often considered a communitarian, espouses the same basic viewpoint very clearly:

I would rather say that the civil society argument is a corrective to the four ideological accounts of the good life than a fifth to stand alongside them. It challenges their singularity but it has no singularity of its own. The phrase "social being" describes men and women who are citizens, producers, consumers, members of the nation, and much else besides—and none of these by nature or because it is the best thing to be. The associational life of civil society is the actual ground where all versions of the good are worked out and tested . . . and proved to be partial, incomplete, ultimately unsatisfying. . . . Ideally, civil society is a setting of settings: all are included, none is preferred.[37]

Walzer clearly distinguishes the civil society from the good society. Indeed, at one point he makes mocking reference to a potential slogan for civil society, "join the associations of your choice,"[38] arguing that it entails a less than morally compelling and mobilizing vision. Walzer regrets that the anti-ideological nature of the civil society makes it unable to inspire citizens, but implies that this feature is necessary to prevent the idealization of the state. I will return to the importance of this point, which reflects a fear, implicit in Walzer's remarks, that the social formation of the good will lead to authoritarianism, if not totalitarianism.[39]

William Sullivan stresses that the realm of associations and organizations that are part of neither the market nor the state makes up the "much-invoked" idea of the civil society.[40] He points out that these aforementioned bodies are not free-standing, but rather "interwoven" with the state and the market, a point well taken.[41] But Sullivan, too, sees no apparent need to draw moral distinctions among the various voluntary associations that comprise civil society. Particularly telling is his description of the various civil virtues which these associations are supposed to promote in their members: "public engagement, reciprocity, mutual trust, tolerance within a general agreement about purposes."[42] Once again, while these values certainly are important, they serve to sustain good citizens and make the civic society work, rather than promote a particular moral vision that a good society seeks to foster.

The definition of civil society, it should be reiterated, is anything but conclusive. And there are some commentators — most of them social conservatives — who pack into their notions of civil society elements of what I have referred to as the good society. Gertrude Himmelfarb, for example, argues that only a renewed and remoralized civil society can effectively curb such immoral behaviors as drug addiction, illegitimacy, neglect of the elderly, and the like.[43]

But the definition of civil society seems to resist such expansions. As the preceding examples suggest, when commentators invoke the concept, they typically do so in a more restrictive manner. Indeed, the very effort by Himmelfarb and others to expand the scope of civil society highlights the need for an additional concept that can capture this added normative element. The good society can well serve in this capacity.

We often can learn a great deal about social doctrines and political theories by examining the alternatives they seek to engage. (For instance, Max Weber's volumes on comparative religion clearly speak to the economic determinism associated with Karl Marx.) The civil society thesis addresses the fear that social formations of the good will be imposed by the state on a wide front. It does so by advocating a great restriction of the public realm, and by opposing collective fostering of virtues (all those not directly subservient to the civic society or liberal state). The crisis that modern societies increasingly have had to face for the last generation is that of the moral vacuum, an emptiness that religious fundamentalism has sought to fill. This challenge is variously referred to as the loss of meaning or virtue, the crisis of culture, and the deterioration of values. This spiritual void, however, cannot long be left unfilled. If not addressed by values that arise out of shared moral dialogue, it will be filled, as we have already seen in large segments of the world, by command and control theocracies. Democratic societies can be expected to continue to be vigilant against the return of overpowering secular governments—a threat countered by a rich fabric of civil institutions. However, given the challenges posed by fundamentalism in the Moslem world, in Israel, and by various Christian, right-wing movements, concerns for the civil society may well need to be supplemented by concern about the nature of the good society. If societies must uphold some substantive values, what will these be beyond the narrow band of largely procedural commitments that civil society presently entails? This is the question the next generation faces, a question flagged by the concept of a good society, a society that fosters a limited set of core values and relies largely on the moral voice rather than upon state coercion.

X

Virtue and the State

A Dialogue Between a Communitarian and a Social Conservative

with Robert P. George

ROBERT GEORGE: In your article, "The Good Society," published in the *Journal of Political Philosophy*, and in your book *The New Golden Rule*, you argue that both communitarians and social conservatives recognize the need for and the legitimacy of social formulations of the good — unlike liberals — and appreciate the cardinal role of the substantive values a society seeks to uphold. You then point to two major differences between communitarians and social conservatives and conclude that communitarian thinking is a third way of thinking. I suspect that you are right that communitarianism is a distinct approach, but the ways you characterize communitarianism actually define, to a significant extent, the social conservative position. Let's explore some points of similarity and difference.

Perhaps I could begin by clarifying one point. As part of your argument that social conservatives favor a strong government, you quote George Will in favor of a strong national government. It is important not to misunderstand what Will and other social conservatives mean here. We favor government that is strong, but small. We are particularly skeptical of large government bureaucracies that are charged to provide domestic social services. This is especially true when it comes to the central (or national) government in a federal system. Even at the state and local levels, however, social conservatives are concerned about the encroachment of government on the functions and prerogatives of families, churches, and other institutions of civil society. Now, critics of social conservatism from the libertarian side deny that we can have government at any level that is strong, yet willing to remain small. Strong government, they say, inevitably means big government. However that may be, I suspect that communitarians would line up with social conservatives on this point against the libertarians.

AMITAI ETZIONI: We seem to agree about my main observation that social conservatives favor strong government. While it is true that many social conservatives favor states' rights, William Kristol and David Brooks also have written about the glory of the nation, as a kind of antidote to the lack of concern with virtue. The British Tories have strenuously opposed devolution to Scotland, Wales, and the City of London, and have argued for a strong unitary government, speaking about the glory of Britain. Indeed, many continental social conservatives throughout recent history have been "Lincolnian," calling for sacrifices for national unity. They have been the champions of nationalism, union, fatherland (and mother church). All this is not to deny that the American social conservatives have been strong and consistent champions of states' rights, but often they have been nationalist at the same time.

RG: The point is that there is no incompatibility between nationalism (and national patriotism) and federalism for people who believe it possible to have government that is both strong and small. Of course, social conservatives disagree among themselves when it comes to a host of issues that are implicated here, at least at the margins. So, for example, those on the side of William Kristol sharply oppose those on the side of Patrick Buchanan regarding questions of isolationism as opposed to engagement in foreign policy. These sides divided bitterly over the Gulf War. They divide over free trade and protectionism. And if you really want to get a ferocious debate going among social conservatives, just mention Lincoln and his legacy — Lincoln's strongest supporters (e.g., Harry Jaffa) and his most uncompromising critics (e.g., M. E. Bradford) are social conservatives.

Turning now to the main point, you write that communitarians "advocate state restraint because they believe that society should be the agent responsible for promoting moral behavior." And you suggest that this distinguishes them from social conservatives who would rely on the coercive power of the state. Here, I think, you exaggerate the differences between communitarians and social conservatives. It is true that social conservatives allow a role — sometimes an important one — for law in upholding public morality, but the primary responsibility for the inculcation and promotion of virtue, as social conservatives see it, lies with families, religious communities, and other institutions of civil society. My own work makes this clear, I think, as does the work of Hadley Arkes, Gerard Bradley, John Finnis, and other leading social conservative intellectuals. My book, *Making Men Moral: Civil Liberties and Public Morality*, opens with the following sentences: "Laws cannot make men moral. Only men can do that; and they can do it only by freely choosing to do the morally right thing for the right reason. Laws can command outward conformity to moral rules, but cannot compel the internal acts of reason and will which make an act of conformity to the requirements of morality a moral act."

What, then, you may ask, is the role of law, as social conservatives see it? Its role, as I say in my book, is "subsidiary" (i.e., helpful). Law is to help people make themselves moral by, among other things, helping to secure or maintain a moral ecology that is conducive to virtue and more or less inhospitable to certain potentially powerfully corrupting and socially damaging forms of vice. In this way, law and the state support families, churches and synagogues, and the other institutions that have the primary role in transmitting virtue. And, indeed, according to the social conservative tradition, it is important that law and the state restrain themselves lest they usurp the authority of these critically important institutions. (We call this the principle of "subsidiarity.") An important part of the social conservative critique of socialist and other "big government" approaches flows from this concern.

Let us take a look at some of the specific examples you have mentioned as areas where social conservatives would rely on state power, while communitarians would look to society. You write that social conservatives would ban abortion, divorce, pornography, and homosexual activities, and would mandate prayers in public schools. Actually, social conservatives would ban outright only abortion (in most cases) and certain kinds of pornography; we would make divorce more difficult to obtain, discourage homosexual acts and heterosexual adultery and fornication, and permit, rather than mandate, prayers in public schools.

AE: Additional examination of the list is a good way to test my thesis that social conservatives are systematically more inclined than communitarians to rely on the state to promote virtue. You agree that social conservatives would ban most abortions and much pornography. You say that they would not ban divorce, but only make it more difficult to obtain. I would accept the use of this language if the state were to rely on its moral voice, exhort people to stay married, send them information about the harm of divorce, and public leaders would remain married. However, the policy proposals that are actively being considered by twenty states and promoted by social conservatives would ban divorces under many conditions, including when the state believes the causes are inappropriate; if the waiting period has not been long enough (draft legislation calls for waiting periods from two to upwards of five years); and if no counseling has taken place.

(And of course in other countries, Italy for instance, divorce is still banned and the ban is hailed by social conservatives.) Communitarians have a different approach, one relying mainly on voluntary means, e.g., voluntary premarital counseling, marriage counseling, "encounter" retreats (all provided by the various religious organizations, especially the Catholic Church, and to some extent by therapists), and a culture that appreciates marriages. Social conservatives are more willing to use the power of the state and the law to limit divorce, albeit not to ban it under all conditions.

Regarding prayers in schools, I suggest that the phrase "permitting" prayers in schools does not fully capture what many social conservatives are fighting for. Voluntary prayers in public schools are now permitted, indeed there is no way of stopping them. (Wits point out that there is a rush of prayers before math exams.) What social conservatives often fight for is institutionalized prayers, conducted by the staff of public schools, in their official capacity as teachers, principals, or officially imported ministers, and in the classroom or assembly framework. While children may be allowed to opt out, prayers conducted as part of the institutional framework give them the imprimatur of the state.

You suggest that social conservatives would "discourage" rather than ban homosexual activities, but you seem to favor closing "bath houses" and "sexual establishments."

Most important is the public policy debate about how to deal with people who abuse controlled substances and other criminals. Welfare liberals tend to blame society for these offenses and suggest that if people were given jobs (better yet, well-paying, meaningful jobs), education, and rehabilitation, and if racism were overcome — then criminal behavior would be minimized. The same liberals tend to oppose increases in punishment administered by law. Social conservatives take the opposite position. They have favored longer prison sentences, less parole, more death sentences, etc. As millions of people are involved, this is a major case in point of a social conservative tendency to rely on the state to keep society good.

The communitarian position on these issues is not developed, but it seems to point to a greater reliance on involvement of the community in fostering social norms ("it takes a village to prevent a crime"), crime watches, restorative justice, and on graduated responses that start with strong elements of rehabilitation and minimal penalties for first offenses by drug abusers and changes the mix of rehabilitation and punishment for repeat offenders.

RG: Let's go back through the issues. First, I'm sure that not all communitarians favor "no-fault" divorce. It was an idea that swept through the states a generation ago, but the evidence that it was a bad idea is mounting. Many people who initially favored it now view it as a mistake. It has, they believe, undermined the institution of marriage in a variety of ways, above all by teaching people that the true value of marriage is instrumental to spousal satisfaction. This, in the end, has many bad consequences, including, ironically, the tendency to impede spousal satisfaction in marriage. And its consequences for children have been truly tragic. In any event, you are right to say that social conservatives (and others!) are looking for alternatives to the "no-fault" policy. One idea is a "covenant marriage" option that would enable people to choose to enter marriages that could not be dissolved according to "no-fault" procedures. ACLU liberals who like to present themselves as proponents of "choice" typically oppose providing this option, but there is no reason in principle why communitarians cannot join social conservatives in supporting it.

As for prayer in school, I do not doubt that some social conservatives would like to return to official, state-composed and staff-led prayers as part of the regular class day. I assure you, however, that this is a distinct minority position within the social conservative camp. Social conservatives are well aware that in many places in the country they would not approve of the prayers that would be chosen. Indeed, the largest social conservative religious denomination, the Southern Baptists, is strictly opposed to such prayers. They favor, as do most social conservatives, opportunities for student-initiated school prayer for those who wish to participate. At the same time, social conservatives do believe that schools and other public institutions should be able to acknowledge God as the ultimate source of basic rights and duties (in line with the Declaration of Independence) and that the philosophy of ethical monotheism should be preferred to that of atheistic materialism.

Social conservatives are vehemently opposed, as well they should be, to the imposition of secularist liberalism in the name of religious neutrality. There is now ample evidence that religiously observant students frequently are denied their right to the free exercise of religion in public schools. Religious beliefs and their expression often suffer discrimination. Sometimes this is the result of ignorance on the part of schoolteachers or administrators; other times it is the fruit of animus. Either way, it is wrong, and social conservatives (joined by old-fashioned liberals such as Nat Hentoff) oppose it. Again, there is no reason why communitarians cannot join them. The key thing here is to accommodate the free exercise of religion in ways that are compatible with the religious freedom of others and respectful of the religious pluralism that exists in many communities.

I do indeed support closing commercial establishments whose purpose is to facilitate illicit sex. This includes legislating against houses of prostitution, "bath houses," and the like. Most social conservatives agree. I also think, as do most social conservatives, that the astonishing spread (and increasingly very public display) of pornography over the past two decades has badly damaged public morality. It encourages men, in particular, to think of women as sexual objects and themselves as "consumers" of the objects of desire. This undermines the capacity of men to love women (and the children they bear) in a mature and unselfish way, thus damaging marriages, families, and society as a whole. To be sure, it is important to avoid fanaticism in regulating material pertaining to sexuality, lest we restrict work of important aesthetic, scientific, or other value; but we are certainly at no risk of doing that at the moment. An $8 billion pornography industry loudly testifies to the fact that we are massively erring in the opposite direction.

It is true that social conservatives favor tough policies against crime and criminals. As an antidote to the liberal criminology of the 1950s and 1960s, this is a good thing. Perhaps we have moved too quickly, however, to embrace inflexible procedures such as mandatory minimum sentences, "three strikes you're out," etc. Here, subject to the proviso that punishment must be truly retributive, there is no reason in principle for social conservatives not to consider some of the ideas that communitarians are trying to develop. By the same token, communitarians should warmly approve of the efforts of evangelical social conservatives — led by Chuck Colson, Pat Nolan, and others who have themselves served time in prison — to secure basic justice and humane treatment for prisoners. Unlike secular "prison reform advocates," the evangelicals make moral demands on the prisoners as well as on prison officials and guards. They are also proving that the rehabilitation of criminals is possible after all, especially where prison administrators are willing to cooperate with those who are prepared to meet the spiritual needs of inmates. When liberal rehabilitation policies failed to work, many social conservatives gave up on the idea of rehabilitation. Colson and others are showing that "where there is faith, there is hope."

On the death penalty, there is a division in the social conservative camp that is often overlooked: many social conservatives, especially though not exclusively Catholics, oppose the death penalty. (Pope John Paul II, a figure revered by Protestant and Catholic social conservatives alike, has personally spoken out strongly against the death penalty.) And, of course, many liberals strongly favor the death penalty — start the list with President Clinton, who ostentatiously returned to Arkansas during his first presidential campaign to sign an order for the execution of a young (and allegedly mentally impaired) man who had been sentenced to death.

A final point on criminal justice: while social conservatives favor strong laws, they also support constitutional guarantees of procedural fairness. Of course, they do not accept the ACLU liberal reading of these guarantees, but that does not mean that they countenance abusive actions by police, prison guards, or other officials.

AE: Responding to your first point, not only do communitarians support the "covenant marriage" option, we seem to have originated the idea. Back in 1993 we called them "supervows" — different name, same concept. But note the nature of covenant marriage: it allows for choice. This is not a case of a strong (but small) government seeking to promote a virtuous citizenry by use of the strong arm of the law; nor is it a case of government neutrality in the face of any question concerning virtue. Rather, covenant marriage involves the government helping to create the conditions for people to choose an option it considers virtuous. I call this "opportuning virtue," and it would seem to entail a new approach to government action in the moral realm: neither coercive nor neutral.

As for the social conservative support for constitutional guarantees of procedural fairness, I very much agree, and this is one of the major differences between social conservatives, who are constitutionalists, and authoritarians whose use of coercion is often discriminatory by ethnic origin, class, or other irrelevant criteria, if not outright arbitrary. But I also note that social conservatives — I refer here not necessarily to scholars like yourself but to more public intellectuals and politically active champions (John DiIulio and Richard Neuhaus, for example), and think tanks such as the Heritage Foundation — have strongly favored not violating procedures but changing them in ways that make the state more powerful. This can be seen in friend-of-the-court briefs that have argued for reversing the Miranda decision or watering it down, for repealing the exclusionary rule, for sharply curtailing appeals of death sentences, and other such changes.

I am not suggesting that reformulating some of these procedures is not called for. Indeed, I have argued for some of them myself. However, it seems that most who engage in a systematic and extensive revision of procedures to increase the power of the state are social conservatives.

RG: On the matter of covenant marriage (or "supervows"), I congratulate communitarians for coming up with the idea. (I first encountered it in 1994 in an article by the social conservative writer Christopher Wolfe.) You are correct to note that covenant marriage has been introduced to provide an alternative to marriages that can legally be dissolved by no-fault divorces. In this sense, as you say, it allows for choice. And I sense from your comment that communitarians perceive some value precisely in people's having a choice between covenant and noncovenant marriages. We may have here a case in which communitarianism truly differs, at the level of moral and political principle, from social conservatism and liberalism. Social conservatives, though supporters of covenant marriage, accept the policy of two tracts of marriage as a compromise, not an ideal. Individuals, couples, and the common good of society as a whole would, we believe, be best served by the simple abolition of no-fault divorce. Social conservatives perceive no value in the availability of a choice of types of marriage as such. So while we have common ground with communitarians in supporting covenant marriage, our reasons for supporting it may differ in an important respect. The orthodox liberal position, on the other hand, is simply to oppose covenant marriage.

Turning now to criminal law enforcement, there is certainly a legitimate debate about the balance between procedural protections and police power. Often trade-offs have to be made, and there is no single uniquely just answer as to how the balance should be struck. Different jurisdictions reasonably and justly strike the balance differently. Britain, for example, has no equivalent of our exclusionary rule, yet freedom survives. The key thing, I think, is to be as fair as possible in allocating the benefits and burdens of striking the balance one way rather than another. Do social conservatives consistently wish to strike the balance in a way that increases state power? It is no doubt true that social conservatives are leading critics of major Warren Court criminal procedure decisions, including Miranda. At the same time, social conservatives have been outspoken critics of law enforcement officials' misbehavior at Waco, Ruby Ridge, and elsewhere. (In his publication *First Things*, Richard Neuhaus published the single most important critique of federal law enforcement abuses at Waco.) Moreover, social conservative journalists — not liberals — have courageously exposed prosecutorial misconduct in connection with a series of apparently false child-sex-abuse allegations. And John DiIulio's writings on law enforcement and prison policy are arguably the most rigorous and nuanced in the vast literatures of these subjects. In some areas his prescriptions would increase state power, in others they would reduce it. In any event, even if it is true that social conservatives tend, overall, to favor an increase in state power when it comes to law enforcement, I doubt that this is a difference of principle with communitarians. Indeed, I suspect that most communitarians would share the view that Warren Court criminal procedure strikes the balance too far in the direction of hampering ordinary law enforcement powers.

AE: Perhaps the key difference between social conservatives and communitarians lies in judgments of what behaviors are considered morally bad, and how bad these behaviors are deemed to be. Of course, social conservatives and communitarians would agree on the moral badness of many things, and would further agree that they cause grave social harm. Drug abuse is certainly one example. But perhaps when it comes to issues such as abortion, pornography, adultery, prostitution, etc., there is only limited consensus among communitarians that all of these things are bad, and even less of a consensus that they are socially harmful enough to warrant the policies of legal restriction that social conservatives favor.

RG: I am inclined to agree. Social conservatives are united on the proposition that these are morally bad (and, in the case of abortion, gravely unjust) behaviors that require action on the legal as well as cultural front. My impression is that communitarians tend to be more ambivalent. In any event, there is nothing like a consensus among them. To be sure, communitarians generally do not view these matters as morally innocent, nor do they suggest that they are not worth worrying about. Many doubt, however, that their social effects are damaging enough to warrant the limitations on personal freedom that social conservatives are prepared to countenance. Moreover, many worry that a preoccupation with these subjects creates a tone of prudishness or even intolerance that is itself damaging to the moral health of society. They buy at least this much of the liberal argument.

AE: It seems to me that the moral agenda of social conservatives (especially the religious ones) is more encompassing while the communitarian one is more focused on a limited set of core values. Focusing the discussion on the substance of the virtues involved is particularly helpful as neither social conservatives nor communitarians consider it appropriate to limit oneself only to procedural considerations. In this context, I would suggest that social conservatives have accorded sex much too much corrosive power and greatly underestimate, for example, the role of impersonal and intergroup violence, especially guns.

I realize that you hold that a society that is decomposing, due to a loss of integrity, driven by sexual promiscuity, is one that is predisposed to violence, i.e., that violence is a derivative rather than a primary cause of social disorder. In part this is an empirical matter. For instance, Scandinavia, which has long been sexually permissive, is much less violent than the United States. And over the last years, as sexual self-indulgence was modeled in the highest office of the land, violent crime has significantly dropped. I am sure you can produce some other examples that lend support to your thesis. But would you submit here to social science evidence? Would a social conservative agree to ban guns if they turn out to be a primary cause of violence? And even if violence is found to be a mere derivative cause, a symptom of another malaise, does this mean it should therefore not be treated in its own right?

RG: I deplore the increasingly common glorification of violence in films, music, and other aspects of contemporary popular culture. It should be clear that most social conservatives share my view. William Bennett, for example, has repeatedly called on the companies who profit from this shameful business to cease and desist. I am not very interested in the question of whether the glorification of illicit sex is worse than the glorification of violence. They are both morally iniquitous and socially damaging. And, as many others have noted, they are connected in various ways: it is no accident, as the Communists used to say, that the purveyors of violence and pornography are very often the same people and companies; nor is it surprising that so much pornography today is violent pornography.

As for whether social conservatives are too concerned about sexual immorality, you are right to suspect that I can produce plenty of social science evidence to support my view that we ought to be very concerned about the social consequences of anarchic sexuality. It is probably enough, however, to rely on common sense and personal observation. Maintaining the integrity of families is crucial to the well-being of children. Yet family integrity is jeopardized by an ideology of "recreational" sexuality that divorces sex from marital unity and treats marital infidelity as a relatively unimportant matter. The spread of such an ideology plainly plays a major role in the family breakdown we have experienced in the United States and which is common in Scandinavian and other European nations as well. It is true that these nations are less violent than the United States (though no one, I hope, is foolish enough to think that sexual permissiveness has the effect of decreasing violence); but it remains to be seen whether they will be resistant to violence and other social pathologies if challenged by stresses from economic or other forms of adversity. If I and other social conservatives are right to believe that irresponsibility and self-indulgence in the area of sexuality, as in other areas, weakens character generally, then that will manifest itself in the life of any sexually permissive people when the strains of adversity come — as surely they will.

I would certainly submit to social science evidence on the question of guns. So far, though, that evidence, as I understand it, shows that gun control, even where it can be rendered workable, is of little effect. Indeed, some social scientists have concluded that gun ownership, and even the right to carry concealed weapons, decreases crime. In any case, it seems to me that this is an area where the law may quite legitimately differ from state to state and even within states. Where I grew up in West Virginia, gun ownership is prevalent, people use their weapons responsibly for hunting and target shooting, and there is little gun crime. The same is true in nearby rural counties of western Maryland and southwestern Pennsylvania. I can see little justification for taking weapons away from these people, even if it turns out to be a good idea to prohibit gun ownership (or some forms of gun ownership) in large cities such as Baltimore, Washington, D.C., Pittsburgh, and Philadelphia.

AE: All said and done, the discussion seems to suggest that moderate social conservatives and strong communitarians are relatively close to one another, but I continue to believe, though subject to some of the caveats you have entered, that strong social conservatives seem to rely more on the state than do communitarians, and that their moral agenda is more encompassing, and thus more restrictive — it provides do's and don'ts about more aspects of human life.

RG: I am grateful for this opportunity to explore the points of commonality and divergence between social conservatives and communitarians. I, too, believe that we have much in common and a great deal to learn from each other. There is obviously much more to say, and many other topics to address, so I hope that we can keep the conversation going and that other social conservatives and communitarians will join us.

XI

Restoring the Moral Voice

Audiences who are quite enthusiastic about the communitarian message, which I carry these days to all who will listen, cringe when I turn to discuss the moral voice. One of my best friends took me aside and gently advised me to speak of "concern" rather than morality, warning that otherwise I would "sound like the Moral Majority." During most call-in radio shows in which I participate, sooner or later some caller exclaims that "nobody should tell us what to do." Studies of an American suburb by sociologist M. P. Baumgartner found a disturbing unwillingness of people to make moral claims on one another. Most people did not feel it was their place to express their convictions when someone did something that was wrong.

At the same time, the overwhelming majority of Americans, public opinion polls show, recognize that our moral fabric has worn rather thin. A typical finding is that while schoolteachers in the 1940s listed their top problems in the classroom as talking out of turn, making noise, cutting line, and littering, they now list drug abuse, alcohol abuse, pregnancy, and suicide. Wanton taking of life, often for a few bucks to buy a vial of crack or to gain a pair of sneakers, is much more common in the United States than it is in other civilized societies or than it used to be in this country. Countless teenagers bring infants into the world to satisfy their ego needs, with little attention to the long-term consequences for the children, themselves, or society.

How can people recognize the enormous moral deficit we face and at the same time be so reluctant to lay moral claims on one another? One reason is that they see immorality not in their friends and neighborhoods but practically every place else. (In the same vein that they find Congress members in general to be corrupt but often reelect "their" representative because he or she is "okay," just as they complain frequently about physicians but find their doctor above reproach.) This phenomenon may be referred to as moral myopia for which there seems to be no ready cure.

In addition, many Americans seem to have internalized the writings of Dale Carnegie on how to win friends and influence in society: you are supposed to work hard at flattering the other person and never chastise anyone. Otherwise, generations of Americans have been told by their parents, you may lose a "friend" and set back your networking. A study found that when college coeds were asked whether or not they would tell their best friend if, in their eyes, the person the friend had chosen to marry was utterly unsuitable, most said they would refrain. They feared losing the friend. They would rather she go ahead and, in effect, hurt herself rather than take the risk of endangering the friendship. This clearly indicates that they ranked their fear of losing a friend above the commitment to help that very friend. Also, Daniel Patrick Moynihan has argued convincingly in his recent article in *The American Scholar*, "Defining Deviance Down," that people have been so bombarded with evidence of social ills that they have developed moral calluses, which make them relatively inured to immorality.

When Americans do turn to contemplate moral reform, many are rather asociological: they believe that our problem is primarily one of individual conscience. If youngsters would be taught again to tell right from wrong by their families and schools, if churches could reach them again, our moral/social order would be on the mend. Americans focus on what is only one, albeit important, component of the moral equation: the inner voice.

In the process, many Americans disregard the crucial role of the community in reinforcing the individual's moral commitments. To document the importance of the community, I must turn to the question: what constitutes a moral person?

I build here on the writings of Harry Frankfurt, Albert Hirschman, and others who argued that humans differ from animals in that, while both species experience impulses, humans have the capacity to pass judgments upon their impulses. I choose my words carefully: it is not suggested that humans can "control" their impulses, but that they can defer responding to them long enough to evaluate the behavior toward which they feel inclined. Once this evaluation takes place, sometimes the judgments win, sometime the impulses. If the judgments would always take precedence, we would be saintly; if the impulses would always win, we would be psychopaths or animals. The human fate is a constant struggle between the noble and the debased parts of human nature. (While I reach this conclusion from social science findings and observations, I am often challenged by those who exclaim, "Why, this is what religion taught us!" or as one heckler cried out, "What about the rest of the catechism?") As I see it, while some may find it surprising that religions contain social truths, I see no reason to doubt that the distillation of centuries of human experience by those entrusted historically with moral education, resulted in some empirically solid, sociologically valid observations.

It is to the struggle between judgments and impulses that the moral voice of the community speaks. The never-ending struggle within the human soul over which course to follow is not limited to intra-individual dialogues between impulses that tempt us to disregard our marital vows, be deceitful, be selfish — and the values we previously internalized, which warn us against yielding to these temptations. In making our moral choices (to be precise, our choices between moral and immoral conduct rather than among moral claims) we are influenced by the approbations and censure of others, especially of those with whom we have close relations — family members, friends, neighbors; in short, our communities. It may not flatter our view of ourselves, but human nature is such that if these community voices speak in unison and with clarity (without being shrill), we are much more likely to follow our inner judgments than if these voices are silent, conflicted, or speak too softly. Hence, the pivotal import of the voice of communities in raising the moral level of their members.

I need to respond to various challenges to this line of argumentation, beyond the general unarticulated uneasiness it seems to evoke in a generation that has largely lost its moral course and voice. Some argue that the reliance on community points to conformism, to "other-directed" individuals who merely seek to satisfy whatever pleases their community. This is not the vision evoked here. The community voice as depicted here is not the only voice that lays claims on individuals as to the course they ought to follow, but rather is a voice that speaks in addition to their inner one. When the community's voice and the inner one are in harmony, this is not a case of conformism, of one "party" yielding to the other, but one of two tributaries flowing into the same channel. (For example, if I firmly believe that it is wrong to leave my children unattended and so do my neighbors, and I stay home, this is hardly an instance of conformism.) If these two voices conflict, I must pass judgment not only vis-à-vis my impulses (should I yield or follow the dictates of my conscience?) but also pass judgment on whether or not I shall heed my fellow community members, or follow my own lead. In short, the very existence of a community moral voice does not necessarily spell conformism. Conformism occurs only if and when one automatically or routinely sets aside personal judgments to grant supremacy to the community. That happens when personal voices are weak — far from a necessary condition for the existence of a community voice. To put it differently, while conformism is a danger so is the absence of the reinforcing effects of the communal voice. The antidote to conformism is hence not to undermine the community's voice but to seek to ensure that the personal one is also firmly instilled.

Above all, it must be noted that while the moral voice urges and counsels us, it is congenitally unable to force us. Whatever friends, neighbors, ministers, or community leaders say, the ultimate judgment call is up to the acting person. (True, under some limited situations, when a community excommunicates or hounds someone, the pressure can be quite intense, but this rarely happens in modern-day communities because individuals are able to move to other communities when they are unduly pressured, since they often are members of two or more communities — say of residence and of work — and hence are able psychologically to draw on one community to ward off excessive pressure from the other.)

Others argue that the community voice is largely lost because of American pluralism. Individuals are subject to the voices of numerous communities, each pulling in a different direction and thus neutralizing one another. Or the cacophony is so high, no clear voice can be heard. The notion that no community is right and all claims have equal standing, especially championed by multiculturalists, further diminishes the claim of the moral voice. While all this is true, there is no way to return to the days of simple, homogenous communities. And those quite often were found to be rather oppressive. The contemporary solution, if not salvation, lies in seeking and developing an evolving framework of shared values, which all subcultures will be expected to endorse and support without losing their distinct identities and subcultures. Thus, Muslim Americans can be free to follow the dictates of their religion, cherish their music and cuisine, and be proud of select parts of their history (no group should be encouraged to embrace all of its history). But at the same time they (and all other communities that make up the American society) need to accept the dignity of the individual, the basic value of liberty, the democratic form of government, and other such core values. On these matters we should expect and encourage all communities to speak in one voice.

Other critics argue that the essence of individual freedom is that every person follows his or her own course and that social institutions leave us alone. (More technically, economists write about the primacy of our preferences and scoff at intellectuals and ideologues who want to impose their "tastes" on others.) In honoring this pivotal value of free society one must be careful not to confuse allusions to freedom from the state, its coercion and controls, with freedom from the moral urging of our fellow community members. One can be as opposed to state intervention and regulation as a diehard libertarian and still see a great deal of merit in people encouraging one another to do what is right. (Technically speaking, the reference here is not to frustrating people and preventing them from acting on their preferences, which is what the coercive state does, but rather appealing to their better self to change or re-order their preferences.)

Indeed, a strong case can be made that it is precisely the bonding together of community members that enable us to remain independent of the state. The anchoring of individuals in viable families, webs of friendships, faith communities, and neighborhoods — in short, in communities — best sustains their ability to resist the pressures of the state. The absence of these social foundations opens isolated individuals to totalitarian pressures. (This, of course, is the point de Tocqueville makes in *Democracy in America*.)

In my discussions with students and others about the moral voice, I have borrowed a leaf from Joel Feinberg's seminal work *Offense to Others*. In his book, Feinberg asks us to imagine we are riding on a full bus that we cannot readily leave. He then presents a series of hypothetical scenes which would cause offense, such as someone playing loud music, scratching a metallic surface, handling what looks like a real grenade, engaging in sexual behavior, and so on.

I am interested not so much in the question of what members of the community find tolerable versus unbearable, but what will make them speak up. I hence asked students and colleagues, "Imagine you are in a supermarket and a mother beats the daylights out of a three-year-old child, would you speak up?" (I say "mother" because I learned that if I just say "someone" most of my respondents state that they would not react because they feared that the other person may clobber them.) Practically everyone I asked responded that they would not speak up. They would at most try to "distract" the mother, "find out what the child really did," and so on. However, when I asked, "Imagine you are resting on the shore of a pristine lake and a picnicking family, about to depart, leaves behind a trail of trash, would you suggest they clean up after themselves?" Here again, many demurred but a fair number were willing to consider saying something.

Possibly, my informal sample is skewed. However, it seems to me something else is at work: we had a consensus-building grand dialogue about the environment. While there are still sharp disagreements about numerous details (for instance, about the relative standing of spotted owls vs. loggers), there is a basic consensus that we must be mindful of the environment and cannot destroy it. However, we have had neither a grand dialogue nor a new consensus about the way to treat children. This would suggest one more reason our moral voice is so feeble and reluctant: too many of us, too often, are no longer confident regarding on behalf of what we are to speak up.

STUDYING THE MORAL VOICE

I must confess, I have little training and experience in developing questionnaires. However, I offer these items in the hope that some of my colleagues will find a series of these kinds of questions of interest and develop them into instruments that will allow us to measure "the moral voice."

A Draft Instrument

1. A blind man is confused and walks into traffic; a teenager jumps in and helps him to cross safely to your side of the street. The blind man walks off, much relieved. The teenager passes by you. Should you say anything? If yes, or no, why? If you choose to

speak, what would you say? Apply these same questions to each of the following scenarios.

2. You are walking down a trail among some very old trees. A young couple is carving their initials into the bark of one of the trees.

3. You are riding home on a bus. Next to you is a person who has not washed in a very long time, and his clothing emits a very foul smell. The bus is very crowded; finding another seat is out of the question.

4. Walking home from the bus station you see a child whose parents you vaguely know from the neighborhood. The child is throwing stones at a cat that is stretching itself next to the sidewalk.

5. You are shopping and see a woman you know from the athletic club to be in good health parking in a space reserved for the handicapped.

6. Two teenagers are hurling abuses at each other and are making threatening motions. A third teenager urges them to cool off and settle their differences in a mature, civil manner. Everyone calms down. You run into the third teenager later.

7. You see a woman leaving her dog in her car, windows rolled up all the way. The day is very hot.

8. You see two nine-year-old children, a boy and a girl, using a spray can to mark a swastika on a mail box.

9. You see a mother slap her two-year-old child hard in the face just down the aisle from you in the supermarket. All the other shoppers pretend not to notice.

10. You are seated in the nonsmoking area of a restaurant. The couple next to you lights up. The servers ignore the situation.

11. You give a ride to a friend, who sits next to you in the front. He does not put on his seat belt. You know this friend well; he does not take kindly to suggestions and tends to view them as personal affronts.

12. You run into your neighbor in the supermarket. He has a small Band-Aid on the inner side of his arm. "Are you all right?" you inquire, pointing to the Band-Aid. He responds that he just donated blood to the community hospital.

The Basic Concept

The single most important difference between individualists[1] and communitarians is their view of the acting agent. For individualists, it is a freestanding person, who in turn engages in forming social arrangements based on his or her preferences, needs, and interests, or on other mechanisms or arrangements of individual choices (voting, for instance). Communitarians view the main agents as groups of people (often communities, although not necessarily residential ones) and individuals who are "encumbered" by their social context. Their choices are assumed to reflect the culture or values of their community, their social formulations of the good. People's choices are assumed to be deeply influenced by marked social forces, often in ways of which they are unaware. The last point is crucial. An individualist can readily concede that a free agent may choose to abide by norms out of self-interest and rational considerations. But this assumes an awareness of external forces and a capacity to deal with them in line with one's *own* independent choices. Communitarians stress that the social context runs much deeper; it influences, unbeknownst to the acting agent, what the person considers to be morally appropriate, and what he or she values.[2]

As a result, social order can rely, to a significant extent, not on compensating the actors for their social efforts nor on policing them but on "socializing" them to believe in the values the social order seeks to uphold. Because the initial socializing that takes place in the home, child care centers, and the school does not suffice, to maintain a social order requires continued reinforcement of internalized values. Communitarians argue that it is here that the moral voice of others plays a crucial role.[3]

To test these concepts, the following must be considered:

1. The importance and depth of the community's culture and the influence of its members on one another;
2. The extent to which a social order can rely on the moral voice; and,
3. The effects of conflicting moral voices.

Interpreting Results

In very preliminary explorations of the subject, we concluded that many respondents either fear that if they spoke up they would be harmed, or use such a fear as a reason to explain why they would not speak up when other motives might be at work. The draft questions above try to deal with these considerations by suggesting nonthreatening situations. It might be necessary, if interviews are conducted, to urge the respondents to assume that there is no danger for those who speak up.

There is reason to believe that there are systematic cultural and historical differences which affect the extent to which people are willing to raise their moral voice, for what kinds of issues, and whether they prefer to praise or criticize. Also, an important distinction exists between a firm moral voice and moralism. The latter implies that *every* item of behavior is scrutinized, which in turn may raise social and moral problems of its own. Quite possibly a middle range is best, that is, communities in which a significant part of the members are willing to raise their voices on a fair number of issues, though not constantly or stridently. Note, though, that there are important cultural differences concerning the optimal level and scope of the moral voice. For instance, level and scope seem to be higher in Japan than in the United States, and lower in the United States in the 1980s than in the 1890s.

A major issue that comes to mind is personal versus societal responsibility for an individual's condition in life. One would be much more likely to raise one's moral voice and chide the person if one assumes that the person chose their condition out of whim or personal indulgence. One would be much less likely to speak up, or address a rather different target, if one assumed that the cause for the person's condition was the socio-economic system, the person's upbringing, and so forth. Empirically, one can investigate this issue by asking respondents about their assumptions regarding social causality and responsibility. One must, though, note that rather major issues follow here on which social scientists themselves are divided. For example, can or should one assume that communities have *one* moral voice, or that the voice is typically divided between those who reflect the dominant culture and those who reject it?

In addition, the question of the moral standing of the values for which the moral voice (or voices) speaks needs to be addressed. This is a surprisingly sticky wicket. Are these values morally sound if a whole community supports them? Cannot whole communities embrace values we hardly consider moral, say a Nazi community? If we grant the possibility that the values of a whole community may be amoral or worse, how do we account for the criteria that we apply in making such judgments? And are they specific to one's culture, as when we express our dismay when China jails dissidents, and when China expresses dismay at our treatment of elderly Americans?[4]

The issues which one (or a community) is willing to address versus those one would rather avoid indicate the substance of the values of the community and their relative standing. We found, for instance, that middle-class, secular individuals are relatively willing to speak up to protect the environment but are not as willing to interfere in social situations. This is, of course, going to vary a great deal from one culture to another.

Finally, for numerous reasons, Americans seem much more inclined to praise and support than to be critical.[5] The results of the test will hence be deeply affected by the number of opportunities for positive response (praising someone who helps the blind or gives blood) versus the number of opportunities for negative response (most of the other items listed above).

Many other issues arise as in all such instruments. My purpose here is merely to help stimulate research along these lines. My colleagues and I would appreciate suggestions on improving the draft questionnaire as well as information about the results of similar surveys and their interpretation.

XII

Cross-Cultural Moral Judgments

The debate between those who argue that we should not pass judgment on the conduct of other people and those who champion universal human rights or other global values is making significant progress. It has achieved several points of broadly based, albeit not universal, cross-cultural consensus. Reviewing these points of near-agreement may enable future deliberations to treat these points as their baseline, seeking for convergence on issues about which the various sides are still far apart.

Thinkers increasingly agree that relativism is a position that has played an important historical role but is difficult now to sustain.[1] Historically, there was good reason to be troubled by the tendency of Western people to view other societies as "primitive," "barbarian," or inferior and to seek to impose their values on other cultures and people. Much of anthropology was in effect dedicated to challenging this Western view and helping members of Western societies understand

and appreciate other cultures. While the need for such didactic work is far from obviated, the danger of a strong bias in the opposite direction has come into evidence during the last decades. I refer to the great reluctance of Western intellectuals to pass judgments on behavior in other cultures such as genital mutilation, child labor, detention without trial, caning, and amputating the limbs of thieves. While such refusals to lay moral claims take many forms, and are deeply anchored in liberalism, the most relevant to the discussion of international relations is cultural relativism, according to which each community should set its own values, and need not make any account to others about the legitimacy of such choices.

If one considers the early Western sense of general superiority (as distinct from having merit in some areas but not in others) as a "thesis," and the rise of cross-cultural relativism as the "antithesis," we seem to be moving into a period of synthesis. There is growing agreement, even in non-Western countries, that some forms of cross-cultural judgments are appropriate. For instance, Bilahari Kausikan of Singapore (whose intellectuals have been strong players in this debate),[2] flatly states, "Human rights have become a legitimate issue in interstate relations. How a country treats its citizens is no longer a matter for its own exclusive determination."[3] He even recognizes, "Others can and do legitimately claim a concern."[4] Yasuaki Onuma, Japan's leading human rights expert, reports that there is increasing recognition that "states can no longer conveniently deny the universality of human rights. Nor can they claim that human rights are exclusively domestic questions . . . the seemingly irreconcilable conflict between universalists and relativists is more theoretical than real. There is actually a wide range of consensus that most of the alleged human rights must be universally protected."[5]

Consensus on the need to protect the environment is a strong example of growing international consensus[6] — allowing of course for great differences in emphasis and willingness to implement policies. The same holds for growing support for an international criminal court, ban on land mines and sex slaves, and protection of some endangered species.

I am not suggesting that the controversy between relativists and universalists is dying or that all agree to some universal notion of the need to respect human dignity (the term "rights" is often avoided by non-Westerners), but only that there is now a mainstream agreement, and those who do not participate in it rapidly are becoming outliers.[7]

Furthermore, there is a growing recognition that the flow *of moral claims does not run in one direction.* While the West increasingly is gaining a following in other countries for its concerns with political freedoms, Asian claims that the West allowed social harmony and moral virtues to deteriorate are not falling on deaf ears. And the claims of many non-Westerners that socio-economic rights also are important are supported by quite a few Western intellectuals and ideologues for various reasons. (They also are included in the German constitution.)

In addition, there is a school of thought that argues that moral claims a society lays on others often can be *justified in the other society's tradition,* albeit drawing on different conceptions and narratives. For instance, Daniel A. Bell argues that Islam does not allow *hudud* — the amputation of a thief's hand — under most circumstances. Hence members of non-Islamic cultures can speak up against it by drawing on intra-Islamic rationales rather than on Westerners' conceptions of human rights;[8] similarly Chinese people may come to freedom of inquiry and the press because they serve the community rather than because they see them as rights in their own right.[9] And Westerners have many sources in their own cultures that lead them to be concerned about socio-economic rights. There is no reason, on the other side of a cultural divide, to object to such intracultural accounting of moral claims, but only if they are far-reaching and well grounded.[10] (For instance, subscribing to human rights because they are "useful" for community purposes may provide sound but insufficient grounding.)

Also, there is some consensus that different societies need not adopt exactly the same regime to be democratic. Thus, just as there are differences among various Western societies (for instance, between the United States and the United Kingdom: the latter has no First Amendment, has a state secret act, and a prohibition on hate speech) so there may be differences among various non-Western societies that are achieving democratic status (for instance, between India and the Philippines).

Finally, there is a growing agreement that there is *a connection between socio-economic and political development.* At least it is agreed that countries whose gross national product per capita is low, state of public health is poor, and education level is minimal will tend to have much greater difficulties in introducing democratic regimes than more fully developed countries.[11] Where may the debate move from here?

NEXT STEPS

The End of Economic Deferral
The argument that underdeveloped countries must defer the introduction of human rights and democratic regimes until they are economically developed, or that saving people from starvation and disease must take priority over political development, should be put to rest because it does not withstand elementary empirical observations and moral criticism. While socio-economic difficulties can hinder political development, these do not make them of lower ethical standing than economic achievements. One also ought to note that countries like China and Singapore are deferring not only so-called "soft" democratic rights such as the right of free expression and assembly, but also protection against detention without trial, curbs on press freedoms, seizures of property,[12] and other elementary human rights. Is it better to be tortured and hanged than to face food shortages?

Moreover, the choice posited is a false one, presented in stark terms that favor those opposed to political development. The fact is that Singapore already has achieved a very high standard of living — a per capita annual income of roughly $14,000 in 1998, the same level that the United States reached only thirteen years before[13] — and yet still feels that it is not sufficiently developed to make room for political freedoms. While there are occasional pockets of food shortages in some parts of China, millions of Chinese now are encouraged to purchase optional consumer goods such as gourmet coffee, designer blue jeans, and name-brand makeup and perfumes. These hardly have a higher moral standing than elementary freedoms.

Also, the argument that economic development will not be possible unless political development is deferred is belied both by the experience of India and of course by the history of the West, in which political and economic development took place simultaneously. Indeed, the opposite may be more accurate—that economic development follows political freedoms and not vice versa. Aryeh Neier notes, "Open societies around the world are flourishing economically to a far greater extent than closed societies or societies that were closed until recently."[14]

The "Need" to Maintain Social Order

Asian political leaders and intellectuals have looked with condescension at the deterioration of the social order in the West and argued that restrictions of political freedoms are needed to sustain social harmony. In a public address, Singapore's Prime Minister, Goh Chok Tong, said, "Western liberals, foreign media, and human rights groups want Singapore to be like their societies, and some Singaporeans mindlessly dance to their tune. . . . We must think for ourselves and decide what is good for Singapore, what will make Singapore stable and successful. Above all else, stay away from policies which have brought a plague of social and economic problems to the United States and Britain."[15] Kevin Y. L. Tan echoes the prime minister when he writes, "The problem as Asians see it is this: How can the West—especially America—preach democracy and human rights as fundamental values when the West can't even get its own house in order."[16]

It should be noted first of all that this argument does not comport with the previous, economic one. The economic development superiority position favors delaying political freedoms; the social argument suggests that they are inherently incompatible with an orderly and virtuous society.

These arguments are not sustainable. First, the deterioration of social order in the West has been a recent development. The American society of the 1950s, for instance, had a strong social order. While it was less democratic than contemporary America (especially in its treatment of minorities and women), it honored basic human rights and political freedoms of the majority. Other free societies in Western Europe had a high level of social order in the 1960s and beyond.

Second, those Asian societies that rely heavily on the state to maintain order act in a rather different way than they imply when they refer to themselves as "communitarian."[17] In contrast, Japan, which is much more democratic, has a strong social order that is based more on family and community, national bonds, and loyalties rather than on state coercion, comes much closer to a model of a society whose members truly are involved and committed to social harmony and moral values. (In recent years there have been some signs of social disorganization in Japan that have alarmed the society's leaders and opinion makers. Still, crime, divorce, and other signs of social decay are low compared to the West.) Coercion is only necessary when people do not voluntarily do what is expected of them. The much lower level of policing in Japan compared to Singapore, without a loss in social order, highlights the difference.

Third, it should be noted that even Japan may put too much weight on social conformity and loyalties. A true communitarian society combines the quest for social order, based largely on voluntary commitment of the members, with socially constructed opportunities for individual and subgroup expressions, and with secure political freedoms. Aside from being right in their own right, such social formations serve to enhance creativity and innovation, and to satisfy deep-seated human needs.

The general idea of combining liberty and order, individual rights and social responsibilities has been stated especially well by Yersu Kim: "Without order, anarchy prevails; without autonomy communities turn into authoritarian states. We must therefore strive for an equilibrium between individual rights and the concern for the common good such that individual rights and respect for the common good enhance each other."[18]

He further explained: "Everyone should be treated with respect, embodying a set of rights which an individual possesses as an attribute of his or her dignity as a human being. At the same time he or she must be recognized as the center of relationships, encompassing family, society, nation and humanity of which he or she is a part. Every individual must therefore be seen as the locus of both rights and responsibilities."[19]

And yet the Asians make a major valid point, which if restated highlights a Western failing. Given the communitarian ideal of balance between social order and individual and subgroup autonomy, the West, especially American society, has veered off in the opposite direction. We have allowed self-interest, self-indulgence, permissiveness, and a sense of entitlement to grow excessively while neglecting the foundations of social and moral order. Hence, a strong case can be made that both kinds of societies are converging on a societal model that combines a higher level of social order than the West recently experienced with a higher level of individual and subgroup autonomy than even Japan currently allows.

Note that in this context it is not helpful to refer to a convergence of East and West, as one may do as a very rough first approximation. Neither "East" nor "West" is of one kind, certainly from the viewpoint of the issues addressed here. The level of policing, social order, and political development of India and Singapore, Japan and China, the Philippines and Burma hardly are the same. And the state of the American society and that of Scandinavia are rather different. Moreover, few would wish to combine the social order deficiencies of several Western societies with the lack of protection of women's rights, poor treatment of minorities, and excessive pressure to conform of several Eastern societies. The cross-cultural dialogue will be best served when the discussion focuses on those virtues and social formations that are legitimate and worth extolling and advancing rather than building on a shorthand that draws on terms such as "East" and "West."

Human Rights: Not an Instrument of Western Oppression

One of the critics of human rights and democratic regimes' most repeated refrains is that human rights are Western ideas, that they have been used as legitimation for Western interventions in the lives of other societies. Adamantia Pollis and Peter Schwab famously refer to human rights as "a Western construct with limited applicability," arguing that "human rights as a twentieth-century concept and as embedded in the United Nations can be traced to the particular experiences of England, France, and the United States."[20] Marnia Lazreg further claims that "the current U.S.-sponsored drive for human rights necessarily reveals itself as a moralistic ideology that satisfies extramoral needs."[21] These arguments must be unpacked and dealt with separately. They mix points that hinder the needed cross-cultural dialogues with those that contribute to the suggested convergence between East and West.

The argument that human rights are Western in origin and hence not suitable to other cultures is a particularly unfortunate one. Virtues either should be considered valid or rejected; the source of an ideal and its legitimacy should not be confused. Westerners should not reject notions of the beauty and peace that harmony entails because they are "Asian"; and human rights should not be rejected by other cultures if they are justifiable, even if they were first formulated in the West. The point can be tested by the following mental experiment. Assume for a moment that recent claims by some African American historians that Western notions of political freedom and democracy actually originated in Africa, in Egypt especially, turn out to be valid. Would that enhance the legitimacy of the democratic ideals? And if yes, only for Africans? Only for North Africans? Clearly, historical accounting has very little to do with the legitimacy of a given virtue.

The second, and more powerful, version of the Eastern argument contends that some Western countries have used others' lack of human rights to legitimate their intervention in other countries. These interventions range from early colonization to the recent landing of U.S. Marines in Haiti and economic sanctions imposed on Cuba. A considerable literature on the subject asks under what conditions such interventions are justified (against a new Hitler?) versus inappropriate (to advance American corporate interests?).[22] One need not address these questions here, however, because they do not deal with the legitimacy of the claim of human rights any more than they deal with the virtue of social order. They concern the means and conditions under which stronger powers may interfere in the affairs of weaker powers. To push the point, one can be radically opposed to any and all economic sanctions, not to mention blockades and invasions, against countries that violate human rights or are disorderly, and still hold liberty and social rules as core virtues.

In short, one needs to separate the legitimacy of certain moral claims across cultures from the ways and means by which they may be advanced. If a society considers it illegitimate to underwrite its moral claims by use of force or economic means, what force do they have? The answer is the force of moral claims.

Cross-Societal Moral Voices

As the notions of the moral voice and moral dialogues are central to my argument but are not widely recognized, they deserve additional elaboration here. The *moral voice* is a peculiar form of motivation that encourages people to adhere to values to which they already subscribe. The term "moral voice" is particularly appropriate because people "hear" it. Thus, when a person who affirms a value is tempted to ignore it, he or she hears a voice urging him or her to do what is right. Hearing the voice does not mean that one will always or even regularly heed it, but it will often affect behavior. For example, a person who at first ignores the voice may later repent and engage in compensatory behavior. As with individuals, communities too may hear moral voices.[23]

Moral dialogues occur when a group of people engage in a process of sorting the values that will guide their lives. Should the sanctity of the unborn child or a woman's right to choose guide our abortion policy? Should the virtue of a color-blind (nondiscriminating) society or that of reverse discrimination (to correct for past and current injustices) guide our employment policies? Built into this concept are tenets that are unacceptable to political theory liberals. These tenets should hence be stated explicitly. Moral dialogues assume that societies need shared formulations of the good and cannot function only on the basis of negotiated settlements of differences between individual and group formulations of the good. Moreover, moral dialogues require that the processes that lead to such shared formulations entail dialogues that concern values and not merely deliberations over empirical facts or logically derived notions.[24] Moral dialogues are not merely a matter of reasonable people coming to terms, but of people of divergent convictions finding a common normative ground.[25]

It is relatively easy to demonstrate that such dialogues take place constantly in well-formed societies, which most democracies are, and that frequently they result (albeit sometimes only after prolonged dialogues) in a new affirmed direction for the respective societies. But can moral dialogues take place internationally, and to what effect?

Moral dialogues occurring across national lines are much more limited in scope, intensity, conclusion, and effect than intranational ones. Nevertheless they point to a process that, if further advanced, can provide a thicker global moral base than currently exists. For example, there is a worldwide dialogue about the extent to which "we" (that is, all nations, and in this sense the people of the world) ought to respect the environment. Of course, the dialogue is affected by numerous non-normative considerations, often dressed up in normative claims. However, the dialogue does affect what people consider morally appropriate. Thus, one reason most countries try to avoid being perceived as environmentally irresponsible is that they do not wish to be considered acting illegitimately in the eyes of nations other than their own. Among the examples frequently given of rising worldwide consensus on specific environmental matters, reflecting the general rising shared commitment to the protection of the environment, are limitations on whaling, on trade in African elephant ivory, on trade in hazardous waste, and on adding to acid rain and ozone layer damage, among others.[26]

Moral voices are applied to superpowers and not merely by them to less powerful countries. (Indeed, some have argued that relying on moral claims is the special province of less powerful nations.[27] A case in point was the worldwide condemnation of the United States following the 1992 Earth Summit in Rio de Janeiro. Here the United States forced a watering-down of the climate control treaty, and refused to sign the biodiversity treaty. These acts drew heavy criticism from all over the world.)

A Communitarian Call for Cross-Cultural Moral Dialogues

To help nourish cross-national moral dialogues, communitarians should favor a step opposite that which cultural relativists have taken: Namely, that moral voices, especially when they truly reflect the people of a society that is raising them, be expressed cross-culturally.

It is necessary to raise moral voices across societal lines in order to identify and articulate a core of globally shared values. The need for, and legitimacy of, laying moral claims on societies other than one's own, to appreciate the drives of other societies when they advance individual rights and shoulder social responsibilities as well as to censor them when they do not, must be recognized. To call on all people to respect the same set of core values does not entail arguing that all have to follow the same path of economic development, enjoy the same music, or exercise the same table manners. At issue are core values such as respecting human dignity by not warring or tolerating genocide, being responsive to all the members of the respective communities rather than serving small elites,[28] and upholding some other select values rather than following a pervasive agenda. Indeed, it is a sociological mistake when international bodies do meet to discuss normative issues for each of the participants to add all that is on their normative wish list to the pile of cross-national moral claims. The long road to a world of shared values will be shortened somewhat if the focus is kept on a limited set of core values.

Rather than muting the cross-cultural moral voice, as the cultural relativists do, all societies should respect the right of others to lay moral claims on them just as they are entitled to do to others. Thus, the West should realize that it is well within its legitimate, world community-building role when it criticizes China for its violation of human rights. And China should be viewed as equally legitimate when it criticizes American society for its neglect of filial duties.

To form cross-cultural judgments requires another layer of accountability: substantive global values, in the sense that they lay a claim on all and are not particular to any one community or society. Thus, as I see it, individual rights do not reflect a Western value, but a global value that lays claims on all people. Far from being deterred or chastened when the Chinese government, or some Asian intellectuals, protest the West's application of this value to Asian cultures and regimes, I see in the furor that such claims generate a recognition of the validity of these claims. And for that same reason, I find their call on the West — for example, to enhance our respect of the elderly — also fully legitimate and compelling.

Cross-cultural moral claims are effective *because* they resonate with values we share, but have been neglected. This is a major reason Asians become distressed when they are criticized for not sufficiently respecting individual rights. If one instead chastised them for using chopsticks instead of forks, they would hardly be perturbed. Similarly, Asians make telling points when they criticize the West about its neglect of social order. Compare the effect of such claims to a call by Muslims on the West to embrace their lax and sexist divorce laws. Nobody would respond in a guilty furor; rather people would ignore such normative appeals or laugh them out of court. Not all cross-cultural moral claims are heard, and it is rather evident which are.

Aside from defensive reactions, there are other signs that the international moral voice does not fall on completely deaf ears. For example, it is reported that, after having ignored human rights issues for years, in Asian countries "human rights [are] no longer dismissed as a tool of foreign oppression but were promoted as a means of asserting Asian distinctiveness."[29] China seems to have reformed some of its most grievous orphanages and labor camps under pressure from Amnesty International and other moral voices.[30] Even in countries such as Cambodia and Myanmar, one now hears voices opposing authoritarian rule in the name of human rights and democracy that come from within and not only from Western critics. Thus an opposition leader recently argued in Cambodia that "no human being should be asked to choose between bread and freedom."[31]

Recognizing the need to raise moral voices globally does not legitimize berating other people cross-culturally any more than it legitimizes berating other members of one's own community. The moral voice is most compelling when it is firm but not screeching, judging but not judgmental, critical but not self-righteous.

We can acknowledge quite readily that those who champion global values themselves do not always heed their call; but this observation does not invalidate the standing of these values. And one might recognize that universal values other than those for which a given party speaks, other values those societies that are being chastised follow quite admirably, may provide a shining example for the rest of the world to follow. But none of these observations argues that bringing strong substantive values to the nascent worldwide dialogue is to be denied; on the contrary, it is a reflection of commitment to these values. At the same time, one must take into account that until a world dialogue of convictions is much more advanced, and a much stronger worldwide core of values is evolved, worldwide shared values cannot serve as a satisfactory frame for societal values.

ULTIMATE VALUES

One can argue quite appropriately that even if a truly democratic global parliament, after properly constructed worldwide megalogues, could formulate public policies, or moral assessments — these would still need to be judged by some other moral criterion than that a worldwide consensus has been reached.

Some liberals and some communitarians have found an escape from relativism in the works of Isaiah Berlin. This is not the place to analyze his position other than to note one point: Berlin basically suggests that while there may not be one set of shared values or a shared definition of the good, societies may agree that certain forms of conduct and social institutions fall outside the tolerable range. That is, there is room for a pluralism of ultimate value, but that it is not boundless.[32]

Berlin's position, as I see it, faces two difficulties. First, it is not clear on what grounds he rules certain behaviors beyond the pale and why these criteria may not be used to further flesh out shared characterizations of the good. Second, the fact is that societies neither behave in this way (they do form core values) nor can they function well without some shared good.

Charles Taylor's often cited position on "overlapping consensus" also deserves attention in this context. His position basically is that while various groups in a society may hold to different ultimate values, they may be able to agree to support the same public policies, albeit on different grounds. This may well be the case, but such consensus is much more fragile and can carry much less weight than one that is based on sharing of a core of ultimate values. Most important, as I repeatedly suggested, while being able to reach consensus is of considerable merit, the question whether the consensus achieved is morally sound cannot be avoided. At least it should not be avoided.

The crowning test may well need to be found elsewhere. I have suggested elsewhere that there is a limited set of deontological values that speak to all people, although in nonfree societies, awareness of these might be suppressed. The Founding Fathers of the American republic recognized those and appealed to them when they referred to "self-evident truths." The world community would do well to build on these and other self-evident moral truths.

XIII

Stakeholders versus Shareholders

Several powerful arguments have been advanced for a shift from a shareholder approach to a stakeholder approach toward corporate governance. These include the pioneering work by R. Edward Freeman,[1] the important analysis based on contract theory by Thomas Donaldson and Thomas Dunfee,[2] as well as works by L. E. Preston[3] and Max Clarkson,[4] the insights of Margaret Blair,[5] and most recently the notions of fairness by Robert A. Phillips.[6] Other fine writings include those by Steven Wallman and others in the *Stetson Law Review*.[7] It should also be noted that British Prime Minister Tony Blair has stated his support for the stakeholder model.[8] Reference here is limited to the literature that focuses on the normative issues raised by the stakeholder approach; there is a larger body of writing that deals with pragmatic merits of taking into account the needs and values of various nonshareholder constituencies out of utilitarian consequentalist considerations. Nell Minow makes the distinction clear in legal terms

when she points to the difference between allowing corporate executives to take into account the needs of constituents other than the
shareholders (e.g., giving money to charity) and — legally entitling
groups other than the shareholders to have a say in the management
of the corporation.[9] This pragmatic literature is not discussed here, as
my interest is limited to adding a normative note to the existing literature that justifies the chartering of stakeholders.

My note is based on the communitarian thinking I have elabo-
rated elsewhere.[10] It points to the idea that all those involved in the
corporation are potentially members of one community; while they
clearly have significantly divergent interests, needs, and values, they
also have some significant shared goals and bonds.

While my main purpose is to help explore whether the claims
stakeholder theory lays are morally defensible, I will also briefly respond to the argument that even if the theory is justified, it could not
be implemented. I should note from the onset that while many consider the stakeholder theory at best a visionary idea, if not outlandish
or damaging, I will show that there are several important precedents
that indicate it is merely a very significant extension of developments
already at hand.

"PRIVATE PROPERTY" AND "INCORPORATION"
AS SOCIAL CONSTRUCTS

My starting point is the elementary observation that the concepts of
"private property" and "incorporation" (the legal and social basis of
corporations) are social constructs, that is, concepts that reflect the
particular values, interests, and needs of the society in which these
concepts are recognized in a given historical period. They are not an
expression of some kind of "natural," self-evident, absolute, incontestable right. Specifically, there is no a priori reason to argue that the
current model of property relations and of governance by shareholders is more natural than any other. In this context, it is worth
reminding, as Berle and Means pointed out long ago, that the notion

that shareholders govern the corporation is largely a fiction; typically, executives have the main power, although shareholders have a measure of influence.[11] Thus the real question is if executives should (and can) be made responsive, to some extent, to groups other than the shareholders.

Most important, as the legitimacy of both private property and the way corporations are owned and managed is conditioned by the society to begin with, society is free and able to change these social arrangements; society gives these licenses and it can take them away or modify them. As Edward S. Mason has pointed out, "The corporation is an evolving entity, and the end of its evolution is by no means in sight. There is every reason to believe that the business corporation a century hence will be a rather different institution from the one we now behold."[12]

To begin, the claim that private property rights are "natural" and hence incontestable, or that those who do contest them are challenging a sanctified law, flies in the face of a wealth of historical and sociological evidence and experience. The evidence shows unmistakably that property, as has often been observed, is not an object nor an innate attribute, but a relationship of one or more persons to specified objects.[13] And the nature of this relationship is determined by the legal system and moral beliefs of the society that defines property. Thus, in some countries individuals cannot own land, oil, or beaches because these are construed to be exclusively public properties. Before the 1980s, many Mexican industries were not allowed to be privately owned. And I know from personal observation that in the early kibbutzim, not only the means of production but also the items of consumption, including the shirt on one's back, were considered communal property.

Moreover, *all* societies set some limits on the extent to which owners can control and benefit from "their" property, and on the specific ways they must go about using it — even for those items a society characterizes as the private property of a given individual. Some societies greatly restrict the extent to which ownership can be transferred from generation to generation (for instance, by imposing hefty estate taxes); others have few such restrictions. Jewish law calls for letting the land lie fallow every seven years. American law imposes numerous restrictions on what people may do with what they consider "their" private property. For instance, if it is declared as an historical trust, owners cannot modify its appearance without prior permission.[14] They cannot use their property in ways that may produce many kinds of pollution or noise above a given amplitude or erect what the community considers eye sores, cause erosion of the soil or flooding or the seeping of chemicals into the water, or threaten endangered species, and so on. Moreover, property laws have been greatly changed over the years as societal values, interests, and needs have evolved.[15] In short, voluminous historical and sociological experience suggests that changing property rights is far from unprecedented, indeed, it is rather common.

All these statements apply with even greater force to the corporation. While the beginning of the notions of private property are shrouded in the mysteries of early history, and most likely prehistory, the corporation is a relatively recent legal and social invention. The permission to incorporate was, to begin with, granted by the state as a charter or license as a matter of privilege, not of right, to some members of society under conditions the state determined (for example, in their petition for incorporation, the organizers of the first manufacturing company in Massachusetts in 1789 asked "to be incorporated 'with such immunities and favors' as the legislators should think necessary").[16] Moreover, as limited liability was introduced as a corporate feature, it granted shareholders an extra privilege of great value. It stands out when shareholders are compared to partners in a business, the main form of amassing capital prior to the existence of corporations. Partners must keep close tabs over their business because if it fails, they may have to sacrifice their personal assets to satisfy those who have claims against the business. This, in turn, limits the extent to which a partnership can grow. In contrast, shareholders' "liability" is limited to the share price, enabling them to invest while they are preoccupied elsewhere, without extensive scrutiny of the enterprise they are "involved" in, and enabling the corporation to amass large amounts of capital.

In short, the comparison of precapitalist partnerships to modern corporations highlights two points already made: corporations are a societal creation, and society grants shareholders a valuable privilege in exchange for which the society can seek some specific consideration.

CORPORATIONS ARE THE PROPERTY OF ALL WHO INVEST IN THEM

While society has legitimate and legal authority to determine who will own, control, and benefit from the corporations it created, it needs to justify the reason it grants this authority to some groups and/or to others. The discussion here focuses on one idea, namely that the right to participate in the governance of a corporation should be shared by all stakeholder groups rather than only by shareholders. The discussion deliberately focuses on the question of whether a compelling case can be made for a *right* to participate rather than a privilege, voluntarily granted by the shareholders should they be so inclined or find it beneficial. That is, the arguments advanced are held to a much higher level of scrutiny because the claim of a right is much stronger than an expression of a desire to be indulged.

The affirmative response to this question is based on the same basic notion that has compelled many to recognize that the corporation should be treated as the property of those who invest capital in it, the shareholders. Or, as it is sometimes put, the corporation "belongs" to the shareholders because they invested their money in it; it is an extension of their private property.[17]

The stakeholder argument, as I see it, accepts the moral legitimacy of the claim that shareholders have the said rights and entitlements, but argues that *the same basic claim can be made by all those who invest in the corporation.* This often includes employees (especially those who worked for a corporation for many years and loyally);

the community (to the extent it provides special investments to a corporation; for instance, if it builds an access road at its own cost, as distinct from providing an environment that is generally favorable to business); creditors (especially large, long-term ones) and, under some conditions, clients. I proceed by briefly discussing what the concept of investment entails, as a moral (and legal) claim rather than merely as an economic concept, before I discuss how one establishes such a claim as a legitimate one.

Investment is defined as the outlay of money for profit. Investment thus differs from a donation or act of charity, in which one gives up the resources one commands without expectations of a specific return. At the same time, investment differs from a sale of one's assets in that investment *forms a relationship* between investors and that in which they invest—a relationship that has a futuristic element because the consummation of the investment relationship presumes continuity, while a sale is often a discrete transaction, complete in and of itself. The underlying difference is that while in the case of a sale, the full compensation is typically collected at the time of the transaction or close to it (or a full commitment is made to provide a specific return at specific dates) and above all, the compensation is considered to complete the transaction—in the case of investment, the return constitutes a future stream of yield which is typically far from secure or specified and which may rise or fall, or even be wholly lost, depending on the ways the investment is used. While sellers typically give up their rights to benefit in the future of the sold property and to have a say in the ways it is used, the opposite is true of investors. They give up some immediate benefits and voice in order to seek a better return in the future. Investors, so to speak, not only have yet to be compensated for their investment, but grant their investment on the condition that they will be able to participate to some extent, and even if indirectly via directors of pension funds and mutual funds, in the decisions that affect what their return may be in the future. Margaret Blair has emphasized the legitimate interest shareholders have in limiting the risk to which their investment is put.[18] Their interest in enhancing the upside is akin to their interest in minimizing the downside, so to speak. In effect, the fact that they invest in shares rather than in bonds reflects their interest in accepting a less secure return for a possibly higher one. Hence, they are keenly interested not merely in minimizing the risks (avoiding bankruptcies or declines in the size of dividends paid and the price of the shares) but also in increasing the upside potential of higher dividends and share prices. Most important for the discussion that follows, the fact that investors draw some benefits in the short run from their investments (typically in the form of dividends) is not and should not be considered a full compensation for the use of their assets and an abdication of their right to participate in the governance of the corporation.

In addition, when one sells an item, unless specific conditions are attached a priori, no future restrictions on its use can be legitimately imposed by the seller. In the case of investment, as one's relationship to the assets continues, one may seek to ensure it is not used for certain purposes, for instance, to make nuclear weapons or to harm the environment, or, in the past, to invest in South Africa. That is, shareholders participate in the decisions concerning the *social* usages of the resources they invest.

The preceding statements are widely accepted, indeed considered incontestable to the point they are rarely even mentioned when the rights of shareholders are discussed. The fact that shareholders receive a flow of dividends (when this is the case) does not preempt their right to participate in the governance of the corporation. This is traditionally explained by saying that shareholders should monitor the corporation because it is their money that is being managed. However, as we already indicated, ownership of corporations, like other laws, is defined by people and societal influences, and both may change the definition. As I see it, shareholders' rights are ultimately based on a conception of fairness: society recognizes that shareholders are provided with no compensation for the use of their assets at the point of investment; that their compensation lies in a future flow of dividends and appreciation of share prices which are expected but explicitly not guaranteed. Hence, the investors have a right to ensure that the tree they helped plant will be properly cultivated so it will bear fruit, hopefully increasing its value.

My main argument is that *from a moral viewpoint this concept of fairness applies to all stakeholders and not merely to shareholders.* While this view may seem visionary, I will show that it is already reflected, albeit to a rather limited extent, in various laws and corporate practices. I proceed to support these two claims by focusing first on employees.

The employees' investment in the corporation, often referred to as human or social capital, is very different in appearance from that of the shareholders but similar in principle. They invest years, sometimes a lifetime, of their labor in the corporation. While an economist may argue that the employees "sell" their labor and are compensated for their work and hence no longer have any rights to the products of their labor, there can be little doubt that a significant part of the employees' compensation lies in the future, in the expectation of being employed and paid in the future. Moreover, workers anticipate, and are often encouraged to believe, that if they work harder and with more dedication and loyalty, the corporation will fare better than it would otherwise. And, they are also encouraged to expect to share in future gains, both in continued flow of wages and in higher wages. Thus, employees have a keen interest in ensuring the future flow of benefits (an issue that often arises in the discussion of job security), the level of benefits the corporation will be able to afford and allot to them in the future (comparable to shareholders' concerns with the size of dividends), and the viability of the corporation (an issue that arises most sharply when corporations are teetering, and most especially when workers are expected to accept cuts in wages and other benefits to help ensure the corporation's future). Like shareholders, the employees' investment in the corporation is endangered when the corporation is managed recklessly or in violation of the law. And, employees, like shareholders, have a social interest in participating in the decisions concerning the asocial and antisocial use of assets they helped create by their "investment."

The notion that employees have some rights akin to shareholders' is far from fanciful. Several theorists have suggested that workers be assigned a fundamental property right to their jobs.[19] John Locke wrote, "Every man has a property in his own person; this nobody has any right to but himself. The labor of his body and the work of his hands, we may say, are properly his. Whatsoever then he removes out of the State that Nature has provided and left it in, he has mixed his labor with, and joined to it something that is his own, and thereby makes it his property."[20] A fair number of court decisions recognize an employee's right to employment by the corporation for which he has been working, based on good faith implied by longevity of satisfactory service.[21] This right may be seen as a precursor or a rather primitive treatment of employees as stakeholders.

Also, in some instances, employees have been granted representation in the governance of the corporations. For example, German companies use codetermination — the requirement to include voting employee representatives on corporate policy-making boards. German workers also have the right to influence decisions at the shop floor level. The popularity of quality of life circles in the United States shows that giving the workers a role in corporate decision making, albeit on a limited level, far from damages its traditional goals.

Communities also invest in corporations through such means as building special access roads at public costs, providing free land, offering loans at below the interest rates, and suspending or granting exemptions from various rules and regulations that apply to others, from pollution controls to noise abatement, from zoning regulations to traffic requirements, among others. Reference is to specific investments on the behest of specific corporations rather than to general investments in an area, to make it attractive for all corporations (for instance, improving the local schools and public safety).

Communities are rarely, if ever, compensated for their investments at the point of investment. Thus, clearly the economic acts at issue do not constitute a sale. Nor do they constitute charity for the corporations. Communities invest in corporations with the implicit understanding that they will benefit from the business in the future —

by job creation, tax collection, or other benefits. Hence, communities have a similar interest to others who invest in the corporations to ensure both the future viability of the corporations they have invested in and that the corporations be managed in ways that will increase rather than diminish their contributions to the community. The notion that a corporation has some obligation to the community is recognized already, albeit to a very limited extent and indirectly, in laws that require corporations to notify communities before they close a local plant or move out of the community in order to allow the communities time to react.

Creditors invest in corporations by providing start-up, working, and expansion capital, not infrequently in amounts that match or exceed that capital provided by shareholders. Creditors especially extend themselves when they provide capital to the corporation when it is at high risk or provide the capital below market rates. The right of large credit investors to participate in the management of corporations they invest in is widely recognized by law in Western Europe. In the United States, the 1933 Glass-Steagall Act mandated the separation of the banking and securities industries. Recently, however, several pieces of legislation have been advanced in Congress to reduce the strictures imposed by the Glass-Steagall Act, reflecting the fact that allowing creditors a voice in corporate governance is not considered particularly visionary or far-fetched.

Finally, *clients* invest in corporations when they continue to purchase a business's products out of loyalty to their source of supply, even when they could either obtain more advantageous terms or products of better quality elsewhere. (Reference is not to brand loyalty by retail consumers but by wholesale clients.) True, in each case an argument can be made that the continued commitment relies on some narrow self-serving grounds. The fact, though, is that such calculations are often difficult to make with any degree of precision. (For instance, if a defect is found in a product, the question whether to seek the product elsewhere or stick with the source will be affected by how long it will take to fix the problem, which is often rather difficult to establish before the repair takes place. Here, loyalty of the client, often a large scale one, to the supplier, will influence the decision of whether or not the client will choose to "invest" in the corporation by sticking it out rather than withdrawing orders.)

For all these stakeholders, the *longer* the relationship, the larger the investment. A worker's investment over a lifetime is much larger than for one who worked for a given corporation for a few months. A client who remains loyal for decades invests more than one who stayed loyal for a year. Even capital investors who did not pull their share out with every down quarter, but kept their investments for years, invest "more" in this sense.

MECHANISMS OF REPRESENTATION: EMPLOYEES

Among those who favor a wider concept of ownership than the shareholder concept, a secondary but important issue arises. It concerns the ways and means of representation of the various stakeholders in the governance of the corporation (as distinct from sharing in the benefits it generates). It has been repeatedly asked how the various constituencies can be represented. The answer for shareholders is obvious, but how may other stakeholders participate in corporate governance?

Before I review the ways various corporate constituencies can be represented, it should be noted that in general, for all groups, the scope of their representation should parallel the scope of their investment. Thus, just as a shareholder who invests larger amounts of capital will typically have more power than one who invests less (by virtue of holding more shares and hence more votes),[22] so an employee who worked many years for the company should have more of a say than one who was recently hired because the long-time employee invested more in the company in terms of what workers invest (sweat equity, as it is sometimes put, whose measure is approximated by counting years at work). Similarly, a community that invested a great deal in a given corporation should have more of a say than one that invested little.

I already listed various mechanisms that are in place that provide for some, albeit rather limited, representation of various stakeholders.

These mechanisms vary a great deal in the extent to which they are institutionalized or exist on an ad hoc basis; the extent of the voice granted (e.g., it is much higher in codetermination than in quality of life circles); and the extent to which participation is ensconced in law or a privilege the corporation may extend or withdraw at will. Twenty-eight states have passed laws that "allow" shareholders to open the doors of their boards and other parts of corporate control to other constituencies, but it is a right shareholders control.[23] By and large, these mechanisms in the United States highlight that stakeholder participation might be possible, but provide rather limited measures of it and on a rather tenuous basis.

A mechanism that would come closer to what is envisioned here would be one in which *employees* would be accorded a specific number of votes, and these votes would be allotted among the employees according to the years they served in the corporation. It might at first seem peculiar that many workers will have more than one vote, but this is, of course, also true of the shareholders and raises no principled issue. The importance of the suggested distribution of votes is that it would keep a correlation between the extent of investment in the corporation and the voice of a given person.

REPRESENTATION OF OTHER CONSTITUENTS

As previously mentioned, *creditors* in other industrial societies are more often represented on corporate boards than they are in the United States. While so far there is no formal, necessary correlation between the amount of credit extended by a given creditor and the number of representatives that creditor has on the corporate board, there seems to be a vague, implicit notion that very substantial creditors will have more of a voice than small ones. The stronger this correlation becomes, the closer we move to a stakeholder model because it seeks to accord representation in line with one's "investments" in the corporation.

Opportunities for and methods of representation of *communities* are much less worked out than those for creditors. Corporations often remove their plants or headquarters from communities that have invested in them, without according any compensation to the community or affording them a voice in this matter or in any other corporate policies, including those that directly affect the community. Moreover, corporations often leave behind burdens on communities they abandoned, in the form of waste, disfigured land, sudden surges in unemployment, and residents who can no longer afford much of what local shops have to offer.

While there is no principled reason for communities to refrain from seeking to encourage corporations to grant them some voice in exchange for specific investments the communities made in these corporations, the main difficulty is that communities compete with one another over the placement of these corporations. The more conditions a community imposes, the less likely it is to attract the desired corporations. Hence, as long as there is no federal legislation that ensures that communities can have a voice in exchange for specific investments in a given corporation, such community representation is unlikely to come about. Granting communities a voice in rough proportion to the size of their investments would also solve the problem of which community is accorded greater decision-making powers, because if two or more communities invest in a given corporation, their "votes" would be divided among themselves in line with the size and duration of their respective investment.

A case can be made that on numerous issues facing the corporation, communities would not want to take sides or have a voice, or should not, because these matters do not affect them directly. One can envision a system in which community representatives would merely serve as observers on some issues, while they would have a vote on others.

Client representation is the most challenging of all. While the investment of employees, main creditors, and contributing communities in a given corporation can be identified, most clients do not invest in a corporation from which they make their purchase and hence should not be entitled to a voice. To put it differently, most clients have no relationship to the corporation whose product they are buying; their typical relationship is not a long-term investment, but a series of sales transactions. Exceptions are large-scale clients, for instance a chain of department stores or the Pentagon, especially those that continue to purchase from a corporation when it runs into one kind of difficulties or another. If and how these should be represented, and how the size of their investment might be calculated, remain open questions.

A neoclassical economist may argue that given the market discipline, corporations that would accord their employees higher wages or benefits than they would gain otherwise (due, for instance, to employee representation on the board), would be driven out of business by corporations that heed the market. Similarly, such an economist may argue that the level of dividends is set by the market; corporations that set a lower rate will not attract the capital they need and those that set a higher rate will lose out to the competition. In short, active participation in the governance of the corporation is either meaningless for the various stakeholders or dangerous for the corporation. But these claims hold at best in some simplified models in the theoretical world of perfect competition. Real corporations have considerable "slack," that is allotted accordingly to cultural factors (for example, American corporations grant more charity than Japanese ones, and not all of it is recaptured in the form of good will that helps the bottom line); political considerations (for instance, the timing of closing of plants is affected by local elections); and others (e.g., executives' demands for bonuses and golden parachutes are affected by whom they consider to be their reference groups — for instance, other executives in their industry or, say, Fortune 500 executives). Some of this slack can be absorbed by accommodating various stakeholders.

STAKEHOLDERS AND THE COMMON GOOD

An argument can be made that while all stakeholders and not only shareholders have fair claims to a voice in corporate governance, recognizing such claims may be damaging to the well-being of the economy, and hence injurious to the common good. Such considerations should outweigh the fairness claim. For instance, it might be argued that workers would seek to maximize their wages and thus damage the ability of the corporation to invest for the long run, that creditors would be more inclined to favor a conservative course, and so on. To examine the effects of granting some measure of representation in corporate governance to all stakeholder groups, which make the corporation much more of a community and democratize its government, would take us into a highly speculative direction as no such corporations exist. However, several preliminary observations can be made. First of all, there is no systematic evidence that corporations in which nonshareholders have been given some rights of representation (for instance, creditors gaining membership on the board or codetermination) have been less successful than others. Moreover, many corporations have increasingly learned to take the needs and demands of nonshareholders into account in their decision making for various pragmatic considerations (e.g., labor peace, good credit rating). The only change suggested here is to make such participation a right rather than a privilege granted by the sufferance of the executives and/or the shareholders.

Last but not least, the myopic tendency of shareholders and executives has often been criticized as damaging to corporations. Workers, whose future is often much more closely tied to a specific corporation than that of shareholders (who can exit with one phone call and very readily find a new investment), may serve as a force to ensure longer run perspectives. Creditors may balance adventurous executives; communities may curb antisocial interests of shareholders. In short, while groups other than shareholders may tilt the corporation into a different course than it would follow if it were responding only to shareholders, it is by no means a foregone conclusion that this course would be less compatible with the common good, even if this good is defined only in narrow economic terms, and even less likely to be injurious if other social considerations are taken into account (for instance, concern for the environment and social peace).

NOTES

Introduction

1. For more information on *The Responsive Community*, please visit the publication's website at www.gwu.edu/~ccps/rcq/index.html.

2. Amitai Etzioni, *The New Golden Rule: Community and Morality in a Democratic Society* (New York: Basic Books, 1997).

3. Amy Gutmann, "Communitarian Critics of Liberalism," *Philosophy and Public Affairs* 14, No. 3 (Summer 1985): 319.

4. Etzioni, *The New Golden Rule*.

5. For more on the principles for dealing with conflicting demands, deemed as our most original contribution to communitarian thinking, see Amitai Etzioni, *The Limits of Privacy* (New York: Basic Books, 1999). On originality, see Daniel A. Bell's review of *The Spirit of Community* (New York: Crown Publishers, Inc., 1993) in the *New York Times Literary Supplement*, 5 November 1994, 5.

I: The Monochrome Society

The author is indebted for research assistance on this chapter to Barbara Fusco and Rachel Mears. The author is also grateful to Philip Selznick and Alan Ehrenhalt for their comments on this chapter. For a previous, but substantially different, publication concerning these ideas, see Amitai Etzioni, "Some Diversity," *Society*, July/August 1998, 59–61, and Amitai Etzioni, Chap. 7 in *The New*

Golden Rule: Community and Morality in a Democratic Society (New York: Basic Books, 1996).

1. Cited in John Leo, "A Dubious 'Diversity' Report," *U.S. News & World Report*, 23 June 1997, 15.

2. Speech by President Clinton Regarding Race Relations in America, The University of California at San Diego, *Federal News Service*, 14 June 1997, White House Briefing section.

3. President Clinton's 2000 State of the Union Address, reprinted in *New York Times*, 28 January 2000, sec. A, p. 16.

4. John F. Harris and John E. Yang, "Clinton Hopes to Prepare Nation for End of Clear White Majority," *Washington Post*, 14 June 1997, sec. A, p. 2.

5. Speech by President Clinton Regarding Race Relations in America.

6. Arthur M. Schlesinger, Jr., *The Disuniting of America* (New York: Norton, 1992), 15, 16.

7. Ibid., 17–18.

8. Ibid., 20. Cited in O. R. Dathorne, *In Europe's Image: The Need for American Multiculturalism* (Westport, Conn.: Bergin & Garvey, 1994), 113.

9. Speech by James Q. Wilson on The History and Future of Democracy, Ronald Reagan Presidential Library, Simi Valley, Calif., 15 November 1999.

10. Dale Maharidge, *The Coming White Minority: California's Eruptions and America's Future* (New York: Times Books/Random House, 1996), 1.

11. Ibid., 11. For an additional telling study see Todd S. Purdum, "Shift in the Mix Alters the Face of California," *New York Times*, 4 July 2000, sec. A, p. 1.

12. Ibid., 10.

13. Ibid., 280–81.

14. John Isbister, "Is America Too White?" in *"What, Then, Is the American, This New Man?"* Washington, D.C., Center for Immigration Studies Center, Paper 13, August 1998, 29.

15. Donald Gabard and Terry Cooper problematize such determinism, specifically common understandings of race based on the existence of genetic differences among the races. They quote R. Cooper and R. David, who note, "No discrete package of gene differences has ever been described between two races, only relative frequencies of one or another trait," and, citing D. R. Williams, Gabard and Cooper write, "It is reported today that there are more genetic variations within the separate races than between them." Donald L. Gabard and Terry L. Cooper, "Race: Constructs and Dilemmas," *Administration & Society* 30, no. 4 (September 1998): 342. (Citing R. Cooper and R. David, "The Biological Concept of Race and Its Application to Public Health and Epidemiology," *Journal of Health Politics, Policy and Law* 2 [1986]: 97–116 at p. 101 and D. R. Williams, "The Concept of Race in Health Services Research: 1966 to 1990," *Health Services Research* 29 (1994): 262–74.)

16. See, for example, James M. Jones, *Prejudice and Racism* (Reading, Mass.: Addison-Wesley, 1972).

17. *Democracy's Next Generation II: A Study of American Youth on Race* (Washington, D.C.: People for the American Way, 1992), 57–58.

18. Ibid.

19. *New York State United Teachers 1991 Education Opinion Survey: Final Report* (Albany, N.Y.: New York State United Teachers, 1991), sec. II, 5, 8.

20. Ibid.

21. Douglas Turner, "Amid the Black–White Divide, Convergence of Some Attitudes," *Buffalo News*, 11 June 1997, sec. A, p. 6.

22. Stephen Covey, "What Americans Agree On," *USA Weekend*, 6 July 1997, 4.

23. *Public Agenda*, "A Lot to be Thankful For: What Parents Want Children to Learn about America," November 1998. Available at http://www.publicagenda.org/specials/thankful/thankful.htm. Accessed 7/14/00.

24. Roper Center Data Review. Survey by the National Opinion Research Center–General Social Survey, 1994. Cited in "Thinking about Ethnicity," *Public Perspective* (February/March 1998): 59.

25. Ibid., 58.

26. *Public Agenda*, "A Lot to be Thankful For."

27. Lawrence Otis Graham, cited in Frank Stasio, anchor, "Lawrence Otis Graham, author of *Our Kind of People*, Discusses the Elitism of Some Upper-Class African-Americans," *NPR Weekend Edition* (20 February 2000).

28. Gerald F. Feib and Joe Davidson, "Shades of Gray: Whites, Blacks Agree on Problems; the Issue Is How to Solve Them," *Wall Street Journal*, 29 September 1994, sec. A, p. 6.

29. Ibid.

30. Alan Wolfe, *One Nation, After All: What Middle-Class Americans Really Think about God, Country, Family, Racism, Welfare, Immigration, Homosexuality, Work, the Right, the Left, and Each Other* (New York: Viking, 1998), 158.

31. "Speaking Out: Teens and Adults See Different Worlds," *Time*/CNN poll from 23 September to 2 October 1997 by Yankelovich Partners, Inc. Cited in *Time*, 24 November 1997, 90. The poll cited compares the views of teens and adults; the percentages cited are the views of the adults only.

32. U.S. Department of Justice, *Sourcebook of Criminal Justice Statistics 1996* (Washington, D.C.: U.S. Government Printing Office, 1997), 115. Cited in Jennifer Hochschild and Reuel R. Rogers, "Race Relations in a Diversifying Nation," forthcoming in *New Directions: African Americans in a Diversifying Nation*, ed. James Jackson (Washington, D.C.: National Policy Association).

33. U.S. Department of Justice, *Sourcebook of Criminal Justice Statistics 1996*, 141.

34. Feib and Davidson, "Shades of Gray," sec. A, p. 1.

35. Ibid., sec. A, p. 6.

36. *Washington Post*/Kaiser Family Foundation/Harvard School of Public

Health Survey Project, *The Four Americas: Government and Social Policy Through the Eyes of America's Multi-racial and Multi-ethnic Society* (Washington, D.C.: *Washington Post*, 1995), 75–76. Cited in Hochschild and Rogers, "Race Relations in a Diversifying Nation."

37. U.S. Department of Justice, *Sourcebook of Criminal Justice Statistics 1996*, 141–45.

38. *Washington Post*/Kaiser Family Foundation/Harvard School of Public Health Survey Project, *The Four Americas*, 73–74.

39. *Public Agenda*, "A Lot to Be Thankful For."

40. For more complete details see "1996 Survey of American Political Culture," *Public Perspective* (February/March 1997): 6–7.

41. Jerelyn Eddings, "Black & White in America," *U.S. News & World Report*, 16 October 1995, 32.

42. Survey by CBS News, *New York Times*, and *Public Agenda*. Available at http://www.publicagenda.org:80/issues/angles—graph.cfm?issue— type = race&id = 202&graph = redflagsl.gif. Accessed 7/14/00.

43. Survey by Voter News Service, November 1998. Cited in "The Shape of the American Electorate at Century's End," *Public Perspective* (December/January 1999): 69.

44. Robert C. Smith and Richard Seltzer, *Contemporary Controversies and the American Racial Divide* (Lanham, Md.: Rowman & Littlefield, 2000), 86, 88, 121, 128.

45. James Davison Hunter and Carl Bowman, *The State of Disunion: 1996 Survey of American Political Culture*, vol. 2, *Summary Tables* (Ivy, Va.: In Medias Res Educational Foundation, 1996), Table 4.E.

46. Hunter and Bowman, *The State of Disunion*, Table 4.C.

47. *Washington Post*/Kaiser Family Foundation/Harvard School of Public Health Survey Project, *The Four Americas*, 73–74.

48. Hunter and Bowman, *The State of Disunion*, Table 94, Table 93.I.

49. James Davison Hunter and Carl Bowman, *The State of Disunion: 1996 Survey of American Political Culture*, vol. 1, *Summary Report* (Ivy, Va.: In Medias Res Educational Foundation, 1996), 34.

50. Hunter and Bowman, *The State of Disunion*, vol. 2, Table 4.J.

51. Survey by Roper Starch Worldwide. Cited in "Thinking about Ethnicity," *Public Perspective* (February/March 1998): 58.

52. Survey by Louis Harris and Associates, 26–29 October 1995. Cited in "Thinking about Ethnicity," *Public Perspective* (February/March 1998): 59.

53. Thirty-one percent of blacks and 33% of whites stated that many whites "dislike blacks." Survey by the Gallup Organization, 5–7 October 1995. Cited in "Thinking about Ethnicity," *Public Perspective* (February/March 1998): 58.

54. Survey by Princeton Survey Research Associates for *Newsweek*, 1–3 February 1995. Cited in "Rethinking Race," *Public Perspective* (June/July 1997): 41.

55. Janet Saltzman Chafetz, "Minorities, Gender, Mythologies, and Moderation," *Responsive Community* 4, no. 1 (Winter 1993/94): 41.

56. E. Thomas McLanahan, "Do 'Disparities' Always Prove the Existence of Discrimination?" *Kansas City Star*, 25 October 1994, sec. B, p. 5.

57. Alan Westin, personal communication, April 1998.

58. John Simons, "Even Amid Boom Times, Some Insecurities Die Hard," *Wall Street Journal*, 10 December 1998, sec. A, p. 10.

59. Alain Corcos, *The Myth of Human Races* (East Lansing, Mich.: Michigan State University Press, 1984), 10–11.

60. Ibid., 12.

61. Ibid.

62. Ibid., 201.

63. Ibid. See also Maurice Berger, *White Lies: Race and the Myths of Whiteness* (New York: Farrar, Straus, Giroux, 1999); Ian Haney-López, *White by Law: The Legal Construction of Race* (New York: New York University Press, 1996); Matthew Frye Jacobson, *Whiteness of a Different Color: European Immigrants and the Alchemy of Race* (Cambridge: Harvard University Press, 1998); Joe L. Kincheloe et al., eds., *White Reign: Deploying Whiteness in America* (New York: St. Martin's Press, 1998); Valerie Melissa Babb, *Whiteness Visible: The Meaning of Whiteness in American Literature and Culture* (New York: New York University Press, 1998); Grace Elizabeth Hale, *Making Whiteness: The Culture of Segregation in the South* (New York: Pantheon Books, 1998).

64. Audrey Smedley, *Race in North America: Origin and Evolution of a Worldview* (Boulder, Colo.: Westview Press, 1993), 22.

65. Ibid.

66. Lawrence A. Hirschfeld, personal communication to Melvin D. Williams. Cited in Melvin D. Williams, *Race for Theory and the Biophobia Hypothesis: Humanics, Humanimals, and Macroanthropology* (Westport, Conn.: Praeger, 1998), 96–97.

67. Jacobsen, *Whiteness of a Different Color*. See also Oscar Handlin, *Race and Nationality in American Life* (Boston: Little, Brown, 1957), 150–53.

68. Debra J. Dickerson, "Roots Come with Strings Attached," *Washington Post*, 7 May 2000, sec. B, pp. 1–2.

69. Todd S. Purdum, "Shift in the Mix Alters the Face of California," *New York Times*, 4 July 2000, sec. A, p. 1.

70. Quoted in Steven A. Holmes, "The Politics of Race and the Census," *New York Times*, 19 March 2000, sec. 4, p. 3.

71. See, for example, Eric Liu, *The Accidental Asian: Notes of a Native Speaker* (New York: Random House, 1998).

72. Lena H. Sun, "Cultural Differences Set Asian Americans Apart: Where Latinos Have Common Threads, They Have None," *Washington Post*, 10 October 1995, sec. A, p. 8.

73. Quoted in John Powers, "The Myth of the Model Minority," *Boston Globe Magazine*, 9 January 1994, 8.

74. Daniel O'Donnell, "Standing on Ceremony," *Ashbury Park Press*, 1 September 1996, sec. D, p. 1.

75. Rodolfo O. de la Garza, "Introduction," in *Ignored Voices: Public Opinion Polls and the Latino Community*, ed. Rodolfo O. de la Garza (Austin, Tex.: Center for Mexican American Studies, 1987), 4.

76. Quoted in Ferdinand M. De Leon and Sally MacDonald, "Name Power— Taking Pride, and Control, in Defining Ourselves," *Seattle Times*, 28 June 1992, sec. A, p. 1.

77. Ibid.

78. Rodolfo O. de la Garza, "Researchers Must Heed New Realities When They Study Latinos in the U.S.," *Chronicle of Higher Education*, 2 June 1993, sec. B, p. 1.

79. Survey by *Washington Post*/Kaiser Family Foundation/Harvard University, June 30–August 30, 1999 cited in *Public Perspective* 11, no. 2 (May/June 2000): 12–13.

80. *Washington Post*/Kaiser Family Foundation/Harvard University National Survey on Latinos in America, June 30–August 30, 1999. Available at http://www.kff.org/content/2000/3023/LatinoFullToplineFinal.PDF. Accessed 7/14/00.

81. Philip Perlmutter, "From E Pluribus Unum to E Unum Pluribus," *American Outlook*, Summer 1999, 53–54.

82. Rodolfo O. de la Garza, Louis DeSipio, F. Chris Garcia, and John Garcia, *Latino Voices: Mexican, Puerto Rican, and Cuban Perspectives on American Politics* (Boulder, Colo.: Westview Press, 1992), 102.

83. Ibid., 110.

84. de la Garza, "Researchers Must Heed New Realities When They Study Latinos in the U.S.," sec. B, p. 1–3.

85. Matt Miller, "Asian-Americans: A Political Enigma," *San Diego Union-Tribune*, 8 September 1996, sec. A, p. 1.

86. Peter A. Morrison and William A. V. Clark, *Demographic Underpinnings of Political Empowerment in Multi-Minority Cities* (Santa Monica, Calif.: RAND, 1993), 3.

87. Peter Skerry, *Mexican Americans: The Ambivalent Minority* (New York: Free Press, 1993), 34.

88. Mirroring many counties in California, between 1992 and 1998, 43 U.S. counties became majority–minority. Overall, 225 counties in the country comprise nonwhite majorities. (Nancy Cleeland, "Beyond 2000: Orange County Diversity," *Los Angeles Times*, 28 September 1998, sec. A, p. 1.)

89. Miller, "Asian-Americans."

90. U.S. Bureau of the Census, *Statistical Abstract of the United States: 1995*, 115th ed. (Washington, D.C.: U.S. Government Printing Office, 1995), 45.

91. Ibid.

92. For an insightful analysis of politics, race, and ethnicity in New York City, see Jim Sleeper, *The Closest of Strangers: Liberalism and the Politics of Race in New York* (New York: W.W. Norton & Company, 1990).

93. U.S. Bureau of the Census, *Statistical Abstract of the United States: 1995*, 46.

94. Ibid., 44; Linda Kanamine, "Dallas Mayor: First for Texas," *USA Today*, 8 May 1995, sec. A, p. 3.

95. U.S. Bureau of the Census, *Statistical Abstract of the United States: 1995*, 46.

96. Ibid., 44.

97. 1992 data from Statistical Compendia Branch, Data User Services Division, Bureau of the Census, *1994 County & City Data Book* (Washington, D.C.: U.S. Government Printing Office, 1994), 2–3. Minorities in the *Data Book* are categorized as black, Hispanic, Asian, and Eskimo or Aleut.

98. Kevin Sack, "In the Rural White South, Seeds of a Biracial Politics," *New York Times*, 30 December 1998, sec. A, p. 1.

99. Henry Weinstein, "Elections '96: 7 Democrats, 4 in GOP Win Governorships," *Los Angeles Times*, 6 November 1996, sec. A, p. 16.

100. Population Projections Program, Population Division, U.S. Census Bureau, *Projections of the Total Resident Population by 5-Year Age Groups, Race, and Hispanic Origin with Special Age Categories: Middle Series, 1999 to 2000; Projections of the Total Resident Population by 5-Year Age Groups, Race, and Hispanic Origin with Special Age Categories: Middle Series, 2050 to 2070; Projections of the Total Resident Population by 5-Year Age Groups, Race, and Hispanic Origin with Special Age Categories: Middle Series, 2075 to 2100.* Available at http://www.census.gov/population/www/projections/natsum-T3.html. Accessed 7/5/00.

101. Roberto Suro, "Mixed Doubles," *American Demographics*, November 1999: 58–59.

102. Statistical Assessment Service, "Can Intermarriage Make You Smarter and Richer?" *Vital STATS*, August 1997. Available at http://www.stats.org/newsletters/9708/interrace2.htm. Accessed 7/3/00.

103. Larry Bivins, "Experts: Increase in Mixed Marriages Gives Mixed Signals that Racism's on Rocks," *Detroit News*, 6 October 1996, sec. B, p. 5.

104. U.S. Census Bureau data, cited in "Interracial Marriages: Percentage of All Marriages That Are Interracial, 1960–1997," *Public Agenda Online*. Available at http://www.publicagenda.org/issues/factfiles—detail.cfm?issue—type=family&list=17. Accessed 7/3/00.

105. Ibid.

106. Christopher Shea, "Intermarriage Rates Found to Be on the Rise," *Chronicle of Higher Education*, 2 May 1997, sec. A, p. 14.

107. "The Melting Pot Survives," *The Economist*, 3 July 1999, 24.

108. "Melting at Last," *The Wilson Quarterly* (Winter 2000): 11.

109. Linda Chavez, Response to 'Is America Too White?' in *"What, Then, Is the American, This New Man?"*

110. Gregory Rodriguez, *From Newcomers to Americans: The Successful Integration of Immigrants into American Society* (Washington, D.C.: National Immigration Forum, 1999).

111. Anne-Marie O'Connor, "Race: Diversity at Work Has Role in Sharp Rise," *Los Angeles Times*, 27 April 1998, sec. A, p. 1.

112. Michael Lind, "The Beige and the Black," *New York Times Magazine*, 16 August 1998, 38.

113. John Fetto, "A Close Race," *American Demographics* (January 2000): 14.

114. Amitai Etzioni, "New Issues: Rethinking Race," *Public Perspective* (June/July 1997): 39–41.

115. U.S. Bureau of the Census, "Table 25: Population by Sex, Race, Residence, and Median Age: 1790 to 1973," *Statistical Abstract of the United States 1974*, 95th ed. (Washington, D.C.: U.S. Government Printing Office, 1974), 26.

116. U.S. Census Bureau, "Quick Table P-1F: Age and Sex of Other Race Population: 1990," *U.S. Census Bureau American FactFinder Web Site*. Available at http://factfinder.census.gov/java—prod/dads.ui.pqr.PopQuickReportPage. Accessed 7/6/00.

117. U.S. Census Bureau, Population Division, Administrative Records and Methodology Research Branch, *Population of States by Modified Race and Hispanic Origin, April 1, 1990* (Washington, D.C.: U.S. Government Printing Office, 1998).

118. Hannah Beech, "Don't You Dare List Them as 'Other,'" *U.S. News & World Report*, 8 April 1996, 56.

119. Gregory Rodriguez, "Do the Multiracial Count?" *Salon*, 15 February 2000. Available at http://www.salon.com/news/feature/2000/02/15/census/index2.html. Accessed 7/3/00.

120. Ibid.

121. House Committee on Government Reform and Oversight, *Census 2000*, 106th Cong., 1st sess., April 23, 1997. Testimony of Bernard L. Ungar, Associate Director, Federal Management and Workforce Issues, General Government Division of United States, General Accounting Office.

122. Quoted in Steven A. Holmes, "The Politics of Race and the Census."

123. More information about the Association of MultiEthnic Americans is available at http://www.ameasite.org/. Accessed 7/3/00.

124. Walter Lee Dozer, "Race: It's No Longer a Matter of Black and White," *Tampa Tribune*, 29 November 1995, sec. "Baylife," p. 1.

125. Geneva Overholser, "Look at Tiger Woods and See the Face of America's Future," *International Herald Tribune*, 22 June 2000, 9.

126. Quoted in Steven A. Holmes, "The Politics of Race and the Census." For

much additional fine discussion see Peter Skerry, *Counting on the Census* (Washington, D.C.: Brookings Institution Press, 2000).

127. Data extrapolated from figures in Population Projections Program, Population Division, Census Bureau, *Projections of the Total Resident Population by 5-Year Age Groups, Race, and Hispanic Origin with Special Age Categories: Middle Series, 2050 to 2070*; and Population Projections Program, Population Division, Census Bureau, *Projections of the Total Resident Population by 5-Year Age Groups, Race, and Hispanic Origin with Special Age Categories: Middle Series, 2075 to 2100*. Available at http://www.census.gov/population/www/projections/natsum-T3.html. Accessed 7/5/00.

128. Ibid.

129. Salim Muwakkil, "Color Bind," *In These Times* 22, no. 8 (22 March 1998): 11.

130. Abigail Thernstrom and Stephan Thernstrom, "Black Progress: How Far We've Come — and How Far We Have to Go," *The Brookings Review* 16, no. 2 (Spring 1998): 12.

131. Henry Louis Gates, Jr., "The Two Nations of Black America," *The Brookings Review* 16, no. 2 (Spring 1998): 7.

132. House Committee on Government Reform and Oversight, Testimony of Bernard L. Ungar. [See note 121 for full bibliographic information.]

133. As Peter Skerry states, ". . . as an animating force in our communities and in our national life, assimilation is alive and well." Peter Skerry, "Do We Really Want Immigrants to Assimilate?" *Society* (March/April 2000): 69. See also, Peter D. Salins, *Assimilation, American Style* (New York: Basic Books, 1997); Charles Taylor, *Multiculturalism and the Politics of Recognition* (Princeton, N.J.: Princeton University Press, 1992); and Daniel Callahan, "Universalism and Particularism: Fighting to a Draw," *Hastings Center Report* 30, no. 1 (2000): 37–44.

134. Roberto Suro, *Strangers Among Us: How Latino Immigration is Transforming America* (New York: Alfred A. Knopf, 1998), 303–04.

135. Peter I. Rose gives us an important understanding of cultural pluralism as first substantially presented by philosopher Horace Kallen in the early 1900s: "The basic premise was that there is strength in diversity, that being proud of one's past and appreciating where one came from complements rather than compromises membership in an ever more heterogeneous society. . . . Kallen saw the orchestra — that is, the society — as consisting of groups of instruments (nationalities) playing their separate parts while together making beautiful music resonant with harmony and good feeling." Peter I. Rose, *Tempest-Tost: Race, Immigration, and the Dilemmas of Diversity* (New York: Oxford University Press, 1997), 65.

136. Etzioni, *The New Golden Rule*, 189–216.

II: Is Shaming Shameful?

1. For the National Public Radio conversation, see Ray Suarez, host, "Good Samaritan Laws," *Talk of the Nation*, 1 October 1998. Transcript #98100102–211.

2. Ibid.

3. Ibid.

4. Letter to the Editor, *Sacramento Bee*, 20 September 1998, sec. F, p. 4.

5. Ann Sjoerdsma, "Is America Too Dangerous for a 'Good Samaritan' Law?" *The Record* (Bergen, N.J.), 16 September 1997. Available at www.bergen.com/morenews/goodsam19970916.htm. Accessed 7/5/00.

6. Dan Kahan, "What Do Alternative Sanctions Mean?" *University of Chicago Law Review* 63 (1996): 635. Cited in "Sentencing Lawbreakers to a Dose of Shame," *CQ Researcher*, 21 March 1997, 252.

7. Jan Hoffman, "Crime and Punishment: Shame Gains Popularity," *New York Times*, 16 January 1997, sec. A, p. 1. Cited in "Sentencing Lawbreakers to a Dose of Shame," *CQ Researcher*, 21 March 1997, 252.

8. Ibid.

9. Doane Hulick, "Molester's Sentence: Photo Ad in Paper," *Arizona Republic*, 9 November 1989, sec. A, p. 1. Cited in Toni M. Massaro, "Shame, Culture, and American Criminal Law," *Michigan Law Review* 89 (1991): 1881.

10. Robert Mintz, "Judge Turns Confessing into a Religious Experience," *National Law Journal*, 6 February 1984, 47. Cited in Massaro, "Shame, Culture, and American Criminal Law:"1888.

11. Pam Belluck, "Forget Prisons. Americans Cry Out for the Pillory," *New York Times*, 4 October 1998, pp. 4, 5.

12. Quoted in "Sentencing Lawbreakers to a Dose of Shame:" 252.

13. Quoted in Tony Allen-Mills, "American Criminals Sentenced to Shame," *Sunday Times*, 20 April 1997.

14. Quoted in memo from American Civil Liberties Union (ACLU Media), "ACLU Answers: Megan's Law," received by fax, 3 December 1996.

15. Ibid.

16. Carl F. Horowitz, "The Shaming Sham," *The American Prospect*, March–April 1997, 71.

17. Suarez, host, "Good Samaritan Laws," *Talk of the Nation*.

18. Quoted in Michael Grunwald, "Shame Makes Comeback in Courtrooms," *Boston Globe*, 28 December 1997, sec. A, p. 1.

19. For more discussion, see J. Ronald Lally, "What to Do About Hitting," *Parents*, July 1994, 64, 66; June Price Tangney, "Recent Advances in the Empirical Study of Shame and Guilt," *American Behavioral Scientist* 38 (1995): 1134–39; June Price Tangney, Patricia Wagner, Carey Fletcher, and Richard Gramzow, "Shamed into Anger? The Relation of Shame and Guilt to Anger

and Self-Reported Aggression," *Journal of Personality and Social Psychology* 62 (1992): 672–75; and Helen Block Lewis, *Shame and Guilt in Neurosis* (New York: International Universities Press, 1971).

20. For related discussion, see essay on social norms in Chapter VIII of this book.

21. Massaro, "Shame, Culture, and American Criminal Law," 1883.

22. Ibid., 1921.

23. Ibid., 1923.

24. Belluck, "Forget Prisons. Americans Cry Out for the Pillory."

25. For more discussion, see John Braithwaite, *Crime, Shame, and Reintegration* (New York: Cambridge University Press, 1989).

26. David Karp, "The Judicial and Judicious Use of Shame Penalties," *Crime and Delinquency*, 44, no. 2 (April 1998): 292.

27. Lawrence M. Friedman, *Crime and Punishment in American History* (New York: Basic Books, 1993), 81.

28. Ibid., 36–37.

29. Quoted in Friedman, *Crime and Punishment in American History*, 37.

30. Amy Gutmann, "Communitarian Critics of Liberalism," *Philosophy and Public Affairs* 14, no. 3 (Summer 1985): 319.

31. Adam Hirsh, "From Pillory to Penitentiary: The Rise of Criminal Incarceration in Early Massachusetts," *Michigan Law Review* 80 (1982): 1179, 1223–24.

32. Friedman, *Crime and Punishment in American History*, 37.

33. Ibid., 75.

III: The Post-Affluent Society

The author would like to acknowledge Frank Lovett for his help with the research for this chapter, and David Karp and Barbara Fusco for their editorial comments. The author remains particularly indebted to comments by Professor Edward F. Diener and David G. Myers. For a critical discussion of the author's position, see Peter Taylor-Gooby, "Comments on Amitai Etzioni: Voluntary Simplicity: Characterization, Select Psychological Implications and Societal Consequences," *Journal of Economic Psychology* 19 (October 1998): 645–50. For the author's response, see Amitai Etzioni, "Response: Reply to Peter Taylor-Gooby," *Journal of Economic Psychology* 19 (October 1998): 651–52.

1. Frank Musgrove notes the paradox that although the counterculture is "marked by frugality and low consumption," it arises specifically in wealthy societies. Frank Musgrove, *Ecstasy and Holiness: Counter Culture and the Open Society* (Bloomington: Indiana University Press, 1974), 17–18, 40–41, 198.

2. Ronald Inglehart, *The Silent Revolution: Changing Values and Political Styles Among Western Publics* (Princeton, N.J.: Princeton University Press, 1977), 3.

3. Similar shifts occurred in most developed nations. Paul R. Abramson and Ronald Inglehart, *Value Change in Global Perspective* (Ann Arbor: University of Michigan Press, 1995), 12–15, 19.

4. Ibid., 12–15.

5. Stanley Lebergott, *Pursuing Happiness: American Consumers in the Twentieth Century* (Princeton, N.J.: Princeton University Press, 1993), appendix A, 147–163.

6. U.S. Census Bureau, *Statistical Abstract of the United States, 1994* Washington, D.C.: U.S. Government Printing Office, 1994), Table 695. See also Roger Rosenblatt, ed., *Consuming Desires: Consumption, Culture, and the Pursuit of Happiness* (Washington, D.C.: Island Press, 1999).

7. See Robert Paehlke, *Environmentalism and the Future of Progressive Politics* (New Haven, Conn.: Yale University Press, 1989) and Juliet Schor, *The Overworked American: The Unexpected Decline of Leisure* (New York: Basic Books, 1991).

8. Cited in Victor Irwin, "Living Lightly Can Mean Greater Independence, Richer Lives," *The Christian Science Monitor*, 21 October 1980, p. 20.

9. See, for instance, Charles Handy, *The Hungry Spirit: Beyond Capitalism: A Quest for Purpose in the Modern World* (New York: Broadway Books, 1998).

10. Nicholas Dawidoff, "The Pop Populist," *New York Times Magazine*, 26 January 1997, 28.

11. Personal observations, 1997, 1998, and 1999.

12. Kara Swisher, "Families: A Couple with Online Connections," *Wall Street Journal*, 6 January 1999, sec. B, p. 1.

13. Ibid.

14. Henry Urbach, "Hide the Money!" *New York Times Magazine*, 13 April 1997, 8.

15. Pilar Viladas, "Inconspicuous Consumption," *New York Times Magazine*, 13 April 1997, 25.

16. David Brooks, "Conscientious Consumption," *The New Yorker*, 23 November 1998, 46–47.

17. Rita Henley Jensen, "Recycling the American Dream," *ABA Journal* 82 (April 1996): 68–72.

18. Faith Popcorn, *Clicking: 16 Trends to Future Fit Your Life, Your Work, and Your Business* (New York: HarperCollins, 1996).

19. Karlyn H. Bowman, "American Fashion Embraces the Casual and the Comfortable," *The Public Perspective*, August/September 1997, 59.

20. Executive Summary from the Merck Family Fund, *Yearning for a Balance: Views of Americans on Consumption, Materialism, and the Environment* (Takoma Park, Md.: Merck Family Fund, 1995).

21. National Public Radio, "Voluntary Simplicity," NPR: *Morning Edition*, 25 February 1997.

22. Carey Goldberg, "Choosing the Joys of a Simplified Life," *New York*

Times, 21 September 1995, sec. C, p. 1; Executive Summary from the Merck Family Fund, *Yearning for a Balance*.

23. Ronald Henkoff, "Is Greed Dead?" *Fortune*, 14 August 1989, 41.

24. "Voluntary Simplicity," *NPR: Morning Edition*.

25. Goldberg, "Choosing the Joys of a Simplified Life," sec. C, p. 1

26. Among men between fifty-five and sixty-four, 85.2% were employed in 1960, while by 1990 only 67.7% were. U.S. Census Bureau, *Statistical Abstract of the United States, 1975* (Washington, D.C.: U.S. Governement Printing Office, 1975), Table 559, and *Statistical Abstract of the United States, 1994*, Tables 615 and 619. The number of persons who had retired by sixty-three doubled between 1960 and 1990 from one-quarter to one-half. See also Charles Strouse, "To Many, Early Retirement is Only a Dream as Workers Turn to Second Careers,"*Miami Herald*, 9 October 1995, sec. A, p. 1.

27. Henkoff, "Is Greed Dead?" 41.

28. Everett Carl Ladd and Larlyn Bowman, "Attitudes towards Economic Equality," as quoted in Robert J. Samuelson, "A Tycoon for Our Times," *Newsweek*, 16 November 1998, 65.

29. Executive Summary from the Merck Family Fund, *Yearning for a Balance*.

30. William L. Bulkeley, "More Career-Switchers Declare, 'Those Who Can, Teach,'" *Wall Street Journal*, 8 April 1997, sec. B, p. 1.

31. The rising pressures on American workers are detailed by Schor, *The Overworked American*.

32. Lydia Saad, "Children, Hard Work Taking Their Toll on Baby Boomers," *Gallup Poll Monthly*, April 1995, 22.

33. Telephone survey of 1,011 Americans by the Gallup Organization, January 19–30, 1994.

34. Duane Elgin, *Voluntary Simplicity* (New York: William Morrow, 1993), 66.

35. Ibid., especially 46–53.

36. Ibid., 201.

37. John de Graaf and Vivia Boe, producers, *Affluenza*, KCTS Television, 1997.

38. www.pbs.org/kcts/affluenza. Accessed 7/6/00.

39. John de Graaf and Vivia Boe, producers, *Escape from Affluenza*, Public Broadcasting System, 8 July 1998.

40. Abby Ellin, "Preludes: Jealousy in a Material World," *New York Times*, 17 October 1999, sec. 3, p. 11.

41. Paul H. Ray, "The Emerging Culture," *American Demographics*, 19 (February 1997): 29, 31.

42. Schor, *The Overworked American*, 81–82.

43. "West Meets East, with a Vengeance," *Chicago Tribune*, 25 September 1994, sec 13, p. 2; see also, "A Great Leap Forward in Shopping," *Los Angeles Times*, 29 January 1996, sec. D, p. 1.

44. David Filipov, "Tinsel? Moscow Buys That," *Boston Globe*, 25 December 1996, sec. A, p. 2.

45. Robert Keatley, "Consumerism is Thriving in Vietnam, Luring U.S. Companies Despite Poverty," *Wall Street Journal*, 13 May 1994, sec. A, p. 7.

46. Fara Warner, "Burma Has Healthy, Up-to-Date Taste for Consumer Goods, Survey Shows," *Wall Street Journal*, 2 August 1996, sec. A, p. 11.

47. Marjorie Miller, "Ugly Americanization?" *Los Angeles Times*, 2 September 1995, sec. E, p. 1.

48. Frank M. Andrews and Stephen B. Withey, *Social Indicators of Well-Being: Americans' Perceptions of Life Quality* (New York: Plenum Press, 1976), 254–255.

49. Jonathan L. Freedman, *Happy People: What Happiness Is, Who Has It, and Why* (New York: Harcourt Brace Jovanovich, 1978).

50. Ed Diener, Ed Sandvik, Larry Seidlitz, and Marissa Diener, "The Relationship between Income and Subjective Well-Being: Relative or Absolute?" *Social Indicators Research* 28 (1993): 195–223.

51. David G. Myers and Ed Diener, "Who Is Happy?" *Psychological Science* 6 (January 1995): 12–13; see also, Diener, Sandvik, et al., "The Relationship between Income and Subjective Well-Being: Relative or Absolute?" 208.

52. Richard A. Easterlin, "Will Raising the Incomes of All Increase the Happiness of All?" *Journal of Economic Behavior and Organization* 27 (1995): 35.

53. Ibid., 41.

54. Ibid.

55. Amartya Sen, *Development as Freedom* (New York: Knopf, 1999).

56. Tim Kasser and Richard M. Ryan, "A Dark Side of the American Dream: Correlates of Financial Success as a Central Life Aspiration," *Journal of Personality and Social Psychology* 65 (1993): 420.

57. Mark Dolliver, "Luxuriating in the Simple Pleasures of Life," *Adweek*, 3 January 2000, 22.

58. Robert H. Frank, *Luxury Fever* (New York: Free Press, 1999).

59. Robert E. Lane, "Does Money Buy Happiness?" *Public Interest*, Fall 1993, 58.

60. Ibid., 56–65.

61. Benjamin M. Friedman, "The Power of the Electronic Herd," *New York Review of Books*, 15 July 1999, 40–44.

62. Jonathan Eig, "Analyze This: As Good Times Roll, What Are Americans Worried about Now? Fresh Low-Grade Anxieties Seem to Pop Up Anew; Frights to Fill the Void; The Stephen King Paradox," *Wall Street Journal*, 8 February 2000, sec. A. p. 1.

63. Elgin, *Voluntary Simplicity*, 25.

64. The addiction of consumption is discussed, however, by Tibor Scitovsky, *The Joyless Economy: The Psychology of Human Satisfaction* (New York: Oxford

University Press, 1992). See also, Barry Schwartz, *The Costs of Living: How Market Freedom Erodes the Best Things in Life* (New York: W.W. Norton and Company, 1994), 154–162.

65. The author notes that Maslow's writings are rather opaque and discursive. What is presented here is an interpretation of Maslow's work rather than a direct derivation. Abraham H. Maslow, *Toward a Psychology of Being* (Princeton, N.J.: Von Nostrand, 1986).

66. It should also be noted that Maslow does not draw a distinction between prosocial self-expression, for example arts, and antisocial, for instance abuse of narcotics.

67. Monique P. Yazigi, "Ideas & Trends: High Society; When You Got It, Flaunt It," *New York Times*, 26 December 1999, sec. 4, p. 1.

68. Brooks, "Conscientious Consumption," 46–47.

69. Alvin Toffler, *Future Shock* (New York: Random House, 1970); Daniel Bell, *The Coming of Post-Industrial Society: A Venture in Social Forecasting* (New York: Basic Books, 1973).

70. Pretty Good Software is an encryption program that is available on the Internet. It was created by Philip Zimmermann. The PGP home page is available at http://www.pgp.com. Accessed 7/6/00.

71. Paul Stern, *Energy Use: The Human Dimension* (New York: W.H. Freeman and Company, 1984), 71–72.

72. Elgin, *Voluntary Simplicity*.

73. Alan Durning, *How Much Is Enough?: The Consumer Society and the Future of the Earth* (New York: W.W. Norton and Company, 1992); Lester W. Milbrath, *Envisioning a Sustainable Society: Learning Our Way Out* (Albany: State University of New York Press, 1989).

74. Joseph A. Pechman, *Federal Tax Policy* (Washington, D.C.: The Brookings Institution, 1987), 6.

75. For instance, note the changes in the Labour Party in the United Kingdom and the Democratic Party in United States in the mid-1990s.

IV: Can Virtual Communities Be Real?

A very brief discussion of some of the points in this chapter has appeared in *Science* magazine, in an essay entitled "Communities: Virtual vs. Real" (*Science*, 18 July 1997, 295). The authors are indebted to Peter Rubin for research assistance and comments on a previous draft of this chapter.

1. See Robert Booth Fowler, *The Dance with Community: The Contemporary Debate in American Political Thought* (Lawrence: University of Kansas Press, 1991).

2. Cited by Colin Bell and Howard Newby in *Community Studies: An Introduction to the Sociology of the Local Community* (New York: Praeger, 1973), 49.

3. See, for example, Steve Jones, *Cybersociety: Computer Mediated*

Communication and Community (Newbury Park, Calif.: Sage, 1995), especially page 138. The book includes reports of people attending funerals, weddings, etc. — basically, the sort of things people do in f2f communities — in a CMC. The WELL (Whole Earth Electronic Links), founded in cyberspace in 1985, is also considered a vibrant community.

4. Bernard Berelson and Gary A. Steiner, *Human Behavior: An Inventory of Scientific Findings* (New York: Harcourt, Brace & World, Inc., 1964).

5. For more information on this variable (which is labeled "diffuse"), see Talcott Parsons, *The Social System* (Glencoe, Ill.: Free Press, 1951).

6. Sherry Turkle, *Life On the Screen: Identity in the Age of the Internet* (New York: Simon and Schuster Trade, 1995).

7. See, for example, Julian Dibbell, "A Rape in Cyberspace," *Village Voice*, 21 December 1993, 36–42.

8. See the MediaMOO website at http://www.cc.gatech.edu/foc/Amy.Bruckman/MediaMOO. Accessed 7/14/00.

9. Jane Mansbridge, *Beyond Adversary Democracy* (New York: Basic Books, 1980), especially Chapter 5, "The Town Meeting." Also Amitai Etzioni, *The New Golden Rule: Community and Morality in a Democratic Society* (New York: Basic Books, 1996), 127.

10. Amitai Etzioni, "An Engineer–Social Science Team at Work," *Technology Review*, January 1975, 26–31.

11. See Amitai Etzioni, "Minerva: An Electronic Town Hall," *Policy Sciences* 3 (December 1972): 457–474.

12. Amitai Etzioni, "Teledemocracy," *Atlantic Monthly*, October 1992, 36–39.

13. William J. Mitchell, author of *City of Bits*, is quoted as having stated that "the more electronic communication expands and diversifies our circles of contacts, the more we are going to want to add the dimension of face to face" (*New York Times*, 25 February 1997, sec. A, p. 12). This may well be true, but it is at least as valid to suggest that those who met in f2f groups are keen to stay in touch via the Internet.

14. For a preliminary discussion of these issues, see a report concerning a community that is eighty percent wired and maintains public access terminals, in Andrew Michael Cohill and Andrea Lee Kavanaugh, eds., *Community Networks: Lessons from Blacksburg, Virginia* (Boston: Artech House, 1997). Also see Goldie Blumenstyk, "An Experiment in 'Virtual Community' Takes Shape in Blacksburg, Va." *The Chronicle of Higher Education*, 17 January 1997, 24.

15. I am indebted to Joanna Cohn for research assistance on the following text, first published in the *New York Times*. (Amitai Etzioni, "E-Communities Build New Ties, but Ties That Bind," *New York Times*, 10 February 2000, sec. E, p. 7).

16. Among the numerous recent publications on the subject, the following deserve special attention: William A. Galston, "Does the Internet Strengthen

Community?" *Report from the Institute for Philosophy & Public Policy*, 19, no. 4 (Fall 1999): 1–8; Sherry Turkle, "Looking toward Cyberspace: Beyond Grounded Technology," *Contemporary Sociology* 28 (1999): 643–48; Barry Wellman and Keith Hampton, "Living Networked On and Offline," *Contemporary Sociology* 28 (1999): 648–54; James B. Rule, "Silver Bullets or Land Rushes? Sociologies of Cyberspace," *Contemporary Sociology* 28 (1999): 661–64; William Sims Bainbridge, "Cyberspace: Sociology's Natural Domain," *Contemporary Sociology* 28 (1999): 664–67; David Holmes, ed., *Virtual Politics: Identity & Community in Cyberspace* (Thousand Oaks, Calif.: Sage Publications, 1997); Rebecca Adams, "The Demise of Territorial Determinism: Online Friendships," in *Placing Friendships in Context*, ed. R.G Adams and G. Allan (Cambridge: Cambridge University Press, 1998), 153–82; and Norman Nie and Lutz Erbring, "Study of the Social Consequences of the Internet," The Stanford Institute for the Quantitative Study of Society, 16 February 2000, available at http://www.stanford.edu/group/sigss/. Accessed 7/14/00. For a criticism of this survey see Amitai Etzioni, "Debating the Societal Effects of the Internet: Connecting with the World," *Public Perspective*, May/June 2000, 42–43.

17. Jerry Guidera, "FTC, States Target Online-Auction Fraud," *Wall Street Journal*, 15 February 2000, sec. B, p. 8.

V: Suffer the Children

The author is indebted to Barbara Fusco for her editorial and research assistance.

1. Roberta Furger, "Internet Filters: The Smut Stops Here. Or Does It? Screening Five Top Web Filters," *PC World*, October 1997, 78.

2. Esther Dyson, *Release 2.0: A Design for Living in the Digital Age* (New York: Broadway Books, 1997), 197–98.

3. For example, Amazon.com, an online bookseller, uses cookies to store information about the types of books a user browses and has ordered in the past. When a user returns to Amazon.com after placing an order, he or she will be greeted, "Hello[Name]. We have recommendations for you in Books, Music, and more." See also, Federal Trade Commission, *Privacy Online: A Report to Congress*, June 1998. Available at http://www.ftc.gov/opa/1998/9807/privacyh.htm. Accessed 7/10/00.

4. Jeri Clausing, "Group Proposes Voluntary Guidelines for Internet Privacy," *New York Times*, 21 July 1998, sec. D, p. 4; Pamela Mendels, "Internet Sites for Children Raise Concerns on Privacy," *New York Times*, 4 July 1998, sec. D, p. 3; Robert O'Harrow, Jr., "Firms Prepare Plan for Protecting Privacy on Internet," *Washington Post*, 20 June 1998, sec. D, p. 3. Also see the Direct Marketing Association's "Privacy Action." Information available at http://www.the-dma.org. Accessed 7/10/00.

5. Rep. Edward J. Markey (D-Mass.), 104th Cong., 2nd sess. *Congressional Record* (29 March 1996.

6. Don Aucoin, "After One Season, TV Ratings Picture is Still Murky," *Boston Globe*, 28 May 1998, sec. E, p. 1.

7. "ACLU Joins Opposition to Tobacco Pact; Says Speech Limits Are Unconstitutional," *ACLU Freedom Network*, 24 March 1998. Available at http://www.aclu.org/news/n032498b.html. Accessed 7/10/00.

8. "Testimony of the American Civil Liberties Union for the Senate Commerce, Science and Transportation Committee Tobacco Hearing on Advertising, Marketing and Labeling," *ACLU Freedom Network*, 3 March 1998. Available at http://www.aclu.org/congress/t030398a.html. Accessed 7/10/00.

9. Ibid.

10. "The Tobacco Settlement is Bad News — Even if You've Never Smoked a Cigarette," *News from the Libertarian Party*, 24 June 1997.

11. "ACLU Hails Victory as California Library Agrees to Remove Internet Filters from Public Computers," *ACLU Freedom Network*, 28 January 1998. Available at http://www.aclu.org/news/n012898d .html. Accessed 7/10/00.

12. Italics added for emphasis by author. "ACLU Hails Victory as California Library Agrees to Remove Internet Filters from Public Computers."

13. Italics added for emphasis by author. "ACLU Enters VA Library Internet Lawsuit on Behalf of Online Speakers," *ACLU Freedom Network*, 6 February 1998. Available at http://www.aclu.org/news/n020698a.html. Accessed 7/10/00.

14. For more discussion on libraries' positions on the subject, see Mark Herring, "Reading Between Librarian's Lines," *Society*, September/October 1999, 26ff.

15. "Access to Electronic Information, Services, and Networks: An Interpretation of the Library Bill of Rights," Available at http://www.ala.org/alaorg/oif/electacc.html. Accessed 7/10/00.

16. American Library Association. *Library Bill of Rights*. Available at http://www.ala.org/work/freedom/lbr.html. Accessed 7/10/00.

17. John Mintz and Saundra Torry, "Internal R.J. Reynolds Documents Detail Cigarette Marketing Aimed at Children," *Washington Post*, 15 January 1998, sec. A, p. 1; John Schwartz, "Documents Indicate Strategy of Targeting Teen Smokers," *Washington Post*, 5 February 1998, sec. A, p. 3.

18. Italics added for emphasis by author. Centers for Disease Control and Prevention's (CDC) Tobacco Information and Prevention Source, web page, "Trends in Smoking Initiation among Adolescents and Young Adults," from CDC's *Morbidity and Mortality Weekly Report*, 21 July 1995, 521–25. Available at http://ww.cdc.gov/nccdphp/osh/ythstart.htm. Accessed 7/10/00.

19. "Paternalism and the Harkin-Bradley Bill: Proposal on Tobacco Advertising Would Violate the First Amendment," *ACLU Freedom Network*, 21 March 1998. Available at http://www.aclu.org/news/n032195.html. Accessed 7/3/00.

20. Aside for the reasons discussed in the text, the ACLU also opposed V-chips

as forms of government censorship. The V-chip discussed in the text is voluntary and not government-imposed.

21. Italics added for emphasis by author. Marjorie Heins, "Screening Out Sex: Kids, Computers, and the New Censors," *The American Prospect* 39 (July/August 1998): 41. It should be noted that in a later article, Heins states that appropriate content level varies by age and maturity level. See Heins, "Rejuvenating Free Expression," *Dissent*, Summer 1999, 43.

22. For more discussion on privacy and children, see Martha Fineman, "Intimacy Outside of the Natural Family: The Limits of Privacy," *Connecticut Law Review* 23 (1991): 955.

23. Personal observation.

24. Italics added for emphasis by author. Cato Institute, "Marketing to Children Does Not Justify Regulation," *Policy Analysis*, 22 January 1998, 19.

25. Ibid., 20.

26. Ibid.

27. Neil Postman, *The Disappearance of Childhood* (New York: Vintage Books, 1982).

28. Janet L. Dolgin, "The Fate of Childhood: Legal Models of Children and the Parent–Child Relationship," *Albany Law Review* 61, no. 2 (1997–1998): 345–431.

29. Arlene S. Skolnick and Jerome H. Skolnick, comp. *Family in Transition: Rethinking Marriage, Sexuality, Child Rearing, and Family Organizations*, 5th ed. (Boston: Little, Brown, 1986), 1–4.

30. For a list of numerous studies on this topic, see Michael S. Wald, "Children's Rights: A Framework for Analysis," *UC Davis Law Review* 12 (1979): 274.

31. Ibid.

32. Joseph Goldstein, "Medical Care for the Child at Risk: On State Supervision of Parental Autonomy," *Yale Law Journal* 86 (1977): 645. As cited in Wald.

33. John O'Neill, *The Missing Child in Liberal Theory: Towards a Covenant Theory of Family, Community Welfare and the Civic State* (Tonawanda, N.Y.: University of Toronto Press, 1994), 64. O'Neill cites John Holt, *Escape From Childhood* (New York: Ballantine Books, 1974) and Bob Franklin, *The Rights of Children* (Oxford: Basil Blackwell, 1986).

34. M.D. Resnick, et al., "Protecting Adolescents from Harm: Findings from the National Longitudinal Study on Adolescent Health," *Journal of the American Medical Association* 278, no. 10 (10 September 1997).

35. "ACLU Joins Opposition to Tobacco Pact," *ACLU Freedom Network*, 24 March 1998.

36. John Stuart Mill, *Principles of Political Economy: With Some of Their Applications to Social Philosophy*, vol. III (Toronto: University of Toronto Press, 1965) 951–52.

VI: Holidays: The Neglected Seedbeds of Virtue

1. Roger D. Abrahams and Richard Bauman, "Ranges of Festival Behavior," in Barbara A. Babcock, ed. *The Reversible World: Symbolic Inversion in Art and Society* (Ithaca, N.Y.: Cornell University Press, 1978); Theodore Humphrey and Lin T. Humphrey, eds. *We Gather Together: Food and Festival in American Life* (Ann Arbor, Mich.: UMI Research Press, 1988); Sheila K. Johnson, "Sociology of Christmas Cards," *Transactions*, 1971; E.M. Litwicki, "Visions of America: Public Holidays and American Culture" (Ph.D. diss., University of Virginia, 1992). Don Handelman, *Models and Mirrors: Towards an Anthropology of Public Events* (Cambridge: Cambridge University Press, 1990); Daniel Dayan and Elihu Katz, *Media Events: The Live Broadcasting of History* (Cambridge, Mass.: Harvard University Press, 1992); Elihu Katz, "Broadcasting Holidays," *Sociological Inquiry* 68, no. 2 (1998): 230–241.

2. *American Heritage Dictionary of the English Language*, 3rd ed. (Boston: Houghton Mifflin Company, 1996), 862. Steven Lukes defines ritual as "*rule-governed activity of a symbolic character which draws the attention of its participants to objects of thought and feeling which they hold to be of special significance*" (Italics in original). Steven Lukes, "Political Ritual and Social Integration," *Sociology* 9 (1975): 291.

3. Emile Durkheim, *The Elementary Forms of Religious Life* (New York: Free Press, 1995). Translated and with an introduction by Karen E. Fields.

4. Durkheim and others frequently refer to rituals rather than to holidays. However, their observations and findings apply to holidays because they are a form of rituals.

5. Steven Lukes, *Emile Durkheim: His Life and Work* (New York: Harper & Row, 1972); Lukes, "Political Ritual": 289–308; Watts Miller, *Durkheim, Morals and Modernity*, (Montreal: McGill-Queen's University Press, 1996); Talcott Parsons, *The Structure of Social Action* (Glencoe, Ill.: Free Press, 1937).

6. Reviewers of a draft of this chapter pointed out, quite correctly, that Durkheim is subject to different interpretations on the points discussed here. Given that the purpose of the chapter is not to sort out the differences among these interpretations but merely to use one of them as a starting point, I will not delve into the question of what is the correct interpretation of Durkheim. See also Lukes, "Political Ritual" 292.

7. Edward Lehman, *Political Society: A Macrosociology of Politics* (New York: Columbia University Press, 1977).

8. Amitai Etzioni and Edward Lehman, "Some Dangers in 'Valid' Social Measurements: Preliminary Notes," *The Annals of the American Academy of Political and Social Science* 373 (1967): 1–15.

9. Gabriel Escobar and Caryle Murphy, "Promise Keepers Answer the Call," *Washington Post*, 5 October 1997, sec. A, p. 1.

10. Edward Shils, "Dreams of Plentitude, Nightmares of Scarcity" in Seymour

Martin Lipset and Philip G. Altbach, ed., *Students in Revolt* (Boston: Houghton Mifflin Company, 1964).

11. Elihu Katz and Tamar Liebes, *The Export of Meaning: Cross-Cultural Readings of "Dallas"* (New York: Oxford University Press, 1990).

12. Durkheim, *The Elementary Forms of Religious Life.*

13. Jack Santino, *All Around the Year: Holidays and Celebrations in American Life* (Urbana: University of Illinois Press, 1994).

14. Robert Bellah, "Civic Religion in America," *Daedalus* 96 (1967): 1–21.

15. Cf. Talcott Parsons, Robert F. Bales, and Edward A. Shils, *Working Papers in the Theory of Action* (New York: Free Press, 1953), 180–81.

16. On this matter, see Joel Best, "The Myth of the Halloween Sadist," *Psychology Today* 19 (1985): 14; Joel Best and Gerald T. Horiuchi, "The Razor Blade in The Apple: The Social Construction of Urban Legends," *Social Problems* 32 (1985): 488–99; Margaret Holmes Williamson, "Family Symbolism in Festivals," in Theodore Caplow et al., eds., *Middletown Families: Fifty Years of Change and Continuity* (Minneapolis: University of Minnesota Press, 1982).

17. Victor Turner, *The Ritual Process: Structure and Anti-Structure* (Ithaca, N.Y.: Cornell University Press, 1985).

18. Sigmund Freud, *Civilization and Its Discontents* (New York: W.W. Norton, 1989). Translated and edited by James Strachey, with a biographical introduction by Peter Gay; Dennis Wrong, *The Problem of Order: What Unites and Divides Society* (New York: Free Press, 1994).

19. Jack Santino, *All Around the Year*, 49.

20. On this concept see Daniel Yankelovich, *Coming to Public Judgment: Making Democracy Work in a Complex World* (Syracuse, N.Y.: Syracuse University Press, 1991).

21. Studied by Theodore Caplow, "Christmas Gifts and Kin Networks," *American Sociological Review* 47 (1982): 383–92; William B. Waits, *The Modern Christmas in America: A Cultural History of Gift-Giving* (New York: New York University Press, 1993); Anna Day Wilde, "Mainstreaming Kwanzaa," *The Public Interest* 119 (1995): 68–79.

22. On layered loyalties see Amitai Etzioni, *The New Golden Rule: Community and Morality in a Democratic Society* (New York: Basic Books, 1996), 202–3.

23. Eve Epstein and Frank James, "The Native American Perspective of Thanksgiving," interview by Bob Edwards, *Morning Edition*, National Public Radio, 24 November 1993. Diana Karter Appelbaum, *Thanksgiving: An American Holiday, an American Tradition.* (New York: Facts on File, 1984).

24. Pam Belluck, "Pilgrims Wear Different Hats in Recast Thanksgiving Tales," *New York Times*, 23 November 1995, sec. A, p. 1; Tara Mack, "Listen Up, Pilgrims: Teachers Modernize Thanksgiving Message," *Washington Post*, 27 November 1996, sec. D., p. 1.

25. Joyce Price, "After Falling Off PC Calendars, Columbus is Back," *Washington Times*, 15 October 1996, sec. A, p. 1.

26. Jack Estes, "The Graying of Bitterness and Pain," *Los Angeles Times*, 30 May 1994, sec. B, p. 7.

27. Michelle Locke, "City with a Radical History Makes Peace with Vietnam Vets," *Los Angeles Times*, 12 November 1995, 4.

28. Mark Caro and Bernie Mixon, "Veterans Get a Big Salute As Holiday is Commemorated Amid Pomp, Protest," *Chicago Tribune*, 12 November 1994, sec. 1, p. 5.

29. Locke, "City with a Radical History."

30. Parsons, *The Structure of Social Action*, 438–41.

31. Diana Karter Appelbaum, *The Glorious Fourth: An American Holiday, an American Tradition* (New York: Facts on File, 1989).

32. Stephen Nissenbaum, *The Battle for Christmas* (New York: Alfred A. Knopf, 1996); Theodore Caplow, et al., eds, *Middletown Families*.

33. Janet Siskind, "The Invention of Thanksgiving: A Ritual of American Nationality," *Critique of Anthropology* 12 (1992): 175.

34. For yet another view see Theodore Caplow, et al. *Middletown Families: Fifty Years of Change and Continuity* . The authors argue that the trend toward family at the center of holidays reflects the fact that family is the institution that is most at risk in the Middletown community.

35. Penne L. Restad, *Christmas in America: A History* (New York: Oxford University Press, 1995). Waits, *The Modern Christmas in America*.

36. Leigh Eric Schmidt, *Consumer Rites: The Buying and Selling of American Holidays* (Princeton, N.J.: Princeton University Press, 1995), 30.

37. Ontario, California Chamber of Commerce, interview with David Carney of The Communitarian Network, 2 July 1996.

38. Amy Adams Squire Stronghart, "Developing Your Own Holiday Traditions," *St. Louis Post-Dispatch*, 27 December 1994, sec. B, p. 7.

39. To conduct the informal survey I queried six anthropologists about all the cultures with which they are familiar, and additionally, scanned the literature regarding the cultures with which I am familiar.

40. Williamson, "Family Symbolism in Festivals," in Caplow, et al., eds., *Middletown Families*, 235.

41. On the implications of this difference see Amitai Etzioni, *The Active Society: A Theory of Societal and Political Process* (New York: Free Press, 1968).

42. William Lloyd Warner, *The Living and the Dead: A Study of Symbolic Life of Americans* (New Haven, Conn.: Yale University Press, 1959).

43. Durkheim, *The Elementary Forms of Religious Life*; for additional discussion see Matthew Schoffeleers and Daniel Meijers, *Religion, Nationalism and Economic Action: Critical Questions on Durkheim and Weber* (Assen, The Netherlands: Van Gorcum, 1978), 35–39.

44. Alessandra Stanley, "December 25 in Russia: The Adoration of the Monetary," *New York Times*, 24 December 1996, sec. A, p. 4.

45. "Reintroduction of Christmas Hailed" in *Daily Report/Soviet Union*, [Foreign Broadcast Information Service Database], New Canaan, Conn.: DataNews, Inc., 7 January 1991.

46. Eric Convey, "Spirituality: Passover by the Book," *Boston Herald*, 26 March 1999, 2.

47. John R. Gillis, *A World of Their Own Making: Myth, Ritual and the Quest for Family Values* (New York: Basic Books, 1996).

48. Schmidt, *Consumer Rites*; Leslie Bella, *The Christmas Imperative: Leisure, Family and Women's Work* (Halifax, Nova Scotia: Fernwood Publishers, 1992).

49. Ralph Linton and Adelin Linton, *We Gather Together: The Story of Thanksgiving* (London: Abelard-Schumann, 1949).

50. Williamson, "Family Symbolism in Festivals," in Caplow, et al., eds., *Middletown Families*, 235.

51. Ianthe Jeanne Dugan, "24-Hour Stock Trading Moves Closer; Nasdaq Board Approves Adding Evening Session," *Washington Post*, 28 May 1999, sec. A, p. 1.

52. Central Conference of American Rabbis, "A Statement of Principles for Reform Judaism Adopted at the 1999 Pittsburgh Convention," May 1999, accessed at http://ccarnet.org/platforms/principles.html. Accessed 7/11/00.

53. Thomas L. Friedman, *The Lexus and the Olive Tree* (New York: Farrar, Straus, Giroux, 1999).

54. Benjamin R. Barber, *Jihad versus McWorld* (New York: Times Books, 1995).

VII: Salem without Witches

There are literally thousands of articles on the factors involved in community formation of different kinds of communities; of the dynamics of communities and how one may build or rebuild communities and much more. It seems gratuitous to cite some and not others. Those interested in finding these works will have no difficulties in locating them in any library or search engine. Amy Gutmann, a liberal philosopher at Princeton University, once quipped, that "communitarian critics want us to live in Salem, but not to believe in witches." [Amy Gutmann, "Communitarian Critics of Liberalism," *Philosophy and Public Affairs* 14, no.3 (Summer 1985): 319.]

1. Personal communication, 8 August 1999.

2. Robert Booth Fowler, *The Dance with Community* (Lawrence: University Press of Kansas, 1991), 142.

3. Colin Bell and Howard Newby, *The Sociology of Community: A Selection of Readings* (London: Frank Cass, 1974), xiii.

4. Colin Bell and Howard Newby, *Community Studies: An Introduction to the Sociology of the Local Community* (New York: Praeger, 1973), 15.

5. Cited in Bell and Newby, *Community Studies*, 49.

6. Amitai Etzioni, *The New Golden Rule: Community and Morality in a Democratic Society* (New York: Basic Books, 1996), 127.

7. These include some needs that are biologically anchored, such as need for caloric intake, and some that are socially but universally implicated, such as need for affection. For additional discussion, see Amitai Etzioni, "Basic Human Needs, Alienation and Inauthenticity," *American Sociological Review* 33, no. 6 (December 1968): 870–84.

8. Elizabeth Frazer, *The Problems of Communitarian Politics: Unity and Conflict* (New York: Oxford University Press, 1999).

9. Amy Gutmann, "Communitarian Critics of Liberalism," *Philosophy and Public Affairs* 14, no. 3 (Summer 1985): 319.

10. Jennifer Reingold, "Executive Pay," *Business Week*, 17 April 2000, 106, 114.

11. Stephen Nathanson, *Economic Justice* (Upper Saddle River, N.J.: Prentice Hall, 1998).

12. For additional discussion and references see Etzioni, *The New Golden Rule*, chap. 4.

13. For a particularly cogent discussion of the role of reason in deliberations of ends and not just of means, see Philip Selznick, *The Moral Commonwealth: Social Theory and the Promise of Community* (Berkeley and Los Angeles: The University of California Press, 1992), especially 524–26.

14. Dennis Wrong illustrates the tendency toward reason in stating: "Many sociologists confine themselves, implicitly at least, to the cognitive rather than the motivational or emotional aspects of interaction, often making tacit assumptions about the latter or simply taking them for granted. Berger and Luckmann explicitly call their vivid account of how actors construct an objective social world that then confronts and constrains them a contribution to the 'society of knowledge.'" Although Wrong speaks directly of sociology, the affinity for the rational applies to many disciplines. [Dennis Wrong, *The Problem of Order* (New York: Free Press, 1994), 60.]

15. James Kuklinski, et. al., "The Cognitive and Affective Bases of Political Tolerance Judgments," *American Journal of Political Science* 35, no. 1 (1991): 22.

16. Jack Knight and James Johnson, "Aggregation and Deliberation: On the Possibility of Democratic Legitimacy," *Political Theory* 22, no. 2 (1994): 289.

17. Ibid., 286.

18. Kuklinski, et al., "Bases of Tolerance," 1.

19. James Q. Wilson, "Interests and Deliberation in the American Republic, or Why James Madison Would Have Never Received the James Madison Award," *PS: Political Science and Politics* (December 1990): 559.

20. James Hunter, *Culture Wars: The Struggle to Define America* (New York: Basic Books, 1991).

21. James Hunter, *Before the Shooting Begins: Searching for Democracy in America's Culture War* (New York: Free Press, 1994), viii.

22. Ibid., 4–5.

23. Jane J. Mansbridge, "The Town Meeting," in *Beyond Adversary Democracy* (Chicago: The University of Chicago Press, 1983), 47–58.

24. For further discussion, see Amitai Etzioni, *The Moral Dimension* (New York: Free Press, 1988), 136–50; Charles Lindbolm, *The Intelligence of Democracy* (New York: Free Press, 1965); Kenneth E. Boulding, "Review of *A Strategy of Decision: Policy Evaluation as a Social Process*," *American Sociological Review* 29, no. 6 (December 1964): 930–31.

25. Bette Hileman, "Fluoridation of Water," *Chemical and Engineering News* 66, no. 31 (1988): 26, 27, 42.

26. For additional discussion see Etzioni, *The New Golden Rule*, chap. 1, "The Elements of a Good Society" and chap. 2, "Order *and* Autonomy?"

27. See such works as Shalom Schwartz, "Are There Universals in the Structure and Contents of Human Values?" *The Journal of Social Issues* 50 (Winter 1994): 19–45, and "Towards a Theory of the Universal Content and Structure of Values: Extensions and Cross-Cultural Replications," *Journal of Personality and Social Psychology* 58 (May 1990): 878–91.

28. Rhoda E. Howard, *Human Rights and the Search for Community* (Boulder, Colo.: Westview Press, 1995).

29. Some evidence is found in *Autonomy and Order: A Communitarian Anthology*, forthcoming volume edited by Edward W. Lehman. See also Shalom Schwartz, "Are There Universals": 19–45; "Towards a Theory of the Universal Content and Structure of Values": 878–91; and Etzioni, *The New Golden Rule*, chap. 8, "The Final Arbiters of Community's Values."

VIII: Social Norms: The Rubicon of Social Science

I am indebted to Eric Posner and Robert Ellickson for their comments on a draft of this chapter, and to Natalie Klein for numerous editorial suggestions.

1. For examples of early law and society works, see Donald Black, *The Behavior of Law* (1976); Lawrence Friedman, *The Legal System* (1975); Robert L. Kidder, *Connecting Law and Society: An Introduction to Research Theory* (1983); and Richard Lempert and Joseph Sanders, *An Invitation to Law and Social Science: Desert, Disputes, and Distribution* (1986).

2. See Cass Sunstein, "Social Norms and Social Roles," *Columbia Law Review* 96 (1996): 903; Sunstein, "Preferences and Politics," *Philosophy & Public Affairs* 20 (1991): 3; Robert C. Ellickson, "Law and Economics Discovers Social Norms," *Journal of Legal Studies* 27 (1998): 537; Lawrence Lessig, "The Regulation of Social Meaning," *University of Chicago Law Review* 62 (1995): 943; Lessig, "The New Chicago School," *Journal of Legal Studies* 27 (1998): 661; Dan Kahan, "Social Influence, Social Meaning, and Deterrence," *Virginia Law Review* 83 (1997): 349 ; Kahan, "What Do Alternative Sanctions Mean?"

University of Chicago Law Review 63 (1996): 591; Eric Posner, "Law, Economics, and Inefficient Norms," *University of Pennsylvania Law Review* 144 (1996): 1697; Richard Epstein, "Enforcing Norms: When the Law Gets in the Way," *The Responsive Community*, Summer 1997, 4; Dennis Chong, "Values versus Interests in the Explanation of Social Conflict," *University of Pennsylvania Law Review* 144 (1996): 2079. For an informal discussion, see Jeffrey Rosen, "The Social Police," *The New Yorker*, 20 & 27 October 1997, 170.

3. Richard Epstein, "Enforcing Norms: When the Law Gets in the Way," *The Responsive Community*, Summer 1997, 4.

4. A reviewer pointed out that there is "no single law and economics." It is of course true that there are significant differences within any school, but what makes them into a paradigm is that these divergent views share certain core assumptions, concepts, and perspectives. When I refer to law and economics, law and society, and law and socio-economics, I mean their shared paradigm.

5. These are the same philosophical assumptions that underlie neoclassical economics but are not specific to economics. For additional discussion see Amitai Etzioni, *The Moral Dimension* (New York: Free Press, 1988).

6. Socio-economics was founded as a discipline in 1989. The International Association of Socioeconomics has all the features of a scholarly association, including an elected group of officers, a journal, and a series of books.

7. David Sills, ed., "Norms," in *International Encyclopedia of the Social Sciences*, vol. 11 (New York: Macmillan Company and Free Press, 1968), 204–13.

8. Robert Ellickson, *Order without Law: How Neighbors Settle Disputes* (Cambridge: Harvard University Press, 1991), 138–39.

9. Epstein, "Enforcing Norms: When the Law Gets in the Way," 7.

10. Tracey Meares, "Drugs: It's a Question of Connections," *Valparaiso University Law Review* 31 (1997): 579, 594.

11. See Robert Cooter, "Law and Unified Social Theory," *Law and Society* 22 (1995): 50.

12. Amartya Sen, "Rational Fools," *Philosophy & Public Affairs* 6 (1977): 317; Lester Thurow, *The Zero-Sum Society* (New York: Basic Books, 1980).

13. Lawrence Lessig, for example, argues that the neoclassical paradigm assumes stable preferences:

> [This assumption is made] [n]ot because economists are so silly as to actually believe they are fixed, but because most of the techniques of economics, like any system of knowledge, function only when certain structures are taken for granted. Usually this discussion is in the context of the evolution of custom, but a custom is no less valuable for our purposes than a direct discussion of social meaning: Custom is just a particular form

of social meaning, less symbolic in general, but generated and transformed by the same mechanisms that affect social meaning. Economists aim to understand both custom's origin and its persistence, and it is in tracking this understanding of a custom's persistence that the most useful parallels to the regulation of social meaning can be drawn.

There is nothing about positing a change in preferences, however, that is inconsistent with even Gary Becker's conceptions of the stability of preferences. As he has explained, what his account presumes is the stability of "metapreferences," not particular preferences.

Lessig, "The Regulation of Social Meaning": 1005 [note 207]. See also Milton Friedman, "The Methodology of Positive Economics," in *Essays in Positive Economics* (Chicago: University of Chicago Press, 1953).

14. I refer to the neoclassical paradigm rather than economics because the former is now widely applied in social sciences that do not deal with economic behavior. See Etzioni, *The Moral Dimension.*

15. See Gary S. Becker and Kevin M. Murphy, "A Theory of Rational Addiction," in Gary S. Becker, ed., *Accounting for Tastes* (Cambridge: Harvard University Press, 1996), 50.

16. See Mark Blaug, "The Empirical Status of Human Capitol Theory: A Slightly Jaundiced Survey," *Journal of Economic Literature* 14 (1976): 837; Etzioni, *The Moral Dimension.*

17. Wassily Leontief, "Interview: Why Economics Needs Input-Output Analysis," *Challenge*, March/April 1985, 27.

18. See Etzioni, *The Moral Dimension*, 141–42.

19. Posner, "Law, Economics, and Inefficient Norms," 1699.

20. Lessig, "The Regulation of Social Meaning," 1044.

21. Sunstein, "Social Norms and Social Roles," 939.

22. Ibid., 935.

23. See Kingsley Davis, *Human Society* (New York: Macmillan Co., 1948).

24. On the difference between treating people as a product of their social status versus the creation of their project, see Arthur Schlesinger, Jr., *The Disuniting of America: Reflections on a Multicultural Society* (1991).

25. Intrinsic affirmation refers to the sense one has when one acts in a manner consistent with one's moral commitments. This sense is often treated, particularly by reductionists, as if it were just another source of satisfaction (i.e., pleasure). However, these acts often entail pain or deferred gratification, and the feelings they generate are far more complex than mere satisfaction. For additional discussion see Etzioni, *The Moral Dimension*, 45ff.

26. See Richard McAdams, "The Origin, Development, and Regulation of Norms," *Michigan Law Review* 96 (1997): 338, 381. See also Robert D. Cooter, "Decentralized Law for a Complex Economy: The Structural Approach

to Adjudicating the New Law Merchant," *University of Pennsylvania Law Review* 144 (1996): 1643, 1662. Shame can be turned into guilt, a point not discussed here.

27. Kahan, "What Do Alternative Sanctions Mean?"

28. Alan Lewis, *The Psychology of Taxation* (New York: St. Martin's Press, 1982).

29. This statement raises an important question: when should social norms be challenged on normative grounds? Dealing with this issue would take the discussion too far off track. For discussion of the selection and critical assessment of core societal values see Amitai Etzioni, *The New Golden Rule* (New York: Basic Books, 1996).

30. The difference between state coercion and social fostering of norms, and the relevance of this distinction to liberalism and to what he calls "soft communitarianism," has been very effectively spelled out by Jonathan Rauch in "Conventional Wisdom," *Reason*, February 2000, 37–41.

31. George Stigler and Gary Becker claim that preferences are fixed. "[O]ne does not argue over tastes," they reason, "for the same reason that one does not argue over the Rocky Mountains—both are there, will be there next year, too, and are the same to all men." Stigler and Becker, "De Gustibus non est Disputandum," *American Economic Review* 67 (1977): 76. More recently, Becker has retreated somewhat from this position; however, it is still very widely held by neoclassical economists.

32. Ellickson, "Law and Economics Discovers Social Norms," 156.

33. Robert Cooter, Law and Unified Social Theory, *Journal of Law and Society* 22 (1995): 50, 61.

34. See Charles Lindblom, *The Intelligence of Democracy: Decision Making through Mutual Adjustment* (New York: Free Press, 1965); Herbert Simon, *Administrative Behavior: A Study of Decision Making Processes in Administrative Organization*, 3rd ed. (New York: Free Press, 1976); Sen, "Rational Fools:" 317.

35. See Tracey Meares and Dan Kahan, "Law and (Norms of) Order in the Inner City," *Law & Society Review* 32 (1998): 805. This article is also a good source for numerous other references to other works on social norms.

36. See *Communitarian Bibliography*, available at http://www.gwu.edu/~ccps/biblio.html for a list of seminal socio-economic works. Accessed 7/13/00.

37. Lawrence Kohlberg, "Moral Development," *in* David Sills, ed., *International Encyclopedia of the Social Sciences* (New York: Macmillan, 1968), 483.

38. Mark C. Hoffman, "Childbearing Antecedents of Moral Internalization" (unpublished manuscript, on file with the author).

39. Personal communication with Professor Wrong.

40. Amitai Etzioni, *A Comparative Analysis of Complex Organizations* (Glencoe, Ill: Free Press, 1961).

41. Robert D. Cooter, review of *Against Legal Centrism* by Robert C. Ellickson, *California Law Review* 81 (1993): 417, 426–27.

42. McAdams, "The Origin, Development, and Regulation of Norms," 376.

43. Ibid., 380–81.

44. Lessig, "The Regulation of Social Meaning," 997.

45. Cooter calls this process internalization as well. Yet the phenomenon he describes is not necessarily compatible with common usage of the term. Cooter, "Decentralized Law for a Complex Economy": 1643.

46. Ibid., 1662.

47. Ibid.

48. Lawrence Kohlberg, "Moral Stages and Moralization," in Thomas Lickona, ed., *Moral Development and Behavior* (New York: Holt, Rinehart and Winston, 1976), 31, 32–35.

49. Note that Kohlberg himself clearly does believe that "moral stage is a good predictor of action." Ibid., 32.

50. Ibid.

51. See Stigler and Becker, "De Gustibus non est Disputandum," 76.

52. While persuasion often flows from authority figures or elites to followers, this need not always be the case. Members of a community can work out a shared position in which peers persuade those who may initially have differed on normative issues, drawing on nonrational means. For additional discussion see examination of moral dialogues in Etzioni, *The Moral Dimension*, 85–118.

53. Stigler and Becker write: "A consumer may indirectly receive utility from a market good, yet the utility depends not only on the quantity of the good but also the consumer's knowledge of its true or alleged properties." Stigler and Becker, "De Gustibus non est Disputandum," 84.

54. Stigler and Becker, "De Gustibus non est Disputandum," 83–84.

55. John Kenneth Galbraith, *The New Industrial State* (Boston: Houghton-Mifflin,1967).

56. Becker acknowledges the significant effect of habits acquired during childhood, and concedes that these may make little sense as the individual grows up. Yet far from conceding the possibility of nonrational behavior, Becker argues that this is the case because "it may not pay to try to greatly change habits as the environment changes." Becker, "Habits, Addictions, and Traditions," in *Accounting for Tastes*, (1996), 118, 127. Again, not a bit of evidence is provided concerning the costs of changing habits as compared to losses incurred by not changing them. See also Lessig, "The Regulation of Social Meaning" (on habits).

57. McAdams, "The Origin, Development, and Regulation of Norms," 358.

58. Ellickson, *Order without Law*, 167. Note that "cooperative" is synonymous with "rational" in the language of the prisoner's dilemma.

59. Robert Axelrod, *The Evolution of Cooperation* (New York: Basic Books, 1984).

60. Robert Cooter, "Normative Failure Theory of Law," *Cornell Law Review* 82 (1997): 947, 950–51.

61. See Robert Shiler, "Stock Prices and Social Dynamics," in *Brookings Papers on Economic Activity* (Washington, D.C.: Brookings Institution, 1984): 457. See also Becker, *Accounting for Tastes*, 226.

62. Douglas C. North, *Structure and Change in Economic History* (New York: W.W. Norton, Inc., 1981).

63. Aaron Wildavksy, "Choosing Preferences by Constructing Institutions: A Cultural Theory of Preference Formation," *American Political Science Review* 81 (1987): 3.

64. Cooter uses this example to illustrate rational reasoning. Actually it is a prime example of persuasion by appeal to values the actor already holds, rather than appeal to facts and logic. See Cooter, "Decentralized Law for a Complex Economy": 1661.

65. Talcott Parsons, *The Structure of Social Action* (New York: McGraw-Hill Book Co., Inc., 1937).

66. This can be empirically demonstrated. In situations where respect for tradition prevails, changing instrumental factors will not modify behavior, or at least, only if this is carried to great extremes. Most people will not eat human flesh, however hungry they are, if they are not members of a culture whose social norms legitimates cannibalism. There are, of course, limited exceptions to this rule under extreme conditions. See Piers Paul Read, *Alive: The Story of the Andes Survivors* (Philadelphia: Lippincott, 1974) for reports of cannibalism among survivors of a plane crash in the remote Andes mountains.

67. Chong, "Values versus Interests in the Explanation of Social Conflict," 2101.

68. Ibid., 2094–95.

69. Ibid., 2132.

70. Lessig, "The Regulation of Social Meaning," 1006 (citation omitted).

71. See Gordon Tullock, *Private Wants, Public Means; an Economic Analysis of the Desirable Scope of Government* (New York: Basic Books, 1970).

72. Amitai Etzioni, "Creating Good Communities and Good Societies," *Contemporary Sociology* 29, no. 1 (January 2000): 188–94 and Etzioni, *The New Golden Rule* (New York: Basic Books, 1996), chap. 8, "The Final Arbiters of Community's Values.

73. For more discussion on the subject, see Etzioni, *The New Golden Rule*, chapt.4, "Sharing Core Values" and chap. 5, "The Moral Voice."

IX: Why the Civil Society Is Not Good Enough
The author is especially indebted to Robert George for comments on a draft of this chapter. Andrew Wilmar provided research assistance and editorial suggestions. The author additionally is grateful to Andrew Altman, David Anderson, Bruce Douglas, and Thomas Spragens, Jr., for their comments on a draft of this

chapter. Much appreciation also goes to Barbara Fusco and Tim Bloser for their help in putting together the final draft of this chapter.

1. The debate took place at a meeting organized by David Blankenhorn at the Institute for American Values.

2. Galston differs with many liberal colleagues, for instance Amy Gutmann, in terms of the scope of such citizen-virtues that he would have the state promote if such cultivation violates the values of a community. Thus, he would respect the Amish culture and not make their children attend public high schools, while Gutmann would override it in the name of the citizen requirements of the liberal state. There is much more to this debate between liberal communitarians and "liberal-liberals," but all I seek to highlight here is that both sides presume that the state limits its virtue-cultivating concerns to citizenship; the difference between the sides is limited to the scope of personal virtues that good citizenship requires. See William Galston, *Liberal Purposes* (Cambridge: Cambridge University Press, 1991) and Amy Gutmann, *Democratic Education* (Princeton, N.J.: Princeton University Press, 1987).

3. Will is seconded by Walter Berns of the American Enterprise Institute, who argues that one cannot fold conservatism's ideals into the notion of "freedom," and by Elliot Cohen, who maintains that the last thing our Founding Fathers envisioned was a "feeble government." See George Will, "Conservative Challenge," *Washington Post*, 17 August 1997, sec. C, p. 7.

William J. Bennett stresses that while there is much to lament about big government, he is deeply troubled by conservatives' "increasing and reckless rhetorical attacks against government itself." He draws on Benjamin Franklin, who is said to have understood that "the strength of the nation depends on the general opinion of the goodness of the government," not a phrase often employed by economic conservatives. See William Bennett, "Rekindling Our Passion for America; Cynicism about Government Programs Cannot be Allowed to Quell Our Love of Country," *Los Angeles Times*, 28 October 1997, sec. B, p. 7.

4. See David Brooks and William Kristol, "What Ails Conservatism," *Wall Street Journal*, 15 September 1997, sec. A, p. 22.

5. See Amitai Etzioni, *The New Golden Rule: Community and Morality in a Democratic Society* (New York: Basic Books, 1996).

6. Quoted in William Lund, "Politics, Virtue, and the Right To Do Wrong: Assessing the Communitarian Critique of Rights," *Journal of Social Philosophy* 28 (1997): 102.

7. Ibid., 108–109.

8. See Etzioni, *The New Golden Rule*, 85–118.

9. Adam B. Seligman, *The Problem of Trust* (Princeton, N.J.: Princeton University Press, 1997).

10. See Etzioni, *The New Golden Rule*, 217–57; Robert Bellah, Richard Madsen, William M. Sullivan, Ann Swidler, and Steven M. Tipton, *The Good*

Society (New York: Vintage, 1991); and Walter Lippman, *An Inquiry into the Principles of the Good Society* (Westport, Conn.: Greenwood Press, 1943).

11. The difference between states and societies is surprisingly often ignored. When the communitarian platform was translated into German, the term "member" was translated as "bürger." When it was pointed out that bürger means "citizen," a participant in the state and not the society per se, it turned out that there is no term that readily allows this distinction to be expressed in German. The word "mitglieder" refers more to a dues-payer or someone who belongs, but does not have the rich evocative power the communitarian notion of membership brings to mind.

12. See Dennis Wrong, *The Problem of Order: What Unites and Divides Society* (New York: Free Press, 1994).

13. John Stuart Mill, *On Liberty*, ed. David Spitz (New York: W.W. Norton, 1975), 71.

14. Alexis de Tocqueville, *Democracy in America*, trans. Henry Reeve, ed. Phillips Bradley (New York: Alfred A. Knopf, 1991), vol. 2, 261.

15. This is a huge subject mentioned but not examined here. For discussion of the author's views relating to the issue at hand, see Etzioni, *The New Golden Rule*, 160–88.

16. For further discussion, see Etzioni, *The New Golden Rule*, 85–159.

17. See, for instance, Robert Sampson, Stephen Raudenbush, and Felton Earls, "Neighborhoods and Violent Crime: A Multilevel Study of Collective Efficacy," *Science*, 15 August 1997.

18. For an excellent analysis of institutions and their role in the good society, see Bellah et al., *The Good Society*.

19. This subject recently has received a great deal of attention in legal scholarship, usually under the heading of "social norms." See, for example, Richard Epstein, "Enforcing Norms: When the Law Gets in the Way," *Responsive Community* 7 (Fall 1997): 4–15.

20. See Avishai Margalit, *The Decent Society*, trans. Naomi Goldblum (Cambridge, Mass.: Harvard University Press, 1996).

21. E. J. Dionne, Jr., "Why Civil Society? Why Now?" *The Brookings Review* 15 (1997): 5.

22. Robert Putnam, "Bowling Alone, Revisited," *The Responsive Community* 5 (Spring 1995): 18–33.

23. See James Davison Hunter, *Culture Wars: The Struggle to Define America* (New York: Basic Books, 1991).

24. See Robert Putnam, *Making Democracy Work: Civic Traditions in Modern Italy* (Princeton, N.J.: Princeton University Press, 1993).

25. Ibid., 90.

26. The relevant differences are instrumental, rather than principled or normative (for example, the relative size of the association, the level of public education of its members, etc.).

27. See Suzanna Sherry, "Without Virtue There Can Be No Liberty," *Minnesota Law Review* 78 (1993): 61. A somewhat similar point is made by the noted civic theorist Benjamin Barber. While Barber is a fan of voluntary associations generally, he warns against those that are so "privatistic, or parochial, or particularistic" that they undermine democracy. He writes: "Parochialism enhances the immediate tie between neighbors by separating them from alien 'others,' but it subverts the wider ties required by democracy — ties that can be nurtured only by an expanding imagination bound to no particular sect or fraternity." See Benjamin Barber, *Strong Democracy: Participatory Politics for a New Age* (Berkeley: University of California Press, 1984), 234–35.

28. See Etzioni, *The New Golden Rule*, 217–57.

29. Hillel Steiner, "Permissiveness Pilloried: A Reply to Amitai Etzioni," *The Journal of Political Philosophy* 7, no. 1 (March 1999): 108.

30. Given the findings of Linda Waite there is good reason for this. See Linda Waite "The Negative Effects of Cohabitation," *The Responsive Community* 10 (Winter 1999/2000): 31–38.

31. Steven Macedo, *Diversity and Distrust: Civic Education in a Multicultural Democracy* (Cambridge, Mass.: Harvard University Press, 1999).

32. Steiner, "Permissiveness Pilloried: A Reply to Amitai Etzioni."

33. Michael Novak, "Seven Tangled Questions," in *To Empower People: From State to Civil Society*, ed. Michael Novak (Washington, D.C.: American Enterprise Institute, 1996), 138.

34. Peter L. Berger and Richard John Neuhaus, "Response," in *To Empower People: From State to Civil Society*, ed. Michael Novak (Washington, D.C.: American Enterprise Institute, 1996), 148–49.

35. Ibid., 149–50.

36. John Rawls, *Political Liberalism* (New York: Columbia University Press, 1996), 382–83.

37. Michael Walzer, "The Concept of Civil Society," in *Toward a Global Civil Society*, ed. Michael Walzer (Providence: Berghahn Books, 1995), 16–17.

38. Ibid., 25.

39. For further discussion and criticism of this conception of civil society, see Jean Cohen, "Interpreting the Notion of Civil Society," in *Toward a Global Civil Society*, ed. Michael Walzer (Providence: Berghahn Books, 1995).

40. William Sullivan, "Institutions and the Infrastructure of Democracy," in *New Communitarian Thinking: Persons, Virtues, Institutions, and Communities*, ed. Amitai Etzioni (Charlottesville: University Press of Virginia, 1995), 173.

41. Ibid., 173.

42. Ibid.

43. See Gertrude Himmelfarb, "The Renewal of Civil Society," in *Culture in Crisis and the Renewal of Civic Life*, eds. T. Williams Boxx and Gary M. Quinlivan (New York: Rowman & Littlefield Publishers, Inc., 1996), 67–75.

XI: Restoring the Moral Voice

1. Individualists include "liberals," laissez-faire conservatives, civil libertarians, most neoclassical economists, rational-choice social scientists, champions of law and economics, among others.

2. Amitai Etzioni, *The New Golden Rule: Community and Morality in a Democratic Society* (New York: Basic Books, 1997).

3. See Dennis H. Wrong, *The Problem of Order: What Divides and Unites Society* (New York: Free Press, 1994); Amitai Etzioni, *The Moral Dimension: Toward a New Economics* (New York: Free Press, 1988).

4. For additional discussion, see Etzioni, *The New Golden Rule*, chap. 8, "The Final Arbiters of Community's Values."

5. See M. P. Baumgartner, *The Moral Order of a Suburb* (New York: Oxford University Press, 1988).

XII: Cross-Cultural Moral Judgments

This chapter draws on ideas originally articulated in "The Final Arbiters of Community's Values" in Chapter 8 of my book, *The New Golden Rule: Community and Morality in a Democratic Society* (New York: Basic Books, 1996).

1. See Ruth Macklin, *Against Relativism* (New York: Oxford University Press, 1999).

2. See for example the work of Singaporean diplomat Kishore Mahbubani, "Asia's Cultural Fusion," *Foreign Affairs* 74, no. 1 (January/February 1995): 100–10, and "The Dangers of Decadence: What the Rest Can Teach the West," *Foreign Affairs* 72, no. 4 (September/October 1993): 10–14. See also the remarks of Singapore's former Prime Minister Lee Kuan Yew, reported by Erik Kuhonta, "On Social and Economic Rights," *Human Rights Dialogue* 2, (September 1995): 3. For a detailed review of exchanges between Singaporeans and Americans, see Donald K. Emmerson, "Singapore and the 'Asian Values' Debate," *Journal of Democracy* 6, no. 4 (October 1995): 95–104.

3. Bilahari Kausikan, "Asia's Different Standard," *Foreign Policy*, 92 (Fall 1993): 24.

4. Ibid.

5. Yasuaki Onuma, "In Quest of Intercivilizational Human Rights: 'Universal' vs. 'Relative' Human Rights Viewed from an Asian Perspective," Center for Asian Pacific Affairs, The Asia Foundation, Occasional Paper No. 2 (March 1996), 8.

6. See Amitai Etzioni, *The New Golden Rule: Community and Morality in a Democratic Society* (New York: Basic Books, 1997), 230–31.

7. Aryeh Neier, "Asia's Unacceptable Standard," *The Responsive Community* 7, no. 3 (Summer 1997): 25–26.

8. Daniel A. Bell, "The East Asian Challenge to Human Rights: Reflections on an East West Dialogue," *Human Rights Quarterly* 18 (August 1996): 664.

9. Ibid., 658.

10. For more discussion, see Daniel A. Bell and Joanne Bauer, eds., *The East Asian Challenge to Human Rights* (New York: Cambridge University Press, 1999).

11. Amartya Sen, *Development as Freedom* (New York: Knopf, 1999). See also Seymour Martin Lipset, et al. "A Comparative Analysis of the Social Requisites of Democracy," *Comparative Political Sociology* 136 (May 1993): 155–56.

12. Kausikan openly states as much. Kausikan, "Asia's Different Standard," 38.

13. Compare numbers in *International Marketing Data and Statistics 2000* (Chicago: Euromonitor International, Inc., 1999), 686; and U.S. Census Bureau, *Statistical Abstract of the United States, 1999* (Washington, D.C.: U.S. Government Printing Office, 1999), 464.

14. Neier, "Asia's Unacceptable Standard," 23.

15. Goh Chok Tong, "Social Values, Singapore Style," *Current History*, December 1994, 422.

16. Kevin Y. L. Tan, "What Asians Think about the West's Response to the Human Rights Debate," *Human Rights Dialogue* 4 (March 1996): 4.

17. See Bell and Bauer, eds., *The East Asian Challenge to Human Rights*. See also *International Conference on Universal Ethics and Asian Values*, Korean National Commission for UNESCO and Korean Society for Future Studies (UNESCO, 1999, unpublished data).

18. Yersu Kim, *A Common Framework for the Ethics of the 21st Century* (Paris: UNESCO, 1999).

19. Ibid.

20. Adamantia Pollis and Peter Schwab, eds. *Human Rights: Cultural and Ideological Perspectives* (New York: Praeger Publishers, 1979), 1, 4.

21. Marnia Lazreg, "Human Rights, State and Ideology: An Historical Perspective," in Pollis and Schwab, eds., *Human Rights*, 41.

22. See, for example, Michael Walzer, *Just and Unjust Wars: A Moral Argument with Historical Illustrations* (New York: Basic Books, 1977).

23. For more discussion, see Etzioni, *The New Golden Rule*, 119–126.

24. For a justification of this point, see Etzioni, *The New Golden Rule*, 102–4, 227–31.

25. See also Amy Gutmann, "The Challenge of Multiculturalism in Political Ethics," *Philosophy and Public Affairs* 22 (Summer 1993): 197ff.

26. Gareth Porter and Janet Welsh Brown, *Global Environmental Politics* (Boulder, Colo.: Westview Press, 1996), 69–105.

27. See Minerva Etzioni, *The Majority of One: Towards a Theory of Regional Compatibility* (Beverly Hills, Calif.: Sage Publications, 1970).

28. See Amitai Etzioni, "The Responsive Community: A Communitarian Perspective," *American Sociological Review* 61 (February 1996): 1–11; and Part 4 of *The Active Society: A Theory of Societal and Political Processes* (New York: Free Press, 1968).

29. Joanne Bauer, "International Human Rights and Asian Commitment," *Human Rights Dialogue* 3 (December 1995): 1.

30. Ibid., 1–2.

31. Cited in "Asia: Who Speaks for the People?" *The Economist*, 27 January 1996, 31.

32. Hans Joas, "Combining Value Pluralism and Moral Universalism: Isaiah Berlin and Beyond," *The Responsive Community* 9, no. 4 (Fall 1999): 17–30.

XIII: Stakeholders versus Shareholders

The author is indebted to Michael Bocian for research assistance and to Margaret Blair for comments on a previous draft of this chapter.

1. R. Edward Freeman, *Strategic Management: A Stakeholder Approach* (Boston: Pittman, 1984).

2. Thomas Donaldson and T. W. Dunfee, "Towards a Unified Conception of Business Ethics: Integrative Social Contracts Theory," *Academy of Management Review* 19 (1994): 252–84.

3. Thomas Donaldson and L. E. Preston, "The Stakeholder Theory of the Corporation: Concepts, Evidence, and Implications," *Academy of Management Review* 20 (1995): 65–91.

4. Max B. E. Clarkson, "A Stakeholder Framework for Analysing and Evaluating Corporate Social Performance," *Academy of Management Review* 20 (1995): 92–117.

5. Margaret M. Blair, *Ownership and Control: Rethinking Corporate Governance for the Twenty-First Century* (Washington, D.C.: Brookings Institution, 1995).

6. Robert A. Phillips, "Stakeholder Theory and a Principle of Fairness," *Business Ethics Quarterly* 7, no. 1 (1997): 51–66.

7. Steven M. H. Wallman, "The Proper Interpretation of Corporate Constituency Statutes and Formulation of Director Duties," *Stetson Law Review* 21, no. 1 (Fall 1991): 163–96.

8. Irwin M. Stelzer, "The Stakeholder Cometh," *Weekly Standard*, 5 (February 1996): 16–17.

9. Nell Minow, "Shareholders, Stakeholders, and Boards of Directors," *Stetson Law Review* 21, no. 1 (Fall 1991): 197–243.

10. Amitai Etzioni, *The New Golden Rule: Community and Morality in a Democratic Society* (New York: Basic Books, 1996).

11. Adolfe A. Berle and Gardiner C. Means, *The Modern Corporation and Private Property* (New York: Macmillan, 1932).

12. Edward S. Mason, "Corporation," in *International Encyclopedia of Social Sciences*, ed. David L. Sills (New York: Macmillan, 1968), 397.

13. William Chambliss and Robert Seidman, *Law, Order, and Power* (Reading, Mass.: Addison-Wesley, 1982), 88–92.

14. Ronald E. Voogt, "'Taking': Real Estate Owners, Rights and Responsibilities," *The Responsive Community* 2, no. 2 (Spring 1992): 7–10.

15. For example, American property law changed during the nineteenth

century from a "natural use" conception of property which favored agrarian uses to a "reasonable use" conception which favored industrial uses. William Chambliss and Robert Seidman, *Law, Order, and Power,* 89–90.

16. E. Merrick Dodd, "The Evolution of Limited Liability in American Industry: Massachusetts," *Harvard Law Review* LXI, no. 8 (September 1948): 1361.

17. Marleen A. O'Connor, "Restructuring the Corporation's Nexus of Contracts: Recognizing a Fiduciary Duty," *North Carolina Law Review* 69 (June 1991): 1189.

18. Margaret M. Blair, *Ownership and Control.*

19. See Rick Molz, "Employee Job Rights: Foundation Considerations," *Journal of Business Ethics* 6 (1987): 449–58.

20. John Locke, *The Second Treatise of Government,* ed. Thomas P. Peardon (New York: Bobbs-Merrill, 1952), 17.

21. For example, see *Cleary v. American Airlines, Inc.* 111 Cal. App. 3d 443, 168 Cal. Rptr. 722 (1980), *Pugh v. See's Candies* 203 Cal. App. 3d 743, 25061 Cal. Rptr. 195 (1981), and *Monge v. Beebe Rubber Co.* 114 N.H. 130, 316 A. 2d 549 (1974).

22. I write typically because nonvoting shares are an exception.

23. Steven M. H. Wallman, "The Proper Interpretation of Corporate Constituency Statutes and Formulation of Director Duties," *Stetson Law Review* XXI, no. 1 (Fall 1991): 163.

INDEX

Clarkson, Max, 246

class differences, 14–16

clients: corporate investment by, 255–56; corporate representation of, 258–59

Clinton, Bill, 3–4, 214

CMC (computer-mediated communications): access to virtual communities by, 82–83; B & R (breakout and reassemble) systems and, 90–91; communal memory and, 94; communication features of, 85–86; comparison of f2f and, 80; cooling-off mechanisms in, 92–93; interactive broadcasting using, 88–89; mixture of f2f and, 94–96

CNN special program (1997), 3

cobbling communication, 87–88

codetermination corporate governance, 254

Colson, Chuck, 214

Columbia University, 14

Columbus Day, 124

The Coming White Minority: California's Eruptions and America's Future (Maharidge), 4

the common good, 259–60

communal memory, 93–94

communication: cooling-off mechanisms/ civility in, 91–93; interactive broadcasting, 86–89; mixed CMC and f2f systems of, 94–96; role of memory/culture in, 93–94; virtual community bonding type of, 80–81; virtual community encompassing knowledge, 83–86

communitarian ideal, 237–38

communitarians: on civil society, 205–6; on core values, 218; covenant marriage idea of, 212, 215–16; cross-cultural moral dialogues promoted by, 242–44; dialogue between social conservative and, 207–20; on encroachment of government, 208; on good society, 188–89; on liberty and order, 193; on moral behavior, 217–18; on no-fault divorce, 212; on promoting virtues, 211–12; on school prayer, 212–13; tolerance level of, 201; view of acting agent by, 229

communities: bonding of, 226; characterization of good society, 142–62; comparing virtual and real, 96–101; corporate investment by, 254–55; corporation representation of, 257–58; defining, 80–82; equality of resource allocation among, 148–49; moral voice of, 223–27; self-policing characteristic of, 97. *See also* civil society; virtual communities

consumerism: correlation of happiness and, 59–64; global experience in, 58; nonmaterialistic satisfaction vs., 72–73; psychological aspects of, 65–66; transition from basic needs to, 50; visibility of, 68

consumption: criticism of, 48–50; as goal of capitalist economies, 48; knowledge age, 69–73; voluntary simplicity alternative to, 49, 50–51

"cookies" (Internet), 103

Cook, Scott, 51

Cooter, Robert, 170, 172, 174, 175, 181

Corcos, Alain, 16–17

corporation property ownership: employee representation in, 256–57; investment and types of, 250–56

Coser, Lewis, 146

covenant marriage, 212, 215–16

creditors: corporate investment by, 255–56; corporate representation by, 257–58

criminal justice system: evaluating existing, 46–47; judicial shaming used by, 37–46; police power/procedural protection balance, 216–17; social conservatives on, 214, 216–17

cross-cultural moral judgments: debate over, 232–35; end of economic deferral and, 235–36; on human rights, 239–40; maintenance of social order and, 236–38; moral dialogues and, 242–44; moral voices and, 240–42; socioeconomic/ political development and, 235

cross-societal moral voice, 240–42

Cuban Americans, 22

"cult of ethnicity," 4

cultural pluralism. *See* multiculturalism

culture: communication role of memory and, 93–94; good society use of, 191–92; moral voice expression and, 230; moral voice as mainstay of, 192–95
culture wars, 152–53
Cyber Patrol, 103

Daley, Richard, 125
The Dance with Community (Fowler), 142
Dasbach, Steve, 105
death penalty, 214
Death of a Salesman (Miller play), 59
"Defining Deviance Down" (Moynihan), 222
deliberation: civility and, 151–52; culture wars contrasted with, 152–53; replaced by moral dialogues, 153–54
democracy: checks and balances of, 91; deliberation and civility of, 151–52
Diener, Ed, 60, 61
Diener, Marissa, 60, 61
DiIulio, John, 217
Dinkins, David, 23
Dionne, E. J., Jr., 196
Direct Marketing Association, 103
divorce (no-fault), 212, 216
Donaldson, Thomas, 246
downshifters movement, 51–53
Dunfee, Thomas, 246
Durkheim, Emile: additions to functional approach by, 138–40; functional approach to holidays by, 114–15, 118, 119, 122; on historical context of holidays, 130; on holidays as public events, 126–27, 128; homogeneous societies studied by, 132–33; symbol/ritual changes unrecognized by, 124
Durning, Alan, 75

Earth Summit (1992), 242
Easterlin, Richard, 62
eBay auctions, 97, 98
economic inequalities, 76–77
education: school prayer issue and, 211; social norm internalization goal of, 176

Elgin, Duane, 56, 65, 75
Ellickson, Robert, 165, 172, 180
Emerson, Ralph Waldo, 56
employee representation, 256–57
Encyclopedia of Sociology, 114
Enough! (O'Neill), 57
environment stewardship, 74–75
Envisioning a Sustainable Society (Milbrath), 75
EPIC (Electronic Privacy Information Center), 106
Epstein, Richard, 163, 166
Escape from Affluenza (TV program), 57
ethnic/racial groups: intermarriage/racial category issue for, 24–30; issues in defining, 33, 262n.15; moderation trend of leadership in, 30–32; of nonwhite states/cities, 22–24; polling on government trust by, 12t–13; polling on identity politics by, 13–16; polling on public policy preferences by, 10–12; polling on social problems of, 9t–10. *See also* racial differences
ethnic/racial leadership moderation, 30–32
Etzioni, Oren, 79
Excite, 100

f2f communications: access to virtual communities by, 82–83; B & R (breakout and reassemble) systems and, 90–91; communal memory and, 94; communication features of, 85–86; comparison of CMC and, 80; cooling-off mechanisms of, 92–93; interactive broadcasting using, 86, 87–88; mixture of CMC and, 94–96
fairness concept, 252–53
Farrakhan, Louis, 27
Feinberg, Joel, 226
female holiday roles, 133–34
female intermarriage rates, 27f
Finkelstein, James A., 68
Finnis, John, 209
First Amendment: four policies regarding children and, 102–4; Internet filtering programs and, 103, 105–6; "Joe Camel"

ads and, 103, 104–5, 106, 111; protecting children through limitation of, 110–12; television V-chips and, 103–4, 106–7, 111

Fowler, Robert Booth, 80, 142
Frankfurt, Harry, 223
Frank, Robert, 63
Frazer, Elizabeth, 146
Freedman, Jonathan, 60
Freeman, R. Edward, 246
Freud, Sigmund, 174, 175
Frey, William, 26
Friedman, Benjamin, 63–64
Friedman, Lawrence M., 44, 45
Fuller, Buckminster, 91

Galbraith, John Kenneth, 177
Gallup Organization poll (1998), 14
Gallup Poll Monthly, 55
Galston, William A., 186
Gates, Bill, 51
Gates, Henry Louis, Jr., 32
Geocities, 80
George, Robert P., 186, 207
George Washington University, 40
Germershausen, Stephen, 39
Gillis, John R., 132
GimmeaBid.com, 99
Giuliani, Rudolph, 23
global consumerism, 58
GO.com, 99
Goh Chok Tong, 236
Golden Rule, 175
Goldstein, Joseph, 109
good citizens: good people vs., 186; personal virtues required of, 186–87, 291n.2
Goode, Wilson, 24
Good Samaritan act, 38
good society: assessing/reducing inequality in, 147–49; characterization of community of, 142–43; compared to civil, 196–201, 204–5; conflict within consensus in, 146–47; exclusivity limited by laws of, 144–45; historic search for, 141–42; moral dialogues of, 149–59; moral justi-fication promoted by, 189–91; moral standing of values in, 159–62, 199; moral voice and liberty in, 192–95; nurturing of virtue by, 191–92; reliance on moral voice by, 155–59; social institutions as instrument of, 195–96; theoretical schools of thought on, 187–89; ultimate values of, 244–45; value and limitations of bonds in, 143–44. *See also* civil society

"The Good Society" (Etzioni), 207
good state, 187
Graham, Lawrence Otis, 8
Gutmann, Amy, 147

Habermas, Jürgen, 203
Harris poll (1990s), 21
Heritage Foundation, 188, 215
Himmelfarb, Gertrude, 205
Hirsch, Adam, 45
Hirschfeld, Lawrence, 17
Hirschman, Albert, 223
Hispanic Americans. *See* Latinos
Hobbes, Thomas, 165
holidays: civil society and theory of, 122–26; comparison of religious and secular, 130–32; cyberspace lack of, 135–37; cycle of, 128–30; defining, 114; Durkheim's functional approach to, 114–15; as "global" indicators, 115–17; importance of maintaining, 136–38; lack of research regarding rituals of, 113–14; lag behind society changes by, 132–35; public vs. private, 126–28; recommitment, 119; as socialization agents, 118–22; sociological theory of, 138–40; of tension management, 119–21; women's roles during, 133–34

Horowitz, Carl F., 40
Howard University, 18
How Much is Enough? (Durning), 75
human capital investment, 253. *See also* investment
human development theories, 175–76

human rights: need for social order and, 236–38; Western moral judgments and, 239–40

Hunter, James Davison, 13, 152

identity politics: of African American leadership, 31; declining influence of, 31–33; engaged in by ethnic groups, 13–16, 31–32; impact on Census "other" category by, 27–29

i-Escrow, 99

illicit sex: closing commercial establishments of, 213; violence and, 218–20

income/well-being correlation: debate over, 59–60; longitudinal study (1971–75) on, 60f; longitudinal study (1981–84) on, 61f; nonmaterialistic satisfaction and, 72–73; research on, 60–66; voluntary simplicity and, 64–66

incorporation, 247–50

individualists, 229

inequalities: assessing/reducing good society, 147–49; global economic, 76–77

Inglehart, Ronald, 49

intellectual property issues, 71–72

intermarriage: Census racial category issue and, 27–30; growth of ethnic groups and, 24–27; rates of female, 27f

internalization of norms, 172–78

International Encyclopedia of Social Sciences, 114

International Institute, 20

International Society of Appraisers, 99

Internet: First Amendment issues and, 103, 105–6; lack of holidays in cyberspace of, 135–38

intrinsic affirmation, 287n.25

intrinsic predispositions, 167–72

investment: community corporate, 254–55; corporate ownership through, 250–52; creditor and client corporate, 255–56; human capital, 253; shareholders vs. stakeholders, 252–54, 256. *See also* corporation property ownership

Investor's Business Daily, 40

Isbister, John, 5

ITV (instruction on television), 95

Iverson, Sherrice, 38

Japan, 237

Jewish holidays, 131–32

"Joe Camel" ads, 103, 104–5, 107, 111

Johnson, James, 151

Journal of Political Philosophy, 207

judicial shaming: during colonial times, 44–45; compared to other punishments, 40–41; conditions required for productive, 42–43; debate over, 37–38, 39–44; distinctions between two kinds of, 44; increasing use of, 39–40; insignia wearing as, 46; reintegrative, 44–46; as response to bad Samaritans, 38–39. *See also* law

Kansas City study (1994), 15

Kant, Immanuel, 143, 151

Kappelhoff, Mark, 39–40

Karp, David, 44

Kausikan, Bilarhari, 233

Kern County library-ACLU lawsuit, 105

Ketchum, Richard, 135

Kim, Yersu, 237–38

Knight, Jack, 151

knowledge age, 69–73

Koch, Ed, 23

Kohlberg, Lawrence, 175, 176

Kristol, William, 187, 208, 209

Kuklinski, James, 151–52

Lampson, Nicholas, 38

Lane, Robert, 63

Laski, Harold, 98

Latino leadership, 32

Latinos: differences among various groups of, 21–22; intermarriage and, 25, 26; polling opinions of, 9t–16; self-identity/characterization of, 18–22

law: exclusivity of good society limited by, 144–45; moral voice vs., 155–59; order and legal centralism of, 165–66; social conservatives on the, 209–10; social

National Endowment for the Humanities, 100
National Foundation for Civic Renewal, 188
nationalism, 208–9
National Latino Political Survey (1989), 20
Nation of Islam, 198
Native American population growth, 25
NCFE (National Campaign for Freedom of Expression), 104
Neier, Aryeh, 236
neoclassicism, 172–73, 177, 286n.13
Net Nanny, 103
Neuhaus, Richard John, 202, 203
Newby, Howard, 142
The New Golden Rule (Etzioni), 207
Newsweek, 14
New Year's Day, 119, 120, 121
New York City ethnic makeup, 23
New York Review of Books, 63
New York Times, 54
Nolan, Pat, 214
nonmaterialistic satisfaction, 72–73
nonwhite states/cities, 22–24
NORC (National Opinion Research Center), 8
North, Douglas, 181
Novak, Michael, 202
NPR (National Public Radio), 37, 38, 41

Oakeshott, Michael, 188
Offense to Others (Feinberg), 226
OMB (Office of Management and Budget), 28–29
one drop rule, 30
O'Neill, Jessie, 57
O'Neill, John, 109
On Liberty (Mill), 192
Online Privacy Alliance, 103
Onuma, Yasuaki, 233
Operation Rescue, 198
opportuning virtue, 215
ownership. *See* corporation property ownership

Packard, Vance, 68
Paehlke, Robert, 49
Parsons, Talcott, 181
patrochialism, 293n.27
Perot, Ross, 91
PGP (Pretty Good Privacy), 70
Phillips, Robert A., 246
Piaget, Jean, 175
Poe, Ted, 42
Politan, Nicholas, 40
political attitudes (racial/ethnic leadership), 30–33
Pollis, Adamantia, 239
Popcorn, Faith, 53
Population Research Center (RAND), 22–23
positive reinforcement theory, 41–42
Posner, Eric A., 168
postmaterialist values, 49
Powell, Colin, 30
preferences, 172–78, 288n.31
Preston, L. E., 246
Princeton Survey Research Associates, 14
principle of subsidiarity, 210
private property, 247–50
The Problems of Communitarian Politics (Frazer), 146
Prohibition failure, 171
Promise Keepers' ritual, 117
Proposals (Simon play), 59
Public Agenda, 10
Public Broadcasting Corporation, 56
Public Perspective poll (1998), 12
public policies: examined by moral dialogues, 153–55; moral voice vs., 155–59
public sphere, 203–4
Pursglove, Kevin, 98
Putnam, Robert, 197, 198, 200

race: changing demographics of U.S., 3–5; issues in defining, 33, 262n.15; social construction of, 16–18. *See also* ethnic/racial groups
racial differences: class differences vs., 14–16; social construction of, 16–18. *See also* ethnic/racial groups

rational choice theory, 179–82
Rawls, John, 151, 203
Reagan, Ronald, 125
recommitment holidays, 119
Record, 38
reintegrative shaming, 44–46
relativism, 161, 232–33
religious social conservative, 188
The Return of Martin Guerre (film), 85
Riordan, Richard, 23
Ripon Society, 198
Rodriguez, Gregory, 26, 29

Sacramento Bee, 38
San Antonio City Council election (1975),
  23
Sandel, Michael, 189
Sandvik, Ed, 60, 61
San Francisco ethnic makeup, 23–24
Santino, Jack, 120
Schlesinger, Arthur M., Jr., 4
Schmidt, Eric, 51
school prayer issue, 211, 212–13
Schor, Juliet, 49
Schwab, Peter, 239
Seidlits, Larry, 60, 61
Semil, Elizabeth, 38, 41
Sen, Amartya, 62
sexual permissiveness, 213, 218–20
shaming. *See* judicial shaming
shareholders: the common good and, 259–
  60; fairness concept applied to, 252–53;
  representation of, 256–57; stakeholders
  vs., 253–54, 256
Sierra Club, 202
Siminoff, David, 51–52
Siminoff, Ellen, 52
Simon, Neil, 59
simple-living movement, 56–57
Skerry, Peter, 23
Smedley, Audrey, 17
Smith, Adam, 188
social capital, 198, 253
social changes: holiday lag behind, 132–
  35; moral voice vs. law to make, 155–
  59. *See also* civil society

social conservatives: on core values, 218;
  criminal law enforcement stance by,
  214, 216–17; dialogue between communitarian and, 207–20; on federalism,
  208; on moral behavior, 217–18; nationalism championed by, 208–9; on promoting virtues, 210–12; on the role law,
  209–10; various schools of thought
  among, 187–88
social institutions: individual freedoms vs.,
  226; virtues in, 195–96
socialization: of acting agent to social order
  norms, 229; nurturing virtue by agencies
  of, 191; role of holidays in, 118–22; social norms and, 174, 176–77
social norms: to construct law/economic
  analysis, 166–67; fixed vs. shaped adherence to, 172–78; intrinsic predispositions
  affected by, 167–72; rediscovery of, 163–
  65; as social order basis, 165–66; socio-
  economics of, 173, 177, 178, 183–85;
  sources of, 178–83. *See also* behavior
social order: cross-cultural moral judgments on, 236–38; moral voice and,
  192–915; socializing acting agent to,
  229; social norm basis of, 165–66
social problems: multiracial category and
  programs for, 32; polls regarding beliefs
  about, 9t–10
socioeconomics: on social norms, 173, 177,
  178, 183–85; of voluntary simplicity, 75–78
Soviet Union, 131
Springsteen, Bruce, 51
Stacey, Margaret, 80
stakeholders model: on the common good,
  259–60; on corporation property ownership, 250–56; fairness concept and,
  252–53; pioneer work on, 246–47; private property and incorporation concepts
  of, 247–50; representation mechanisms
  in, 256–59; stakeholders vs. shareholders
  and, 253–54, 256
Star of David, 40, 42
state: community bonding and independence from, 226; differences between society and, 292n.11; good, 187; values
  fostered by societies vs., 194–95

Warren Court criminal procedure, 216, 217

Washington Post/Kaiser Family Foundation/ Harvard school of Public Health Survey Project, 10

Web sites. *See* Internet

Westerman, William, 20

Western moral judgments: cross-cultural relativism of, 232–34; differences among, 234–35; human rights and, 239–40. *See also* cross-cultural moral judgments

white majority decline: intermarriage and, 24–30; predictions on U.S., 3–5; ramifications of, 5–16

Whiteness of a Different Color: European Immigrants and the Alchemy of Race (Jacobson), 18

Wilder, L. Douglas, 24

Will, George, 187, 208

Williamson, Oliver, 129, 165

Wilson, James Q., 4, 152

Withey, Stephen B., 60

Wolfe, Alan, 8

women's holiday roles, 133–34

Woods, Tiger, 27, 30

World Economic Forum, 51

Wright, Erik Olin, 141

Wrong, Dennis, 173–74

X-Stop, 103

Yahoo!, 100

Other Books by A M I T A I   E T Z I O N I

The Limits of Privacy (1999)

The New Golden Rule: Community and Morality in a Democratic Society (1996)

The Spirit of Community: The Reinvention of American Society (1993)

A Responsive Society (1991)

The Moral Dimension: Toward a New Economics (1988)

Capital Corruption: The New Attack on American Democracy (1984)

An Immodest Agenda: Rebuilding America before the Twenty-First Century (1983)

Genetic Fix: The Next Technological Revolution (1973)

The Active Society: A Theory of Societal and Political Processes (1968)

Political Unification: A Comparative Study of Leaders and Forces (1965)

Modern Organizations (1964)

A Comparative Analysis of Complex Organizations (1961)

NEW FORUM BOOKS

New Forum Books makes available to general readers outstanding original interdisciplinary scholarship with a special focus on the juncture of culture, law, and politics. New Forum Books is guided by the conviction that law and politics not only reflect culture but help to shape it. Authors include leading political scientists, sociologists, legal scholars, philosophers, theologians, historians, and economists writing for nonspecialist readers and scholars across a range of fields. Looking at questions such as political equality, the concept of rights, the problem of virtue in liberal politics, crime and punishment, population, poverty, economic development, and the international legal and political order, New Forum Books seeks to explain — not explain away — the difficult issues we face today.

PAUL EDWARD GOTTFRIED
After Liberalism: Mass Democracy in the Managerial State

PETER BERKOWITZ
Virtue and the Making of Modern Liberalism

JOHN E. COONS AND PATRICK M. BRENNAN
By Nature Equal: The Anatomy of a Western Insight

DAVID NOVAK
Covenantal Rights: A Study in Jewish Political Theory

CHARLES L. GLENN
The Ambiguous Embrace: Government and Faith-Based Schools and Social Agencies

PETER BAUER
From Subsistence to Exchange and Other Essays

ROBERT P. GEORGE, ED.
Great Cases in Constitutional Law

AMITAI ETZIONI
The Monochrome Society